Critical Criminological Perspectives

Series Editors
Reece Walters, Faculty of Law, Deakin University, Burwood, VIC, Australia
Deborah H. Drake, Department of Social Policy & Criminology, The Open University, Milton Keynes, UK

The Palgrave Critical Criminological Perspectives book series aims to showcase the importance of critical criminological thinking when examining problems of crime, social harm and criminal and social justice. Critical perspectives have been instrumental in creating new research agendas and areas of criminological interest. By challenging state defined concepts of crime and rejecting positive analyses of criminality, critical criminological approaches continually push the boundaries and scope of criminology, creating new areas of focus and developing new ways of thinking about, and responding to, issues of social concern at local, national and global levels. Recent years have witnessed a flourishing of critical criminological narratives and this series seeks to capture the original and innovative ways that these discourses are engaging with contemporary issues of crime and justice. For further information on the series and to submit a proposal for consideration, please get in touch with the Editor: Josephine Taylor, Josephine.Taylor@palgrave.com.

Heather Panter · Angela Dwyer
Editors

Transgender People and Criminal Justice

An Examination of Issues in Victimology, Policing, Sentencing, and Prisons

palgrave
macmillan

Editors
Heather Panter
School of Justice Studies
Liverpool Centre for Advanced Policing Studies
Liverpool John Moores University
Liverpool, UK

Angela Dwyer
School of Social Sciences
University of Tasmania
Glen Waverley, VIC, Australia

ISSN 2731-0604 ISSN 2731-0612 (electronic)
Critical Criminological Perspectives
ISBN 978-3-031-29892-9 ISBN 978-3-031-29893-6 (eBook)
https://doi.org/10.1007/978-3-031-29893-6

This Palgrave Macmillan imprint is published by the registered company Springer Nature Switzerland AG
The registered company address is: Gewerbestrasse 11, 6330 Cham, Switzerland

Contents

Contributors

Annette Brömdal Faculty of Business, Education, Law and Arts, School of Education, Institute for Resilient Regions, Centre for Health Research, University of Southern Queensland, Toowoomba, QLD, Australia

April Carrillo Department of Political Science, Criminal Justice, College of Arts and Sciences, University of South Dakota, Vermillion, SD, USA

Kirsty A. Clark Department of Medicine, Health and Society, Institute for Public Policy Studies, Vanderbilt University, Nashville, TN, USA

Noel Cross School of Justice Studies, Criminal Justice, Liverpool John Moores University, Liverpool, UK

Kirstie Daken Faculty of Health, Engineering and Sciences, School of Psychology and Wellbeing, Institute for Resilient Regions, Centre for Health Research, University of Southern Queensland, Ipswich, QLD, Australia

Joseph Debattista Metro North Public Health Unit, Metro North Hospital and Health Service, Brisbane, QLD, Australia

Carol du Plessis Faculty of Health, Engineering and Sciences, School of Psychology and Wellbeing, Institute for Resilient Regions, Centre for Health Research, University of Southern Queensland, Ipswich, QLD, Australia

Angela Dwyer School of Social Sciences, Tasmanian Institute of Law Enforcement Studies, University of Tasmania, Glen Waverley, VIC, Australia

Yarin Eski Vrije Universiteit Amsterdam, Amsterdam, Netherlands

Jessica Gildersleeve Faculty of Business, Education, Law and Arts, School of Humanities and Communication, Institute for Resilient Regions, Centre for Health Research, University of Southern Queensland, Toowoomba, QLD, Australia

Sherree Halliwell Faculty of Business, Education, Law and Arts, School of Humanities and Communication, Institute for Resilient Regions, Centre for Health Research, University of Southern Queensland, Toowoomba, QLD, Australia

Andrew Hickey Faculty of Business, Education, Law and Arts, School of Humanities and Communication, University of Southern Queensland, Toowoomba, QLD, Australia

Jaclyn M. W. Hughto Departments of Behavioural and Social Sciences and Epidemiology, School of Public Health, Centre for Health Equity Research, Brown University, Providence, RI, USA

DeShaun LaChance Illinois Department of Human Rights, Chicago, IL, USA

Amy B. Mullens Faculty of Health, Engineering and Sciences, School of Psychology and Wellbeing, Institute for Resilient Regions, Centre for Health Research, University of Southern Queensland, Ipswich, QLD, Australia;
Faculty of Health, School of Psychology and Counselling, Queensland University of Technology, Kelvin Grove, QLD, Australia

Heather Panter School of Justice Studies, Liverpool Centre for Advanced Policing Studies, Liverpool John Moores University, Liverpool, UK

Tania M. Phillips Faculty of Health, Engineering and Sciences, School of Psychology and Wellbeing, Institute for Resilient Regions, Centre for Health Research, University of Southern Queensland, Ipswich, QLD, Australia

Tait Sanders Faculty of Health, Engineering and Sciences, School of Psychology and Wellbeing, Institute for Resilient Regions, Centre for Health Research, University of Southern Queensland, Ipswich, QLD, Australia

Sarah Sramota Vrije Universiteit Amsterdam, Amsterdam, Netherlands

Jace Valcore College of Public Service, Criminal Justice, University of Houston Downtown, Houston, TX, USA

List of Tables

1

Framework for Viewing Transgender Victimological Experiences in Global Criminal Processing Systems

Angela Dwyer and Heather Panter

Introduction

During the publication of this book, the homicide case of Brianna Ghey was widely circulated across global headlines. Brianna, a 16-year-old, was found murdered in a park in Cheshire England with multiple stab wounds. Initially, her story was described as a "targeted attack" carried out by two 15-year-old fellow students by media outlets and the police. Once Brianna's transgender identity became known by news outlets, she was continually misgendered and deadnamed. While the police in the

A. Dwyer (✉)
School of Social Sciences, University of Tasmania, Glen Waverley, VIC, Australia
e-mail: angela.dwyer@utas.edu.au

H. Panter
School of Justice Studies, Liverpool Centre for Advanced Policing Studies, Liverpool John Moores University, Liverpool, UK
e-mail: h.a.panter@ljmu.ac.uk

H. Panter and A. Dwyer (eds.), *Transgender People and Criminal Justice*, Critical Criminological Perspectives, https://doi.org/10.1007/978-3-031-29893-6_1

ongoing homicide investigation have stated that the incident was not "hate-related", the way the case has been presented to the public has not quelled discontent held by transgender community members and transgender advocates regarding larger transphobic sentiments within the United Kingdom.

Just within the past few years, social hostility towards transgender people has grown in the United Kingdom, despite outward generic appearances of improvement in social acceptance. Advocates (as illustrated in the Brianna Ghey case) have stressed the overt transphobic social rhetoric that exists with the media, within the criminal processing systems, and within society in general. While Brianna's identity may or may not be relevant to the circumstances of her murder, the discussions around her case within criminal justice and the media/ public usage of her deadname identity are unethical and unwarranted. Unfortunately, Brianna's story is far too common across criminal processing systems.

Globally, we are seeing an increase in anti-transgender rhetoric and an increase in violence with 327 transgender people murdered due to their gender identity from October 2021 to September 2022 (ILGA-Europe, 2023). Notably, 36% of those murdered occurred in Europe alone (ILGA-Europe, 2023). When examining these homicides specifically, issues surrounding the intersectionality of misogyny, racism, and xenophobia cannot be disregarded. Further, transgender communities face unique barriers that should be explored independently, not just regarding victimhood, but also regarding other interactions through criminal processing systems hence the importance of this book.

Book Objectives

There are few people who have enough privilege to emerge unscathed from formal contact with criminal processing systems, even those who are victim/survivors. We have significant evidence demonstrating that these systems lead mostly to incarceration of vulnerable, disadvantaged people en masse and "have not resulted in significant reductions in crime rates, nor has it produced safety" (Mogul et al. 2011, p. xii). However, there is no clearer demonstration of harm being inflicted by criminal processing systems than examining the experiences of transgender people with these systems. People who identify as transgender experience some of the most dehumanising and discriminatory practices from workers and others within every part of criminal processing systems around the world (Mogul et al., 2011; Stanley & Smith, 2011).

In recent years, some deeply disturbing stories about the experiences of transgender people with police have drawn public attention, including those where police perpetrated sexual assault against the transgender person when processing them for custody (Bohm & Hodgson, 2022), and those where police were called to assist the person and the interaction ended with the person deceased (Powell, 2022). These experiences could only be eclipsed by their encounters in prison, where transgender people are routinely placed in prisons that do not match with their gender identity and subjected to multiple serious harms (like being denied access to basic healthcare requirements: see Bohm & Hodgson, 2022) that too often lead to their suicide (Gregoire, 2020). Although court experiences for transgender people are less extreme than what can occur with police and in prisons, they are no less discriminatory and stressful, with these experiences often replete with misgendering and deadnaming (Richardson, 2020).

These are just some of the reasons why it is imperative that we continue dialogue around the treatment of transgender people in criminal processing systems, and why we sought to compile this text. In a supposedly progressive contemporary moment, we have less visibility than ever about the number of transgender people being arrested, charged, and detained by police, being processed through the courts, and being subject to periods of detention—simply because governments do not appear to care enough to collect these statistics (Mogul et al., 2011). Legislation regulating and criminalising transgender people continues to exist, and it is even expanding. Being transgender and displaying gender identity in opposition to their assigned sex at birth is a capital offence in some countries. While these are the more extreme exceptions (thankfully), there is no doubt that transgender people continue to be subject to a vast array of legislative frameworks, even if those frameworks do not specifically target them as transgender people. Similarly, transgender young people are subject to ever-expanding sanctions for slight digressions from normative behaviours in schooling environments, something that is seeing a lot of transgender young people racking up long lists of offences before they have even completed their schooling. These sanctions are more often than not being applied at burgeoning levels to transgender adults and young people of colour.

These are the parameters that we explore in this text. There exist limited published works specifically examining the unique issues that transgender identities face globally in respect of different features of the criminal processing system. At the time of writing, researchers and practitioners faced a challenging task with attempting to find information and research about these issues and consolidate their knowledge and awareness of the key concerns. Often scholars must rely upon sparse publications across multiple journals (often blocked by paywalls) in each unique strand of the criminal processing system: law; policing; courts; and prisons. And often this research rarely, if ever, considers the contexts of community reintegration and rehabilitation in these discussions. As such, this collective multi-authored work, through each chapter, walks readers through unique issues in each strand of the criminal processing system through empirical and theoretical contributions. This collection of papers distinctively examines emergent issues related to transgender experiences with criminal processing systems.

The first few chapters of the text explore the experiences of transgender people that skirt around the edge of criminal processing systems. At first glance, discussions in these chapters appear somewhat disconnected from these systems, but authors show unequivocally how they manifestly funnel transgender people into these systems unnecessarily and consequently produce outcomes for them ranging from uncomfortable to catastrophic. The authors elaborate how broader understandings of transgender people as criminal or deviant can influence how the public think about, how politicians act with regard to, how legislation is conceptualised around, and how institutions work with transgender people. This includes how political rhetoric can lead to legislation expunging them from public spaces, how their bodies are criminalised in international law, and how transgender young people are funnelled into school-to-prison pipelines as young people. Importantly, horrific crimes against transgender people, be they adults (Brandon Teena) or young people (Larry King), are made possible by uninformed, conservative public social commentary about transgender people. These crimes stand as examples of the inherent, ever-present dangers transgender people face when they move about in public and institutional spaces, and their appearances and behaviours are seen as transgressing cisnormative social expectations, and how there is an urgent need to focus on the outcomes of systems and institutions even when they are tenuously linked with criminal processing systems.

The latter chapters in the text then move to examining the experiences of transgender people with explicit parts of criminal processing systems, including how they are policed in public spaces as product of colonisation, and how they are treated in courts, in prisons, and in death when their deaths are investigated by police as homicides. It is imperative that the focus of future work continues these discussions in every part of the world precisely because of the apparent lack of justice that we see emerging out of any part of formalised criminal processing systems. Cases like the New Jersey 7 demonstrate that, even when gender-non-conforming people defend themselves from hate violence, they can be charged with very serious offences—by the very system supposedly designed to protect victim/survivors like them. Even police treatment of transgender people after they have died warrants further research attention given that the misgendering of transgender murder victims has been found to contribute to longer times until the case is resolved, if they are resolved at all.

With these diverse foci, the text provides suitable discussions for academics, but also for criminal justice practitioners, and policymakers to provide insight on how to improve transgender experiences within the criminal processing system. This is also reflected in our authors in this text. While many of our authors are aligned with universities, they represent established transgender scholars, in addition to former criminal justice practitioners, people who work/volunteer as transgender equality rights activists and policy influencers, and people who conduct research for/with non-profit groups. Our discussions emerge out of specific areas around the globe, including the United States, Australia, and Europe, but issues examined touch on every part of the globe, including Asia, Africa, the Americas, and Oceania.

Despite this diversity, there is a set of overarching theoretical concepts, that the text is grounded in, and about which we have a shared understanding, particularly a critically queer criminological framework informed by a decolonising, Southern criminological focus. The following discussion therefore outlines the conceptual framework of the volume while introducing key definitional terms to readers, such as how we define "transgender". Following this, the introduction provides a brief overview of each chapter in the text. Finally, we conclude noting the future research foci for criminal processing systems around the world.

A Critical, Queer, Decolonising Conceptual Lens

The work in this volume aligns with critical criminologies because it has a keen interest in charting how these systems exacerbate unequal power dynamics, and crime is produced by structural inequalities (DeKeseredy, 2010). Ryan (2022, p. 7) summarises the perspective of critical criminologies about crime: "Most people in detention are there because they are poor, Black, female, queer, gender non-conforming, brown, mentally ill, chemically addicted, indigenous, abandoned by their families and the state, or some combination of the above". Critical criminologists challenge the basis of crime, and the criminal processing systems organised around the notion of punishment as an end in itself, with a focus instead on social justice and human rights. They argue that criminal processing systems create only harm—not justice or rehabilitation (Ryan, 2022). Although discussing cultural criminologies in this instance, Ferrell (1999) astutely summarises the perspective of critical criminologists who critique criminal processing systems. He notes that these systems are structured, and practitioners working within them interact with people, in ways where sometimes criminalisation "stands as an end in itself, successfully dehumanising or delegitimating those targeted, though no formal legal charges are brought against them" (Ferrell, 1999, p. 405). This is more than evident in police interactions with transgender people where their chief aim is to humiliate them in public spaces by pulling off their wigs (Dwyer, 2012). The work unfolding in this text is grounded in these conceptualisations of crime and criminal processing systems.

Queer criminologies align closely with critical criminological ways of thinking. Just like critical criminologists, queer criminologists have a focused interest on highlighting human rights and social justice. They suggest that the notion of justice is not evidenced in how criminal processing systems are structured and organised, and that we "need to interrogate the ways that gender, sexuality, race, and class collide with harsh penal policy and aggressive law enforcement" (Richie, 2005, p. 80). However, queer criminologists highlight a more specific focus than a broader agenda of human rights and social justice. They dedicate their work to a concerted focus on how heteronormative and cisnormative expectations of social behaviour shape outcomes for LGBTQ+ people. The especially crucial element of queer criminological thinking for this text is how researchers conceptualise gender as a key element of oppression, as a multidimensional concept with a scope extending beyond a simple binary system of gender (Kean, 2021). Gender can be heteronormative in how people expect and assume that a masculine man would be partnered with a feminine woman—and all other manifestations of gender are non-heteronormative and marginalised against this norm. Importantly, gender can also be cisnormative—that is, the assumption that the sex a person was assigned at birth (e.g. female) aligns with how that person displays their gender identity (e.g. femininity) in everyday life. Gender identity is a term that describes how a person experiences and feels their gender at a deep, personal, individual level, and sometimes this gender aligns with birth sex, and other times gender identity may not correspond with their physicality or their sex assigned at birth . When a person experiences their gender identity in a way that fails to correspond with their physicality, this can be interpreted by other people as a form of deviance. The reason for these types of thinking stem from the concept of cisnormativity, a concept developed to explain the expectation that people represent this alignment, with non-cisnormative people—non-binary, genderqueer, and transgender people—marginalised as abnormal. Queer criminologists argue that the power of heteronormative and cisnormative expectations that people are socialised into mean that

LGBTQ+ people are at higher risk of being incarcerated, and again these ideas are centralised in the work of authors in this text.

This critical, queer criminological focus is further informed by a decolonising, Southern criminological focus. The different conceptualisations that we currently work through to understand criminal processing systems, even those in critical and queer criminologies (Ball & Dwyer, 2017), are products of Global North theorists and researchers (Cunneen & Tauri, 2016). The Americas and Europe are largely where our ideas about crime come from, and queer political theorisation is no exception. Recognition of the especial vulnerabilities and disadvantages experienced by those living in colonised nations is rarely elaborated in criminological thinking (Agozino, 2003). Even our understandings of sex, sexuality, and gender are developed out of theorisations of mostly white, male scholars (Brown et al., 2010; Dworkin et al., 2016). For instance, emerging out of an intensive focus on political advocacy relating to LGBTIQ people's lives in Australia, scholars unfortunately can make assumptions around shared experiences across communities, which simultaneously marginalises and excludes the experiences of brotherboys and sistergirls (AHRC, 2011; Hill et al., 2021). The United States has one of the largest surveys in the world of transgender people, the US Transgender Survey (James et al., 2016), which is for the most part a survey conducted in online spaces. We are yet to see any survey of transgender people at the same level in many colonised nations, just as we are yet to see any survey of this level focused on the lives of Aboriginal and Torres Strait Islander sistergirls and brotherboys in Australia as colonised First Nations people in what most would recognise as a Global North country. It is therefore imperative that we provide a space for these conversations to happen, and for the experiences of transgender people from colonial contexts to be documented and understood.

With these important conceptualisations being centred in our work, we draw on particular understandings of essential terms used in this book to elaborate the issues. "Sex" is commonly conflated with "gender", and we recognise that "sex" is indeed a label assigned on a person at the time of birth by medical practitioners, so we have therefore suggested to our authors to employ wording that indicates they are talking about how these labels are "assigned at birth". This is to ensure that authors indicate clearly that they are not discussing gender and gender identity. The core term "transgender" is one of the most important terms for this text. A transgender person is someone whose gender identity does not align with their sex assigned at birth. However, our thinking around this term is much broader and more fluid than this singular word enables. Many experiences may be encapsulated in this term: non-binary, genderqueer, gender fluid, agender, bigender, transsexual, and gender non-conforming. Someone who identifies as non-binary may have completely different experiences to someone identifying as gender non-conforming. Our understanding of transgender, like that of Rodgers, Asquith, and Dwyer (2017, p. 2), also incorporates "non-Western formulations of non-cisgenders, such as Two-Spirit", in addition to people who identify as brotherboy and sistergirl. Importantly, we recognise that transgender experience is a personal process that is medicalised and pathologised by medical practitioners and institutions, with experiences often conceptualised in finite, essentialist ways based on physicality. We acknowledge this as a powerful form of stigmatisation and affirm that languages and identities used to identify as a transgender person are fluid and shifting.

Finally, we have encouraged our authors in this book to move away from using the term "criminal justice system". As critical, queer criminological scholars, invested in raising up the perspectives of those whose lives become even more deeply impoverished and vulnerable *because of* interactions with these systems, we argue strongly that there is no justice that can come out of these systems. Like Ryan (2022, p. 7) notes, justice and rehabilitation have very little to do with criminal processing systems because "[j]ustice deals with root causes: punishment and confinement do not" (Ryan, 2022, p. 7). It is our view that there is no semblance of justice in any form in the complex machinations of criminal processing systems: they only perpetrate and perpetuate harm against transgender and other vulnerable people.

Book Overview

The book begins with a discussion of the politico-legal regulation of transgender people in the contemporary moment. In this chapter explores this with reference to the treatment of transgender people within "LGBT free zones" in Poland from a social-legal justice perspective. This chapter, "Understanding Cultural Policing and Segregation of LGBTQ+ Communities in Poland", examines the political influences the right-wing conservative and populist PiS party has upon current political discourse in Poland and the policing of LGBTQ+ people. This chapter specifically examines legalised transphobic cultures and how these have triggered hetero-nationalist sentiments through cisnormativity. Chapter 2, "Exclusion and ignorance: international legal recognition and criminalisation responses to transgender communities in the context of political economy", examines definitions and enforcement of criminal laws which target transgender people specifically from across the world. This legal chapter examines discriminatory legal frameworks while contextualising criminalisation within wider social, economic, and political frameworks drawing out contrasts between law definition and the enforcement of said laws.

Moving on from legal and political regulation of transgender people, Chapters 3 and 4 explore the regulation of transgender lives by formalised, state-sanctioned institutions. Chapter 3 examines the regulation of transgender young people through the school-to-prison pipeline. "Transgender and gender non-conforming young people and the school to prison pipeline: too crucial to ignore" outlines forms of abuse and violence present in school spaces and suggests ways to stop transgender and gender non-conforming young folx from entering the school-to-prison pipeline. Drawing upon data from the United States, Australia, New Zealand, United Kingdom, and Brazil, this chapter also provides an overview of the detrimental effects of transphobic school bullying and describes how transgender and non-conforming young people become incarcerated. Shifting from regulation in school spaces, Chapter 4, "Policing Transgender "Policing Transgender People", examines key concerns impacting police interactions with adult transgender people, including issues such as being profiled as sex workers as an entry point to police experiences and the violence experienced from police. This includes examination of inappropriate searches, custody issues, and misgendering by police officers when they are being processed into the criminal processing system. Drawing upon case study examples, this chapter highlights how these experiences occur.

Chapters 5 and 6 shift to a focus on the regulation and treatment of transgender people in the contexts of police investigation and court processes. Chapter 5, "US Transgender Homicides (2013–2020): Characteristics of Homicide and Police Disclosure During Criminal Investigations", empirically examines 166 transgender homicides in the United States to elaborate themes present in homicide investigations and how victims are portrayed in reports by police investigators. Using content analysis of open-source media reports alongside official data sources (i.e. government reports, police reports, etc.), the vast majority of transgender homicide victims were described as "black" or "mixed" (78.31%), as a transgender woman (86.74%), and were more likely to die from gunshot wounds (63.25%). Homicide investigators misgendered/deadnamed them in the media 59.29% of the time (67 times out of 166 cases). Chapter 6, "Disorder in the court: transgender folx experiences of criminal legal practitioner failings", shifts to examining documented accounts of transgender folx in the courtroom and with legal practitioners. Drawing on the voices and narratives of transgender folx with courtroom, the chapter shows that transgender folx are repeatedly disrespected, deadnamed, and misgendered, with courtroom practitioners shown to be at the very least impolite, but also deliberately targeting folx because of their gender identity. These interactions can create complications for the person, as outing them in open court can result in later violence and, in some cases, the weaponisation of their gender identity altered case outcomes.

Chapter 7, ""Never let anyone say that a good fight for the fight for good wasn't a good fight indeed": The enactment of agency through military metaphor by one Australian incarcerated transgender woman", examines the story of Natasha Keating, a transgender woman who was incarcerated in two male carceral settings in Australia. Using 121 letters of complaint and self-advocacy authored by Natasha, the authors provide an in-depth analysis of the discursive strategies employed by Natasha to construct an affirming self-identity and effect social change within a carceral system designed to curtail self-determination. Through an empathetic and impassioned letter-writing approach leveraging military metaphors, the letters showcase the significant implications that Natasha's activism, self-agentism, and self-determination had in naming and seeking to dismantle the systems of oppression experienced by incarcerated transgender women.

Taken together, the chapters in this volume begin to unpack the very crucial importance of focusing explicitly on the experiences that transgender people have with criminal processing systems, and how they are funnelled into these systems through a range of different social institutions. They show the very deep, impactful harms that transgender people are experiencing as they move in and out of criminal processing systems as offenders, victims, witnesses, and family members. They highlight the urgent need to focus our energies on a range of reforms with the parts of criminal processing systems, in addition to a focus on decolonisation more broadly. They demonstrate how much more work is yet to be done if we are ever going to educate young people to a point where hate-filled violence against transgender people—anywhere—is the exception rather than the rule in the lives of transgender people around the world.

References

Agozino, B. (2003). *Counter colonial criminology: A critique of imperialist reason.* Pluto Press.

Australian Human Rights Commission. (2011). *Brotherboys, sistergirls and LGBT Aboriginal and Torres Strait Islander peoples.* https://humanrights.gov.au/our-work/lgbti/brotherboys-sistergirls-and-lgbt-aboriginal-and-torres-strait-islander-peoples

Ball, M., & Dwyer, A. (2017). Queer criminology and the global south: Setting queer and southern criminologies into dialogue. In K. Carrington, R. Hogg, J. Scott, & M. Sozzo (Eds.), *Handbook criminology and the global south* (pp. 121–138). Palgrave.

Bohm, A., & Hodgson, B. (2022). Three trans women stories illustrate a wider problem. *New York Civil Liberties Union.* Retrieved April

1, 2022, from https://www.nyclu.org/en/news/three-trans-womens-stories-illustrate-wider-problem

Brown, G., Browne, K., Elmhirst, R., & Hutta, S. (2010). Sexualities in/of the global south. *Geography Compass, 4*(10), 1567–1579.

Cunneen, C., & Tauri, J. (2016). *Indigenous criminology*. Policy Press.

DeKeseredy, W. (2010). *Contemporary critical criminology*. Routledge.

Dworkin, S. L., Lerum, K., & Zakaras, J. M. (2016). Sexuality in the global south: 50 years of published research in the Journal of Sex Research-inclusions, omissions, and future possibilities. *Journal of Sex Research, 53*(9), 1059–1064.

Dwyer, A. (2012). Policing visible sexual/gender diversity as a program of governance. *International Journal for crime, justice and social democracy, 1*(1), 14–26.

Ferrell, J. (1999). Cultural criminology. *Annual Review of Sociology, 25*, 395–418.

Gregoire, P. (2020, October 6). Veronica Baxter's death in custody: A trans woman neglected in a male prison. *Sydney Criminal Lawyers*. Retrieved April 1, 2022, from https://www.sydneycriminallawyers.com.au/blog/veronica-baxters-death-in-custody-a-trans-woman-neglected-in-a-male-prison/

Hill, B., Uink, B., Dodd, J., Bonson, D., Eades, A., & Bennett, S. (2021). *Breaking the silence: Insights into the lived experiences of WA Aboriginal/LGBTIQ+ people: Community summary report 2021*. Kurongkurl Katitjin, Edith Cowan University. Retrieved April 1, 2022, from https://www.ecu.edu.au/centres/kurongkurl-katitjin/research/current-projects-and-past-projects/breaking-the-silence

ILGA – Europe. (2023). Trans Murder Monitoring: October 2021–September 2022. ILGA-Europe.

James, S., Herman, J., Rankin, S., Keisling, M., Mottet, L., & Anafi, M. A. (2016). The report of the 2015 US transgender survey. National Center for Transgender Equality.

Kean, E. (2021). Advancing a critical trans framework for education. *Curriculum Inquiry, 51*(2), 261–286.

Powell, L. (2022, August 26). HRC mourns the passing of Maddie Hofmann, transgender woman killed by police in Malvern, PA. *Human Rights Campaign*. Retrieved April 1, 2022, from https://www.hrc.org/news/hrc-mourns-the-passing-of-maddie-hofmann-transgender-woman-killed-by-police-in-malvern-pa

Richardson, H. (2020, September 28). Police launch new online form to curb misgendering, discrimination of Queensland's LGBTI community. *ABC*

News. Retrieved April 1, 2022, from https://www.abc.net.au/news/2020-09-28/queensland-police-reporting-pronouns-transgender-trauma/12698442

Richie, B. E. (2005). Queering antiprison work: African American lesbians in the juvenile justice system. In J. Sudbury (Ed.), *Global Lockdown* (pp. 73–85). Routledge.

Stanley, Eric A., and Nat Smith, eds. 2011. Captive Genders: Trans Embodiment and the Prison Industrial Complex. AK.

2

Understanding Cultural Policing and Segregation of LGBTQ+ Communities in Poland

Sarah Sramota and Yarin Eski

Introduction

"LGBT rights are the canary in the coal mine", as a recent headline stated, which is an idiomatic reference to the fact that Dutch LGBTQ+ activists have been warning about Vladimir Putin's totalitarianism for eight years, now physically apparent in his war against Russia (Spauwen, 2022): "Minorities often see more clearly how power behaves than people who are comfortable in the mainstream" (Spauwen, 2022: id.—online source). Ukranian LGBTQ+ communities fear for their lives since Putin's invasion of their country (Greenhalgh, 2022). Weaponisation of such national(ist) hate against LGBTQ+ communities, including against transgender identities (Binnie, 2014; Konopka et al., 2020), is being used more frequently by regimes whose respect for human rights is doubtful, as seen in Kyrgyzstan and Belarus earlier in 2022 (Erkebaeva, 2022). The

S. Sramota · Y. Eski (✉)
Vrije Universiteit Amsterdam, Amsterdam, Netherlands
e-mail: y.eski@vu.nl

H. Panter and A. Dwyer (eds.), *Transgender People and Criminal Justice*, Critical Criminological Perspectives, https://doi.org/10.1007/978-3-031-29893-6_2

role of resistance against LGBTQ+ identities, as a symbol of Western-European values, in Russia's justification of the war on Ukraine is, too, striking and should not be neglected (De Hingh, 2022).

The lingering risk of such anti-LGBTQ+ sentiments and what it says about nearing totalitarianism seems to be on the rise not just outside of the European Union, but also inside. As of the wake of 2022, the attention given to the position of LGBTQ+ people in Hungary, Slovakia but also Poland is negligible (Bucholc, 2022; Wesolowsky, 2021), despite the fact that at the end of 2019, the European Parliament (EP) passed a resolution that condemns the practices of public discrimination against LGBTQ+ people in Poland by creating 'LGBT-free zones'. During her State of the Union speech in September 2020, Ursula von der Leyen labelled the 'LGBT-free zones' as 'humanity free zones' and said the European Commission (EC) would soon present a new strategy to strengthen LGBTQ+ rights. Consequently, the EC had denied funds to six Polish towns that have declared themselves to be free of LGBTQ+ ideology (Pronczuk, 2020). Nevertheless, during the summer of 2022, a rise of specifically transphobic political rhetoric has been observed, inciting fear among transgender communities about the role their identities will (continue to) play in the electoral competition (Ciobanu, 2022).

One of the authors of this chapter, Sarah Sramota, is a queer person of Jewish descent, who has grown up in the Netherlands, seldom having experienced any discrimination based on either of these identities. However, because of how LGBTQ+ communities in Poland are treated xenophobically, and in relating it to the horrible fates that Jewish and LGBTQ+ communities have faced throughout history, the discrimination is an undeniable and felt reality. Discussions with family about the discriminatory rhetoric Polish authorities would use against LGBTQ+ people made her father react with the following: "This is like Hitler's time". Her Czech father spent several months of his early childhood in the ghetto of Theresienstadt, which was established by the German SS nearby Prague during World War II. Feelings of being unwanted as a Jewish individual back then are the same ones LGBTQ+ communities currently feel in Poland, a country only two national borders away from the Netherlands.

Clearly, the authors are personally invested in problematising the treatment of LGBTQ+ communities within the LGBT-free zones in Poland. It would be pretentious to state that this chapter voicing those marginalised and often unheard communities in Poland contains value-neutrality. So, and resembling criminological studies of state-corporate crime (Tombs & Whyte, 2003), this chapter is "inseparable from partisanship" and it is about "being answerable to the 'other'" and the "being answerable to the relatively powerless" (Tombs & Whyte, 2003, p. 230). In this case, the powerless are the othered, marginalised and voiceless LGBTQ+ communities who have been subjected to apartheid and segregation policing practices. Our aim is to critically dissect the harms that LGBTQ+ communities do endure within the socio-legal realm of these policed zones. Our partisan, critical criminological contribution to this volume shall consist of, first, describing the specific context of 'LGBT-free zones' in Poland. Then, the specific Polish context in relation to the EU shall be discussed, in which the emergence of these 'free zones' is embedded as institutionalised and symbolic discrimination of LGBTQ+ communities. Afterwards, the Polish context will be placed in the wider socio-political context of the European Union (EU) and the rise of European populism. The discussion, finally, works towards a broader understanding of what we considered a policing of LGBTQ+ segregation *inside* but *without* the EU.

'LGBT-Free Zones': Scapegoating Sexual and Gender Minorities

The spring of 2019 can be marked as the dawn of a new wave of LGBTQ+ discrimination in Poland. After the liberal mayor of Warsaw had signed a progressive declaration in support of sexual minority rights, the conservative Polish government launched a hate campaign against the spread of the 'LGBT ideology', leading to the emergence of dozens of local and regional so-called LGBT-free zones across the country (Bea, 2020), and being also fuelled by already lingering but existing transphobia (Konopka et al., 2020). How these zones fit within the Polish history of political homophobia (O'Dwyer & Vermeersch, 2016) and populism (Wodak, 2015), what the politically exploited concept of 'LGBT ideology' is and how these elements have led to legal declarations of 'zones free of LGBT ideology', will be explored in the following, including what the legal and societal implications of such 'LGBT-free zones' are.

In the spring of 2019, in the wake of an election-filled year—with European elections taking place in May and the parliamentary elections in October—Polish political parties were setting up their campaigns (Markowski, 2020). The *2019 Warsaw Declaration of the Community of Democracies* served for the populist right-wing and national-conservative PiS-party as an excellent opportunity to strategically prioritise a sensitive topic on the political agenda during this very crucial period: the LGBTQ+ communities in Poland.

The political party PiS (Prawo i Sprawiedliwość; *Law and Order*) is a right-wing populist and national-conservative party. It is Poland's biggest political party, winning consecutively the 2015 and 2019 parliamentary elections, and, as part of the United Right coalition, obtaining an absolute majority of the votes (Markowski, 2020). Furthermore, PiS, which has been established in 2001 by the brothers Kaczyński, has delivered the country's president in 2005 (Lech Kaczyński), 2015 and 2020 (Andrzej Duda). Hence, the party's political and societal impact in Poland is undeniable.

The PiS-party's prioritising was considered an "attack on LGBT [that] was triggered by the Declaration, but that was just a welcome excuse", Polish scholar Agnieszka Graff said in an interview with investigative news platform Balkan Insight (Ciobanu, 2019b). It was a very strategic move leading up to the parliamentary elections in October 2019, when the PiS-party mobilised their conservative constituency against LGBTQ+ communities. This was not the first time that the PiS-party secured their win through politics of fear; during the previous parliamentary elections of 2014, amidst the European refugee crisis, the party had done exactly the same by running a political hate campaign against refugees. However, Graff said "that topic is now dead, so they are onto another scapegoat" (Ciobanu, 2019b).

Engaging in politics of fear is an established electoral strategy of (old and new) populist political parties across and outside the EU (Wodak,

2015). These parties simplify complex issues and look for a culprit to blame for the concerns (Pelinka, 2013). This enables these parties to create easy-to-grasp election topic and revolve their entire political campaign around fearmongering against one scapegoat of choice (Vieten & Poynting, 2016). In uniting their voters against a common threat—usually a scapegoat—they shape a collective identity (Wodak, 2015; Marchlewska et al., 2018). Populist politicians, in that sense, have become identity entrepreneurs that assure their leadership and authority by removing the power of marginalised social groups away from them and relocating it into their own hands (Reicher & Haslam, 2016; Shayegh et al., 2021). In the discourse of the 2019 campaign against LGBT communities, it becomes apparent that we see the protection of religious values and nationalist politics emerging and causing friction with ideals embodied in 'liberalisation' and 'modernisation' that is feared by the conservative PiS-party (cf. Reicher & Haslam, 2016; see also Graff, 2006, 2010). LGBTQ+ communities are, in the eyes of Polish right-wing, nationalist-populist political movements, what Bauman (2000)—himself a Polish national—and Lash (2003) would have considered the blurring and weakening of strong institutions, such as religious communities and traditional families. Contrary to the sociological observations that describe the change from modern to late modern societies, the ruling PiS-party experiences LGBTQ+ identities as an example of losing grip on the facets that have historically constituted the sense of a national collective identity in Poland (for a similar argument Graff, 2006, 2010). Therefore, in the political discourse, the PiS-party frames itself both as a victim and as a defender (Hadjari, 2019): they are according to themselves, and by extension the Poles, victims of a foreign liberal threat, which they define as 'the LGBT ideology'.

'LGBT Ideology' and Polish National Identity

According to the PiS-party, the 'LGBT ideology' seeks to disrupt the foundations of Polish national unity, and they are the strong defenders of the national identity against it (Ciobanu, 2019b). In a country that is socio-culturally ridden with homophobic and transphobic tendencies

(Bucholc, 2022; Konopka et al., 2020), it proved to be a fruitful electoral strategy, as the ruling PiS-party received almost 45% of the popular vote (Ciobanu, 2019b). It also showed the victims of the fear of cultural modernisation: LGBTQ+ communities themselves.

In political rhetoric of the 2019 LGBTQ+ hate campaign, sexual and gender minorities are arguably not referred to as a group of people, but as an ideology: the 'LGBT ideology'. This LGBT ideology is politically framed as being a foreign, liberal threat to traditional Christian family values and to marriage as a union between a man and a woman, which is codified in Article 18 of the Polish Constitution. During his re-election campaign in the summer of 2020, ruling President Andrzej Duda (PiS) said this 'ideology' was more destructive than communism (BBC News, 2020).

There is a difference between homosexuality and the LGBT ideology. Activists who promote the LGBT ideology attack the national institutions of family and marriage and try to destroy the bonds between parents and their children. This happens in school, for example. They wait till the teacher walks out and teach children about sexualization and techniques of masturbation; parents are confused. The local treaties [see below] are here to defend the municipality and protect the Constitution; they do not support any legal acts against LGBT people. Nikodem Bernaciak, press speaker for Ordo Iuris (personal communication, December 2019).[1]

The quote highlights that the use of the impersonal term 'LGBT ideology' is a political move, but it also dehumanises members of LGBT communities (Panter, 2021), while it also tests the boundaries of the law and may justify violation of human rights, simply by claiming that 'it is not about people'. However, at the EU level and regarding the LGBTQ+ 'free zones' and 'ideology', Ursula von der Leyen said during her first State of the Union speech in September 2020: "Being yourself is not your ideology. It's your identity" (Von der Leyen, 2020). It was a direct

[1] Above quote was retrieved from an interview for a Dutch news medium in December 2019 with Nikodem Bernaciak of Ordo Iuris, which is a big conservative, anti-choice private lobby organisation, that seeks to 'protect the Polish Constitution' and influence European and national policy through legal expertise.

EU critique on the nationalist Polish PiS-party, re-emphasising the 'free zones' are targeting actual people, not an idea or ideology.

Poland Inside and Against the EU? A Historical Overview

More than citizens from any other country in Eastern Europe, Poles do not have a clear collective national history (Borowik, 2017; Hadjari, 2019; Hall, 2015; Keinz, 2011; Zielińska, 2015). Since the seventeenth century, the borders of what we now call 'Poland' have changed so many times, and that it is almost impossible to define a single territory that can be seen as traditionally/historically 'Polish'. Attacks from and occupations by neighbouring countries left the population with "an understandable feeling of historical injustice" (Hadjari, 2019). The only factor historically uniting the inhabitants of current Polish territory is their belief in the Catholic Church. Now, religion is the key component of the Polish national identity, with approximately 95% of the population identifying themselves as Roman Catholic believers (Zielińska, 2015). In other words: in Poland religion and nationality are inextricably interlinked (Hall, 2015).

During the communist rule of Poland between 1944 and 1989, the regime had put efforts into 'privatising' the Church. By moving religious practices to the private sphere, the regime strived to minimise the role of religion in people's live and consequently achieve atheisation of society (Borowik, 2017). However, the impact was the opposite: "Communist efforts strengthened the linkage between Catholicism and the national identity of Poles" (Borowik, 2017, p. 315). After the fall of Eastern-European socialist regimes in 1989, the Catholic Church took one of the leading roles in reshaping civil society, facilitating collective resistance against the foreign socialist rule (Hall, 2015; Keinz, 2011). Note that during communist rule, some traditional Christian norms had been overthrown by the regime: abortion had been decriminalised and traditional gender roles were challenged by communist notions of radical equality (Keinz, 2011).

After the fall of communism in the 1990s, abortion was illegalised again under influence of the Church (Ramet, 2006). Since 1997, the 'natural institutions' of marriage—a union between man and women—and family were protected in Article 18 of the Polish Constitution. During that period, opposition to sexual minorities was not a politically salient issue (Tarta, 2015). This changed at the beginning of this millennium, however, when Poland became a member of the European Union. Note that LGBTQ+ rights were not a substantial part during the 2004 enlargement negotiations (Slootmaeckers & Touquet, 2016), but the political backlash around LGBTQ+ rights during that period was striking (see Graff, 2006, 2010). The public discourse did not revolve around specific EU efforts to persuade Poland to adopt certain progressive policies (O'Dwyer, 2012). The link between homosexuality and Europe in the political rhetoric had rather symbolic origins. In 2004, the former Polish President Lech Kaczyński, who was at that time the mayor of Warsaw, banned an Equality March in his city—which then took place anyway—and condemned earlier marches in other towns. He then bombarded the LGBTQ+ issue to a key theme in his presidential campaign of 2005 and used it to highlight Polish sovereignty and independence from the European Union. Polish conservative, religious nationalism was juxtaposed against progressive European values, symbolised by the normalisation of reprehensible practices such as homosexuality (Graff, 2006). Similar dynamics occurred during the parliamentary election campaign of the PiS-party in 2019 and the presidential elections in 2020.

The Polish relationship with the European Union is not only one of tension. After all, Poland is a member of the EU, enjoying full membership rights and benefitting from a great amount of funds including cohesion—and agricultural funds. Out of the entire EU, Poland financially benefits the most from their EU membership, absolutely as well as compared to their expenditures (European Commission, Directorate General 'Budget', 2020). Furthermore, roughly two million Polish workers benefit from the open European labour market (Statistics Poland, 2013). This leads us to believe that there must be certain benefits for the European Union and its member states to invest in the development of the Polish economy, and that the Polish government must see benefits of EU membership as well, despite ongoing issues over human rights.

Between 2007 and 2014, Poland was ruled by two liberal coalitions led by the Civic Platform (currently the biggest opposition party against PiS), with the liberal, Europe-oriented politician Donald Tusk as Prime Minister (who was the President of the European Council between 2014 and 2019). Parallel to that, during the second half of the 2000s, the hostile climate for LGBTQ+ communities began to stabilise. The LGBTQ+ movement became more powerful and the political discourse less homophobic (O'Dwyer, 2012). Despite the electoral wins of the right-wing conservative PiS-party in 2015 and 2019, and the remaining influence of the Catholic Church in civil society, Polish society is slowly but steadily liberalising and modernising, especially in metropolitan areas. A vast majority of the population still identifies as Catholic, but there is a secularisation trend when it comes to the role of religious values and practices in daily life (Marody & Mandes, 2017). And though they are still well below EU average, people's attitudes regarding 'traditional' topics are changing. In 2015, only 32% of Polish citizens believed LGBTQ+ people should have the same rights as cishet people, but only four years later, it was 49% (European Commission, 2019). With regard to transgender people and their rights, attitudes of Polish citizens are often somewhat more positive and supportive than negative (Brown et al., 2020). Paradoxically, it is exactly this climate that has facilitated the most recent wave of political homophobia and the emergence of local LGBT-free zones in (most) conservative parts of Poland.

Though it seems evident that this attack on LBGT communities in 2019 has developed from the ongoing value conflict between Poland and the EU, it is believed that there are other political more motives at stake. Political homophobia is seldom self-contained, meaning that it may be strategically used to distract from bigger political issues (Panter, 2021). Aside from the value crisis the country is experiencing, Poland is also facing a crisis of the judicial system. Since the PiS-party gained power in 2015, it has put effort into establishing political control over the members of the country's Constitutional Court (e.g. by lowering the judges' retirement age) so the party could fill the empty seats with loyalists (Pech & Keleman, 2020). This has led to ongoing pressures from the

European Judicial Court (EDJ) and other EU institutions, widespread protests and even the start of an Article 7 procedure, because of the violation of the rule of law (which has been on hold since 2018). On the one hand, it might seem contra-intuitive that a government with a record in violating the rule of law would proceed onto publicly violating human rights as well. On the other hand, however, the striking anti-LGBT hate campaign and the international attention it has yielded might have been used as a tool to disguise that the Polish *trias politica* is collapsing.

Legal Declarations, Policing LGBTQ+ and Societal Harms

Since August 2019 during the Polish parliamentary elections, an estimated hundred local and regional authorities (mostly in the highly religious South-East of Poland) have adopted several legal declarations to 'stop the spread of the LGBT ideology' and 'protect the Polish Constitution'. These included types of declarations in various regions, with adopted documents specifically mentioning the harmful impact of the spread of the 'LGBT ideology' (Janiszewski, 2021). Technically, these declarations entail the exact opposite of the progressive declaration in Warsaw of 2019: (1) to prevent any legislation being made that could protect and/or support rights of LGBTQ+ communities and (2) to ban sex education in school to protect children from being exposed to the "harmful" LGBT ideology.

The other text, referred to as the 'family charter' (Ordo, 2020), does not mention 'LGBT ideology', yet encourages local government to promote traditional family values, based on a template initiated by the Ordo Iuris lobby. Ordo Iuris is an ultra-conservative, Catholic organisation and think tank aiming to protect Polish traditional (family) values, using their legal expertise and a law-oriented approach (Ciobanu, 2021). Ordo Iuris claims that their…

Charter of the Rights of the Family has been elaborated by Ordo Iuris experts in cooperation with over 20 Polish social organisations. It is a declaration that aims to promote the constitutional principles of protection of the family, marriage, parenthood and motherhood (Article 18 of the Constitution), protection of family life (Article 47) and protection of children against demoralisation (Article 72) (Ordo, 2020: online source).

Local and regional authorities that have adopted such declarations have gained the label 'LGBT-free zones' or 'zones free of LGBT ideology', in reference to stickers that were distributed by the populist conservative newspaper Gazeta Polska during the summer of 2019 to mark certain neighbourhoods in Polish cities as "dangerous" (Janiszewski, 2021). Note that these 'LGBT-free zones' do not mean that people identifying as LGBTQ+ are not allowed to enter these regions or municipalities. However, it is a powerful symbolic term, one that has also been used for the good by (international) media, politicians and activists, to create visibility and raise awareness of the hostile and unsafe climate for LGBTQ+ people, and their vulnerable position for the law.

The policing implications of the introduction of 'LGBT-free zones' in a multitude of Polish regions vary significantly and has become problematic during protests against them (Ciobanu, 2020a). During one of these protests, 10 August 2020, mass arrests took place in Warsaw, followed by several violent actions by police. Police violence against LGBTQ+ activists is referred to as the "Polish Stonewall", resembling the violent attacks against the Bialystok equality parade of 2019 (Ciobanu, 2019a). One of the victims of the protest policing actions stated:

> The government has chosen us as a target and it is using a big machine, including public institutions and the media, to attack us. (Ciobanu, 2019a: online source)

Another LGBTQ+ activist protestor, one who created an "Atlas of Hate" map (Gawron, 2022)[2] that exposed 'LGBT-free zones' in Poland (almost a third of the country), stated that the policing "system responding to civil disobedience [is] abusing the penal and petty offences codes" (Gawron, 2022). In fact, the map-making LGBTQ+ activists risked being brought in front of a court, as in Spring 2020, multiple Polish municipalities announced their plans to sue the activists who created the map for defamation (Ciobanu, 2020b).

---

[2] Please consider: https://atlasnienawisci.pl.

Several sources indicate (Janiszewski, 2021; Sramota, 2019; Winiewski et al., 2021) that as of the start of the most recent hate campaign in 2019, the living conditions of non-cishet people in Poland have worsened. A recurring national survey on the social situation of LGBTQ+ people in Poland indicates that their mental health has declined compared to previous years, especially in regions that have been declared 'free of LGBT ideology' (Winiewski et al., 2021). The increase in experiences of discrimination, violence and rejection breaches the positive ongoing trend from the past years, reflecting the impact of the latest hate campaign and establishment of 'LGBT-free zones' (Winiewski et al., 2021). Other evidence for a rise in aggression against LGBTQ+ people is mainly anecdotal, and it remains difficult to infer causality between the adoption of the declarations and increasing violence against LGBTQ+ people (Janiszewski, 2021).

Nevertheless, the hostile environment Polish LGBTQ+ people must navigate deserves—and—has been given - attention. In the wake of 2021, the organisation Kampania Przeciw Homofobii (KPH; Campaign Against Homophobia) launched a campaign called #InfringementNOW to instigate the start of an infringement procedure by the European Union, to formally confirm the breach of human rights by Polish authorities. The aim of the campaign was to bombard responsible EU commissioners with Tweets containing stories of Polish LGBTQ+ people and their personal experiences with homophobia, discrimination, violence and rejection. They describe the dehumanising effects of the use of 'LGBT ideology' rhetoric and the hostile environments that force LGBTQ+ people to live in fear of being attacked or prosecuted.

Sramota (2019), of the authors, has gained access to several Polish people who identify as LGBTQ+ through her journalistic internship. Their stories share a similar pattern of fear, dehumanisation and experiences with violence and discrimination. For example, a twenty-five-year-old bisexual woman described how she does not identify with a so-called ideology and argued that the term is used to justify discriminatory practices. A nineteen-year-old gay man described that he has been verbally and physically abused in his small hometown and feels much safer in the city of Lublin. He feels that the declarations confirm a broader societal sentiment and invite others to use violence against LGBTQ+ people.

Such abuse is (and related traumatic feelings are) amplified into severe secondary victimisation in instances political leadership keeps on stigmatising, as happened when the conservative PiS-party leader Jaroslav Kaczyński publicly "reject[ed] West views on transgender issues" during the recent Warsaw and Kyiv Pride march of 25 June, 2022, claiming "we want to maintain normality" (AP News, 2022: online source). The severity of such public rejection of LGBTQ+ lives and identities through legal declarations, 'free zones' and conservative political rhetoric even has had fatal consequences. Young trans-activist Milo Mazurkiewicz took their life on 6 May 2019, after having posted on Facebook a few days before the following:

> I'm fed up being treated like a piece of shit. [...] fed up with people (psychologists, doctors, therapists) telling me I can't be who I am because I don't look like that. [...] Treating me as if it was all in my head and telling me I need papers proving it. [...] Telling me that it's good that my chosen name is neutral-sounding, that it's good my body is not extremely feminine, that's it's good I haven't come out at work (yet). Telling me that maybe I should stop being (trying to be) myself and wait until other doctors and therapists decide I can. I'm fed up of all of that. Sometimes it makes me fight even more, sometimes it makes me want to end it all and stop my life right here. Sometimes it's just makes me want to cry (ONeil, 2019: online source).

Strikingly, the suicide of Mazurkiewicz has occurred alongside the positive experiences of medical tourists from all over Europe frequenting Poland to avoid waiting lists and undergo relatively cheap gender affirmation surgery in specialised private clinics (Graham, 2022; Roberts, 2022; Ryan, 2021). Yet, while this medical infrastructure exists, Polish transgender people, due to financial reasons, must rely on the national healthcare system, where they lack protection from discrimination by medical staff (Mazurczak et al., 2019). Furthermore, they face various financial, legal and administrative burdens (Ciobanu, 2022). For example, Ciobanu (2022) highlights how a Polish transgender woman, albeit medically advanced in her gender affirmation process, will probably never be recognised as a woman by the law, as that requires a civil law procedure where she sues her parents, as well as a divorce from her wife (as same-sex marriage is not recognised) (see also Mazurczak et al., 2019).

Besides abovementioned challenges, the establishment of Polish 'LGBT-free zones' and the associated discourse can be perceived as a symbolic reflection of a societal tension between progressive liberalism and conservative nationalism, that causes real societal harms and even death. The resolutions do not criminalise any form of (sexual) activities or gender expression, nor do they explicitly justify or encourage offences *against* LGBTQ+ people. However, while assessing the effects and implications of LGBTQ+ zones, a focus on legal harms does not suffice. People with a minority status may experience so-called anticipatory stressors due to their stigmatised identity, reflected in a person's persistent state of vigilance in the expectation of a potential threat (Toman, 2019). The personal stories of Polish LGBTQ+ people may indicate that the hateful and dehumanising rhetoric associated with (living in) 'LGBT-free zones', as well as acts of violence they have experienced, invokes feelings of continuous fear and hypervigilance, with all its consequences for the quality of life and mental health of Polish LGBTQ+ people.

Implications of a Value Conflict

Several European institutions have condemned the existence of 'LGBT-free zones', labelling them as discriminatory and in breach with human rights and European values. During her State of the Union speech in September 2020, Ursula von der Leyen labelled the 'LGBT-free zones' as 'humanity free zones' and said the EC would soon present a new strategy to strengthen LGBTQ+ rights. Several months later, the European Parliament would vote over a symbolic resolution, declaring the entire EU an "LGBTIQ freedom zone" (European Parliament, 2021). In September 2021, the EU had launched an infringement procedure against Poland over the issue of 'LGBT-free zones'. Hungary awaits the same fate because of their 'anti-LGBT law' (European Commission, 2021b).

The foremost sanctions that Polish regions, counties and municipalities may currently face are financial by nature. During the summer of 2020, the EC had denied funds to six Polish towns that have declared themselves to be "free from LGBT ideology" (Pronczuk, 2020). Further EU warnings to continue denying up to 126 million euros of funds to local governments urged Polish regional authorities to action. The majority of 'LGBT-free' regions have formally rejected the declarations used to proclaim 'LGBT-free zones' (BBC News, 2021; see also The Atlas of Hate). Some local governments have gone as far as labelling themselves regions of 'established tolerance' (e.g. the Subcarpathian Voivodeship, see The Atlas of Hate), or adjusting the content of the resolutions to meet the requirements of the EU to continue negotiations with regard to funding (Maciuszczak, 2021). However, considering the symbolic nature of the original document and the harm that has already been caused, the practical implications for the well-being of LGBTQ+ people are doubtful. These doubts are furthermore underpinned by recent statements by PiS-party leader Jaroslav Kaczynski targeting and ridiculing gender minorities (Ciobanu, 2022). It is speculated that "[he] is testing the demonising of transgender people in Poland as a way to rally support ahead of next year's election" (Ciobanu, 2022, online source).

(Western) EU Politics Versus Eastern-European Populism?

Since the establishment of the European Coal and Steel Community (ECSC) in 1951 as a union with a solely economic purpose, a lot has changed: "The EU identifies and presents itself as an organisation focused on 'fundamental values' and as a defender and guardian of fundamental rights" (Slootmaeckers & Touquet, 2016, p. 19). Since the 1990s onwards, the promotion of fundamental (human) rights has become an increasingly important focus of European foreign politics and enlargement policy (Slootmaeckers & Touquet, 2016). According to the Copenhagen Criteria of 1993, a country is eligible for EU membership when it has a functioning market economy and stable institutions to guarantee the commitment to the values of human dignity, freedom, democracy, equality and rule of law. It must accept a set of human rights, as protected since 1951 by the EU Charter of Fundamental Rights.

Despite their marginal role in formal EU politics, the fundamental rights of LGBTQ+ people have gained a powerful symbolic position in what it means to be 'European' (Ayoub & Paternotte, 2014a). Europe has provided national LGBTQ+ movements with opportunities for transnational organisation and granted them normative tools to claim agency and exercise their rights (Ayoub & Paternotte, 2014b; Rupp, 2014). From a more top-down perspective, and through the adaptation of declarations, directives and guidelines, they have become a salient matter in EU-expansion negotiations (Slootmaeckers & Touquet, 2016). Since 2000, sexual orientation is specifically mentioned in the EU Charter of Fundamental rights, and since 2009, this Charter is legally binding. In 2013, the Union has adopted the 'fundamentals first' approach to EU-expansion, stressing the importance of stable institutions and commitment to European rights and values as membership requirements. Now, the Polish stance towards LGBTQ+ rights could be considered a litmus test for evidencing to have a general level of modernisation and commitment to human rights c.q. European values (Graff, 2010).

What have the EU's efforts to protect sexual and gender minorities in new member states yielded? Slootmaeckers and Touquet (2016) concluded that the more prominent LGBTQ+ rights issues became with each expansion, the bigger the impact was on the new member state. Some scholars have rightly questioned the effectiveness of EU's 'social learning' strategy on policy changes in the new member states (O'Dwyer, 2010; Godzisz, 2019). Rather than leading to progressive legal reforms, the attention drawn to LGBTQ+ rights caused political backlash on a national level and re-emphasised a fault line that divides 'civilised' and 'modern' Western Europe from 'traditionalist' and 'conservative' countries of the former East-Block (Tarta, 2015). These latter countries are "offered redemption and help in their attempts to Europeanize" (Slootmaeckers et al., 2016, p. 6). In turn, Eastern-European nationalist and populist politicians use the LGBTQ+ issue to operationalise, even weaponise this schism between East and West Europe (Mole, 2011). Through it, they re-invent their national identity and sovereignty through 'political homophobia' (Mole, 2016; also see Graff, 2006, 2010). Paradoxically, it seems that the EU's value-based expansion strategy has not led to the expansion of liberal thinking as well, but rather to its corrosion, as politically initiated homo- and transphobic practices in the EU are presented as liberal resistance.

Compared to Western-European countries, there are indications made claiming that the states of the former East-Block score low on the acceptance of LGBTQ+ communities (European Commission, 2019). Several reasons have been pointed out for this. A first reason would be that the processes of liberalisation and modernisation that characterised Western-European societies in second half of the twentieth century has had a slow(er) start in developing democracies in Eastern Europe (Kaldor & Vejvoda, 1997). Countries under communist rule until 1989 only have been established democracies for thirty years, compared to countries of the West, that have a democratic tradition of at least 75 years. It has been explained, however, that efforts of the EU to promote and protect rights of sexual and gender minorities through the enlargement process to the East have not yielded the desired results and might have even contributed to temporarily a more hostile climate for LGBTQ+ communities (Tarta, 2015).

Yet to understand where the moral backlog of some countries of the former East-Block originates from, the role of a crucial stakeholder must be considered: the Roman Catholic Church (see Casanova, 1994; Dericquebourg, 2015; Graff, 2010; Mole, 2016; Sremac & Ganzevoort, 2015; Tarta, 2015; Zaccaria, 2015; Zielińska, 2015). The relationship between the Catholic religion and human rights is a complex one. Social and economic (human) rights, firmly grounded in values of human dignity and solidarity, have religious origins and are therefore openly supported by Churches across Europe (Dericquebourg, 2015; Zaccaria, 2015). However, tensions as reflected in emerging 'culture wars' (Tarta, 2015) between religious and modern values of 'third generation human rights' that originate from liberal, secular ideas of the Enlightenment—these include values of (individual) freedom and equality, and include women's rights, reproductive rights or LGBTQ+ rights. The promotion and protection of these rights, as it ought to be in liberal democracies, seem to be incompatible with some Catholic beliefs and traditions (Zielińska, 2015).

Through clashes of values in countries across Europe with a strong religious tradition, the Catholic Church is (re)claiming its spot in civil society and politics (see Casanova, 1994; for Polish context, see Żuk & Żuk, 2019). In Ireland, for example, conflicts around abortion law have led all the way to the European Court of Human Rights (Erdman, 2014), and in 2016, Italy was the only country in Western Europe that did not recognise civil partnerships between people of the same sex (Zaccaria, 2015). National populist sentiments there are in tandem with a strong religious identity. However, it is in several countries in Eastern Europe, especially Hungary, Romania, Croatia or Poland, where the Catholic religion is an important component of the national identity (Sremac & Ganzevoort, 2015; Żuk & Żuk, 2019). Unlike most Western-European countries, Eastern-European countries usually did not emerge from ethnically homogenous states and therefore historically lack the sense of a national identity (Mole, 2016). Having the same religion compensates for this (Tarta, 2015). Thus, promoting religious values and opposing 'morally reprehensible' modern values, as the protection of LGBTQ+ rights is, are perceived as an act to protect sovereignty and national identity of the state (Graff, 2010). With this, political LGBTQ+ phobia is "…more about cultural identity and national pride than about sexual orientation or public morality" (Graff, 2010, p. 584).

When LGBTQ+ rights issues become politically salient (e.g. during the EU enlargement negations), heteronationalist rhetoric starts to dominate the political discourse (see Graff, 2006). Heteronationalism—or, more broadly, sexual nationalism (see Sremac & Ganzevoort, 2015)—comprises how heteronormativity intertwines with the national identity of a state (Hague, 1997, cited in Panter, 2021). This means, despite the common belief that the modernisation of Europe goes hand in hand with secularisation, the Catholic Church still successfully claims their place in civil society and politics (Casanova, 1994) by shaping a frictional relationship between individual nation states and the EU and its human rights (politics). It is particularly countries of the former East-Block with strong Catholic traditions and cultures that have joined the EU as a 'value union' where frictions and conflict result from confrontations between religious nationalism and LGBTQ+ rights.

Although discrimination and harassment of LGBTQ+ communities remain a daily reality throughout the EU, it is in several specific Eastern-European countries, where populist state politics (indirectly) facilitate, support and promote discriminatory practices against LGBTQ+ people: banning pride marches, condemning cultural practices or obstructing proposed anti-discrimination laws are but a few examples (United Nations Human Rights, 2013). Particularly problematic is the trend in a variety of former East-Bloc countries to actively ban same-sex marriage, as opposed to its formal recognition in 'Western' countries (Mos, 2020). In 2014, the Slovak parliament conveniently reached a two-third majority necessary to pass a constitutional amendment that would confirm marriage as an exclusive union between exclusively men and women (Zeldin, 2014). Fitting the notion of anti-liberal and populist resistance, this ban is framed as a precautionary measure, "...meant to protect the Slovak nation against imminent pressure from abroad, in particular from the European Union" (Mos, 2020, p. 397). Bans like these cannot be understood without considering the international context and motives, next to domestic demands and attitudes (Mos, 2020). In fact, directly preceded by Croatia (2013), and followed by Armenia (2015) and Georgia (2018), the Slovak constitutional ban on same-sex marriage and adoption is not self-contained but fits a wider phenomenon. Note, however, that this amendment has not received popular support in the 2015 referendum that was designed to strengthen it due to insufficient turnout (Rousek, 2015).

Among the most prominent examples of rising Eastern-European populism is Hungary where recently two controversial laws have been passed. As of May 2020, amendments to existing birth, death and marriage laws prevent the legal registration of sex change, banning the formal recognition of transgender and intersex people (Knight & Gall, 2020). Furthermore, international controversy arose when MPs of Hungarian President Orban's party Fidesz proposed amendments to a seemingly innocent Anti-Paedophilia Act. It turned out the legal proposal was passed containing a ban on the portrayal or 'promotion' of homosexuality and gender reassignment to minors and 'tightening up regulation' regarding sexual education in schools (Rankin, 2021). Resembling the Polish case, Fidesz officials frame these regulations as measures to protect Hungarian children from harmful, pedophilic practices (Rankin, 2021); they instead facilitate toxic tabooisation, stigmatisation and discrimination against non-cishet identities.

In sum, the Polish xenophobic cultural policing of its LGBTQ+ citizens is part of the rising Eastern-European nationalist populism clashing with EU's acknowledgement and protection of LGBTQ+ communities and their rights. What Bucholc (2022) has considered as "the symbolic dimension of the Polish anti-LGBTQ+ campaign" (Bucholc, 2022, p. 14), countries' cultural policing (cf. Comarrof & Comarrof, 2004) and wider Eastern-European policing and its politicisation of LGBTQ+ identities, reflect a conflict between the national identity and a transnational enemy (Hanley, 2017). How othering politics by such Eastern-European nationalist populism is met with counter-othering by the EU shall now be discussed.

The EU Politics of Policing LGBTQ+ in Poland: Discussion and Conclusion

This chapter has shed light on the policing of LGBTQ+ communities out of "free zones" in Poland, and how such xenophobic policing relates to the broader socio-political discourse between specifically Poland and the EU, and wider, between Eastern and Western Europe. For the Polish government, the turn to excluding LGBTQ+ communities is a consequence of how LBGTQ+ people are considered. They are a minority group of others (Said, 1977), often considered strangers that must be excluded from society, as everyone is afraid and nobody seems to know how to prevent their, considered, unpredictable behaviour; they are dangerous and risky others (Hudson, 2009: 19).

In this case, LGBTQ+ community members in Poland threaten the heteronormative and nationalist ideas about gender and sex. Although treated as strangers, as outsiders, as if they are external, risky others, Polish LGBTQ+ communities remain internally present in Poland, and they are thus a "danger" from within. Often, we understand colonisation as dominating an external, foreign group and in a faraway land; something that happened ages ago (Zimmerman, 2013).

However, LGBTQ+ communities and their treatment as a "policeable" domestic threat against Polish family values as codified in laws rather reflect a fearful othering that is enabling and enabled by *native* colonialism happening *today* in Poland. By restricting them from areas, much like how the previous apartheid regime in South-Africa echoes through in gated communities (Ramoroka & Tsheola, 2014), they are contemporarily colonised *inside* national borders (cf. Etkind, 2013; Gregory, 2004; Wolpe, 1975), in this case of Poland. The segregation of LGBTQ+ communities that effectively produces such internal, contemporary colonised spaces, has also been observed in India (Debnath, 2017), where LGBTQ+ communities share the same faith as those in Poland.

Such apartheid policing of Polish LGBTQ+ communities is itself condemned and criminalised by the European Union because such segregation is in severe conflict with EU values. Meaning, Poland is othered by the EU an internal threat to the EU. The EU counter-others Poland's othering, reflecting a strong EU fortress thinking (Peers, 1998) directed inwardly. The EU polices "rogue" EU states that do not comply with EU laws and regulation that safeguard the EU values of 'inclusion, tolerance, justice, solidarity and non-discrimination', and that 'are an integral part of our European way of life' as the European Commission website states (European Commission, 2021a—online source).

What the EU does not tackle by condemning the Polish xenophobic and apartheid policing of LGBTQ+ communities are the deeper lying societal causes, such as poverty, that drive much LGBTQ+ phobia (cf. Burns, 2008). By not tackling those deeper origins of fear and hate, the richer parts of the EU reside in a comfortably numb 'saviour' bubble while remaining incapable of trying to 'imagine (let alone solve) the pervasive problems of their poorer fellow [EU] citizens' (Currid-Halkett, 2017, p. 189), of which LGBTQ+ phobia and LGBTQ+ policing are an effect of deeper, existential fears that find their origin in (relative) poverty. Wealthier EU states where citizens blame other EU citizens of intolerance and being non-emancipated—which is itself a structural violence and a perverted intolerance (Žižek, 2009)—remain 'wilfully ignorant' of the fact 'that many of these decisions, veiled in morality, are practical and realistic outcomes of socioeconomic position' (Currid-Halkett, 2017, p. 196).

This suggests that the EU's reaction to Poland's othering and apartheid policing of LGBTQ+ communities is in and of itself othering, and that othering reflects how the EU wants to exert and keeps on exerting its symbolic supranational superiority, which considered EU-internal colonisation, as seen elsewhere (cf. Eski, 2020; Gregory, 2004). So, paradoxically, whereas the Polish government colonises its own citizens they consider risky others, and police through laws and legal cultures through formalistic double-speak, the EU fortress asserts itself through European symbolical politics, acting as a protagonist of democracy, freedom and tolerance. As much as Poland targets minorities, Poland is targeted by the EU as minority. In that sense, the EU's answer to the violations of these basic principles of the value union should be seen as a test of credibility, "whether it can act in a way that shows it cares more about people than politics" (Paradys, 2021).

In reaction to such internal EU colonisation of Poland, Poland seems to persist in its resistance to the EU values not only by falling even further (back) into heteronationalistic othering of LGBTQ+ communities, but also by its ongoing undermining of independent courts and judges (Kovács & Scheppele, 2018) and by prohibiting abortion laws (Hussein et al., 2018). In other words, the very fact the EU is symbolically penalising Poland for its apartheid-resembling LGBTQ+ policing and politics, seems to establish more and stronger LGBTQ+ discriminatory criminalisation (see De Hingh, 2022).

While this vicious paradox is born out of fear of the other, in the EU politics of policing LGBTQ+ communities in Poland, however, Polish LGBTQ+ communities themselves are left behind in a void. They are trapped in a vicious circle where both sides of the discourse use LGBTQ+ people as pawns to make moves against each other, constantly reinforcing their argument that the other narrative is bad. LGBTQ+ communities are disillusioned and victimised by their own government, while being symbolically utilised by a far-away EU supranational organisation that pushes through a (aggressive!) progressive agenda through which the EU asserts its power. Either way, Polish LGBTQ+ communities cannot go anywhere, but are policed into somewhere in-between being on the one side, nationally discriminated against, and on the other side supranationally supported. Such in-betweenness is also referred to as liminality, which can be experienced individually, socio-culturally and societally (Horvath et al., 2015; Turner, 1969). In that sense, LGBTQ+ communities in Poland are policed by both Poland and the EU into specific socio-cultural and political (symbolical) liminality. They are not allowed to be neither totally themselves in Poland, nor can they "be" on a European level where they are accepted. In such liminality, feelings of nothingness and being vulnerable increase. Once such desperation is completed, it is not that far stretched anymore to compare the LGBTQ+ cultural policing and segregation with that of the Jewish people's dehumanisation during the Nazi occupation, which is a most dangerous and mass-lethal form of apartheid policy that happened in Poland before (Browning, 1986), one that must not happen under any circumstances.

References

AP News. (2022, June 27). Poland's leader rejects West views on transgender issues. Retrieved December 19, 2022, from https://apnews.com/article/poland-gay-rights-warsaw-jaroslaw-kaczynski-441e0921b309b61a46c6784c4e458d58

Ayoub, P. M., & Paternotte, D. (2014a). Introduction. In P. M. Paternotte & D. Ayoub (Eds.), *LGBT activism and the making of Europe: A rainbow Europe?* (pp. 1–25). Palgrave Macmillan.

Ayoub, P. M., & Paternotte, D. (2014b). Conclusion. In P. M. Paternotte & D. Ayoub (Eds.), *LGBT activism and the making of Europe: A rainbow Europe?* (pp. 233–240). Palgrave Macmillan.

Bauman, Z. (2000). *Liquid modernity*. Polity Press.

BBC News. (2020, June 14). Polish election: Andrzej Duda says LGBT 'ideology' worse than communism. *BBC News*. Retrieved December 19, 2022, from https://www.bbc.com/news/world-europe-53039864

BBC News. (2021, September 28). Three Polish regions scrap anti-LGBT resolutions. *BBC News*. Retrieved December 19, 2022, from https://www.bbc.com/news/world-europe-58714658

Bea, B. (2020, October 21). Europe's sanctions dilemma: How to punish Hungary without hurting Hungarians? *Balkan Insight*. Retrieved December 19, 2022, from https://balkaninsight.com/2020/10/21/europes-sanctions-dilemma-how-to-punish-hungary-without-hurting-hungarians/

Binnie, J. (2014). Neoliberalism, class, gender and lesbian, gay, bisexual, transgender and queer politics in Poland. *International Journal of Politics, Culture, and Society, 27*(2), 241–257.

Borowik, I. (2017). Religion in Poland between tradition and modernity, or religious continuity and change in conditions of transformation. In S. Ramet & I. Borowik (Eds.), *Religion, politics, and values in Poland: Continuity and change since 1989* (pp. 185–207). Palgrave Macmillan.

Brown, J., Fleming, J., & Silvestri, M. (2020). Policewomen's perceptions of occupational culture in the changing policing environment of England and Wales: A study in liminality. *The Police Journal, 94*(3), 259–281.

Browning, C. R. (1986). Nazi ghettoization policy in Poland: 1939–41. *Central European History, 19*(4), 343–368.

Bucholc, M. (2022). The anti-LGBTIQ campaign in Poland: The established, the outsiders, and the legal performance of exclusion. *Law & Policy, 44*(1), 4–22.

Burns, J. K. (2008). Xenophobia-evolved 'outgroup' hatred or product of a toxic social environment? *South African Journal of Psychiatry, 14*(4), 120–121.

Casanova, J. (1994). *Public religions in the modern world*. University of Chicago Press.

Ciobanu, C. (2019a). Polish right-wing emboldened by ruling party agenda. *Balkan Insight*. Retrieved December 19, 2022, from https://balkaninsight.com/2019/07/31/polish-far-right-emboldened/

Ciobanu, C. (2019b). 'Foreign ideology': Poland's populists target LGBT rights. *Balkan Insight*. Retrieved December 19, 2022, from https://balkaninsight.com/2019/06/26/save-the-children/

Ciobanu, C. (2020a). Mass arrest of LGBT people marks turning point for Poland. *Balkan Insight*. Retrieved December 19, 2022, from https://balkaninsight.com/2020/08/13/mass-arrest-of-lgbt-people-marks-turning-point-for-poland/

Ciobanu, C. (2020b). Polish activists face legal action over 'atlas of hate'. *Balkan Insight*. Retrieved December 19, 2022, from https://balkaninsight.com/2020/03/04/polish-activists-face-legal-action-over-atlas-of-hate/

Ciobanu, C. (2021). Ordo Iuris: The ultra-conservative organisation transforming Poland. *Balkan Insight*. Retrieved December 19, 2022,

from https://balkaninsight.com/2021/06/22/ordo-iuris-the-ultra-conservative-organisation-transforming-poland/
Ciobanu, C. (2022). In bid to boost poll numbers, Poland's ruling party targets trans people. *Balkan Insight*. Retrieved December 19, 2022, from https://balkaninsight.com/2022/08/03/in-bid-to-boost-poll-numbers-polands-ruling-party-targets-trans-people/
Comaroff, J., & Comaroff, J. (2004). Policing culture, cultural policing: Law and social order in postcolonial South Africa. *Law & Social Inquiry, 29*(3), 513–545.
Currid-Halkett, E. (2017). *The sum of small things*. Princeton University Press.
De Hingh, V. (2022, March 23). Rusland valt Oekraïne binnen met tanks, raketten en homohaat. *De Correspondent*. Retrieved December 19, 2022, from https://decorrespondent.nl/13227/rusland-valt-oekraine-binnen-met-tanks-raketten-en-homohaat/20292578768187-3936472c
Debnath, K. (2017). LGBT identity: The illustration of "othering" in India. *Sexuality, Gender & Policy, 1*(1), 89–100.
Dericquebourg, R. (2015). Religion and human rights in France. In G. Črpić & H. Ziebertz (Eds.), *Religion and human rights: An International Perspective* (pp. 31–44). Springer.
Erdman, J. N. (2014). Procedural abortion rights: Ireland and the European Court of Human Rights. *Reproductive Health Matters, 22*(44), 22–30.
Erkebaeva, A. (2022). The weaponization of homophobia in Kyrgyzstan and Belarus. *Eurasianet*. Retrieved December 19, 2022, from https://eurasianet.org/perspectives-the-weaponization-of-homophobia-in-kyrgyzstan-and-belarus
Eski, Y. (2020). Policing the Eastern Bloc other in Northwestern European port zones. In V. Nagy & K. Kerezsi (Eds.), *A critical approach to Police science: New perspectives in post-transitional policing studies* (pp. 355–378). Eleven International Publishing.
Etkind, A. (2013). *Internal colonization: Russia's imperial experience*. Wiley.
European Commission. (2019). *Special Eurobarometer 493: Discrimination in the EU (including LGBTI)*. Retrieved December 19, 2022, from https://data.europa.eu/data/datasets/s2251_91_4_493_eng?locale=en
European Commission, Directorate General 'Budget'. (2020). *EU expenditure and revenue 2014–2020*. European Union Open Data Portal.
European Commission. (2021a). The EU values. Retrieved December 19, 2022, from https://ec.europa.eu/component-library/eu/about/eu-values/
European Commission. (2021b, July 15). *EU founding values: Commission starts legal action against Hungary and Poland for violations of fundamental*

rights of LGBTIQ people. Retrieved December 19, 2022, from https://digital-strategy.ec.europa.eu/en/news/eu-founding-values-commission-starts-legal-action-against-hungary-and-poland-violations-fundamental

European Parliament. (2021, March 11). *Declaration of the EU as an LGBTIQ Freedom Zone.* Retrieved December 19, 2022, from https://www.europarl.europa.eu/doceo/document/TA-9-2021-0089_EN.html#:~:text=Hereby%20declares%20the%20European%20Union,3

Gawron, J. (2022). *Atlas of Hate.* Retrieved December 19, 2022, from https://atlasnienawisci.pl/

Główny Urząd Statystyczny [Statistics Poland; Central Statistical Office]. (2013). *Informacja o rozmiarach i kierunkach emigracji z Polski w latach 2004–2012* [Information about the scope and directions for Polish emigration between 2004 and 2012]. Retrieved December 19, 2022, from https://stat.gov.pl/

Godzisz, P. (2019). The Europeanization of anti-LGBT hate crime laws in the Western Balkans. *Crime, Law, and Social Change: An Interdisciplinary Journal, 71*(3), 291–306.

Graff, A. (2006). We are (not all) homophobes: A report from Poland. *Feminist Studies, 32*(2), 434–449.

Graff, A. (2010). Looking at pictures of gay men: Political uses of homophobia in contemporary Poland. *Public Culture, 22*(3), 583–603.

Graham, H. (2022). Five-year NHS waiting lists leaving North East transgender people's lives 'in limbo'. Retrieved December 19, 2022, from https://www.chroniclelive.co.uk/news/north-east-news/trans-waiting-lists-nhs-treatment

Greenhalgh, H. (2022). LGBTQ+'ers in Oekraïne vrezen voor gevolgen Russische invasie: 'Blijven zal onmogelijk zijn'. Retrieved December 19, 2022, from https://www.mo.be/analyse/LGBTQ+-ers-oekra-ne-vrezen-voor-gevolgen-russische-invasie-blijven-zal-onmogelijk-zijn

Gregory, D. (2004). *The colonial present: Afghanistan, Palestine, Iraq.* Wiley-Blackwell.

Hadjari, U. (2019, December 31). The demagogue's cocktail of victimhood and strength. *The Atlantic.* Retrieved December 19, 2022, from https://alturi.org/news_items/the-demagogues-cocktail-of-victimhood-and-strength/

Hague, E. (1997). Rape, power and masculinity: The construction of gender and national identities in the war of Bosnia-Herzegovina. In R. Lentin (Ed.), *Gender and catastrophe* (pp. 59–70). Zed Books.

Hall, D. (2015). Antagonism in the making: Religion and homosexuality in post communist Poland. In S. Sremac & R. R. Ganzevoort (Eds.), *Religious and sexual nationalisms in central and eastern Europe*. Brill.

Hanley, T. (2017). Homophobia in Poland and Hungary: Assessing its political motives and influences. In J. A. Pino & K. Karamanakis (Eds.), *Body Politics: What's the state got to do with it*. Eagle Print Collegiate Press.

Horvath, A., Thomassen, B. & Wydra, H. (Eds.). (2015). *Breaking boundaries: Varieties of liminality*. Berghahn Books.

Hudson, B. (2009). Security and the 'risky other': Doing justice in a world of strangers. In M. Hildebrandt, A. Makinwa, & A. Oehmichen (Eds.), *Controlling security in a culture of fear* (pp. 15–34). Boom Legal Publishers.

Hussein, J., Cottingham, J., Nowicka, W., & Kismodi, E. (2018). Abortion in Poland: Politics, progression and regression. *Reproductive Health Matters: An International Journal on Sexual and Reproductive Health and Rights., 26*(52), 11–14.

Janiszewski, J. (2021, April 15). Neither in nor out: The paradox of Poland's 'LGBT-free' zones. *Balkan Insight*. Retrieved December 19, 2022, from https://balkaninsight.com/2021/04/15/neither-in-nor-out-the-paradox-of-polands-lgbt-free-zones/

Kaldor, M., & Vejvoda, I. (1997). Democratization in central and east European countries. *International Affairs, 73*(1), 59–82.

Keinz, A. (2011). European desires and national bedrooms? Negotiating "normalcy" in postsocialist Poland. *Central European History, 44*(1), 92–117.

Knight, K., & Gall, L. (2020, May 21). Hungary ends legal recognition for transgender and intersex people. *Human Rights Watch*. Retrieved December 19, 2022, from https://www.hrw.org/news/2020/05/21/hungary-ends-legal-recognition-transgender-and-intersex-people

Konopka, K., Prusik, M., & Szulawski, M. (2020). Two sexes, two genders only: Measuring attitudes toward transgender individuals in Poland. *Sex Roles, 82*(9), 600–621.

Kovács, K., & Scheppele, K. L. (2018). The fragility of an independent judiciary: Lessons from Hungary and Poland—and the European Union. *Communist and Post-Communist Studies, 51*(3), 189–200.

Lash, S. (2003). Reflexivity as non-linearity. *Theory, Culture & Society, 20*(2), 49–57.

Maciuszczak, T. (2021, September 27). PiS już nie ma problemu z LGBT, tylko broni "podstawowych praw i wolności". *Dziennik Wschodni*. Retrieved

December 19, 2022, from https://www.dziennikwschodni.pl/polityka/lubelski-pis-juz-nie-ma-problemu-z-lgbt-solidarna-polska-nazywa-to-dawaniem-palca,n,1000296182.html

Marchlewska, M., Cichocka, A., Panayiotou, O., Castellanos, K., & Batayneh, J. (2018). Populism as identity politics: Perceived in-group disadvantage, collective narcissism, and support for populism. *Social Psychological and Personality Science, 9*(2), 151–162.

Markowski, R. (2020). Plurality support for democratic decay: The 2019 Polish parliamentary election. *West European Politics, 43*(7), 1513–1525.

Marody, M., & Mandes, S. (2017). Polish religious values as reflected in the European values study. In S. Ramet & I. Borowik (Eds.), *Religion, politics, and values in Poland* (pp. 231–255). Palgrave Macmillan.

Mazurczak, A., Mrowicki, M., & Adamczewska-Stachura, A. (2019). *The legal situation of non-heterosexual and transgender persons in Poland: International standards for the protection of LGBT persons human rights and compliance therewith from standpoint of the Commissioner for Human Rights.* Commissioner for Human Rights. Retrieved December 19, 2022, from https://bip.brpo.gov.pl/sites/default/files/Raport_synthesist_LGBT_legal_situation.pdf

Mole, R. C. M. (2011). Nationality and sexuality: Homophobic discourse and the "national threat" in contemporary Latvia. *Nations and Nationalism, 17*(3), 540–560.

Mole, R. C. M. (2016). Nationalism and homophobia in Central and Eastern Europe. In K. Slootmaeckers, H. Touquet, & P. Vermeersch (Eds.), *The EU enlargement and gay politics* (pp. 99–121). Palgrave Macmillan.

Mos, M. (2020). The anticipatory politics of homophobia: Explaining constitutional bans on same-sex marriage in post-communist Europe. *East European Politics, 36*(3), 395–416.

O'Dwyer, C., & Vermeersch, P. (2016). From pride to politics: Niche-party politics and LGBT rights in Poland. In K. Slootmaeckers, H. Touquet, & P. Vermeersch (Eds.), *The EU enlargement and gay politics* (pp. 123–145). Palgrave Macmillan.

O'Dwyer, C. (2012). Does the EU help or hinder gay-rights movements in post-communist Europe? The case of Poland. *East European Politics, 28*(4), 332–352.

ONeil, D. (2019). LGBTI people pay loving tribute with powerful video for late trans friend. *Meaws*. Retrieved December 19, 2022, from https://meaws.com/blogs/lgbti-people-pay-loving-tribute-with-powerful-video-for-late-trans-friend/

Ordo, I. (2020). Are there LGBT-free zones in Poland? *Report*. Retrieved December 19, 2022, from https://en.ordoiuris.pl/family-and-marriage/are-there-lgbt-free-zones-poland-report

Panter, H. (2021). LGBT+ genocide: Understanding hetero-nationalism and the politics of psychological silence. In Y. Eski (Ed.), *Genocide & Victimology* (pp. 69–85). Routledge.

Paradys, E. (2021, June 17). Europe must act on Hungary's anti-LGBT law. The EU's credibility is at stake. *Euronews*. Retrieved December 19, 2022, from https://www.euronews.com/2021/06/16/europe-must-act-on-hungary-s-anti-lgbt-law-the-eu-s-credibility-is-at-stake

Pech, L., & Keleman, D. R. (2020). If you think the U.S. is having a constitutional crisis, you should see what is happening in Poland. *Washington Post*. Retrieved December 19, 2022, from https://www.washingtonpost.com/politics/2020/01/25/if-you-think-us-is-having-constitutional-crisis-you-should-see-what-is-happening-poland/

Peers, S. (1998). Building fortress Europe: The development of EU migration law. *Common Market Law Review, 35*(6), 1235–1272.

Pelinka, A. (2013). Right-wing populism: Concept and typology. In R. Wodak, M. Khosravnik, & B. Mral (Eds.), *Right-wing populism in Europe: Politics and discourse* (pp. 3–22). Bloomsbury.

Pronczuk, M. (2020, July 30). Polish towns that declared themselves 'L.G.B.T. free' are denied E.U. funds. *New York Times*. Retrieved December 19, 2022, from https://www.nytimes.com/2020/07/30/world/europe/LGBT-free-poland-EU-funds.html

Ramet, S. (2006). Thy will be done: The Catholic Church and politics in Poland since 1989. In T. Byrnes & P. Katzenstein (Eds.), *Religion in an expanding Europe* (pp. 117–147). Cambridge University Press.

Ramoroka, T., & Tsheola, J. (2014). Gated-communities and the privatization of public spaces in urban South Africa: Democratic social integration or exclusion? *Journal of Geography and Regional Planning, 7*(4), 58–68.

Rankin, J. (2021, June 15). Hungary passes law banning LGBT content in schools or kids' TV. *The Guardian*. Retrieved December 19, 2022, from https://www.theguardian.com/world/2021/jun/15/hungary-passes-law-banning-lbgt-content-in-schools

Reicher, S., & Haslam, S. A. (2016, November 19). The politics of hope: Donald Trump as an entrepreneur of identity. *Scientific American*. Retrieved December 19, 2022, from https://www.scientificamerican.com/article/the-politics-of-hope-donald-trump-as-an-entrepreneur-of-identity/

Roberts, H. (2022). Transgender man with 42GG breasts finally has them removed in operation costing £3,000 after raising money by carrying out 'dares' on TikTok—including eating worms, chillies and dog biscuits. Retrieved December 19, 2022, from https://www.dailymail.co.uk/femail/article-11043611/Transgender-man-42GG-breasts-completes-TikTok-dares-raise-3-000-surgery-Poland.html

Rousek, L. (2015, February 8). Slovakia referendum on gay-adoption ban fails. *The Wall Street Journal*. Retrieved December 19, 2022, from https://www.wsj.com/articles/slovakia-referendum-on-gay-adoption-ban-fails-1423355269

Rupp L. J. (2014). The European origins of transnational organizing: The international committee for sexual equality. In P. M. Ayoub & D. Paternotte (Eds.), *LGBT activism and the making of Europe: A rainbow Europe?* Palgrave Macmillan.

Ryan, O. (2021). 'We can't keep sending trans people abroad for major surgery with no aftercare when they get home'. *The Journal*. Retrieved December 19, 2022, from https://www.thejournal.ie/transgender-surgery-options-ireland-5370886-Mar2021/

Said, E. (1977). *Orientalism.* Penguin.

Shayegh, J., Storey, L., Turner, R. N., & Barry, J. (2021). A social identity approach to how elite outgroups are invoked by politicians and the media in nativist populism. *Political Psychology, 43*(6), 1009–1025.

Slootmaeckers, K., & Touquet, H. (2016). The co-evolution of EU's Eastern enlargement and LGBT politics: An ever gayer union? In K. Slootmaeckers, H. Touquet, & P. Vermeersch (Eds.), *The EU enlargement and gay politics* (pp. 19–44). Palgrave Macmillan.

Slootmaeckers, K., Touquet, H., & Vermeersch, P. (2016). Introduction: EU enlargement and LGBT rights-beyond symbolism? In K. Slootmaeckers, H. Touquet, & P. Vermeersch (Eds.), *The EU enlargement and gay politics* (pp. 1–16). Palgrave Macmillan.

Spauwen, N. (2022). Lhbti-rechten zijn de kanarie in de kolenmijn. Retrieved December 19, 2022, from https://fd.nl/opinie/1432015/lhbti-rechten-zijn-de-kanarie-in-de-kolenmijn

Sramota, S. (2019, December 18). Europees Parlement steunt LHBT'ers in Polen: 'Dit is publieke discriminatie'. *NOS*. Retrieved December 19, 2022, from https://nos.nl/artikel/2315328-europees-parlement-steunt-lhbt-ers-in-polen-dit-is-publieke-discriminatie

Sremac, S., & Ganzevoort, R. (2015). The interplay of religious and sexual nationalisms in central and Eastern Europe. In S. Sremac & R. R.

Ganzevoort (Eds.), *Religious and Sexual Nationalisms in Central and Eastern Europe*. Brill.

Tarta, M. (2015). European culture wars: sexual nationalism between Euro-Christian and Euro-Secular civil religion in Poland and Romania. In S. Sremac & R. R. Ganzevoort (Eds.), *Religious and Sexual Nationalisms in Central and Eastern Europe*. Brill.

Toman, L. (2019). Navigating medical culture and LGBTQ+ identity. *The Clinical Teacher, 16*(4), 335–338.

Tombs, S., & Whyte, D. (2003). Unmasking the crimes of the powerful. *Critical Criminology, 11*(3), 217–236.

Turner, V. (1969). Liminality and communitas. In V. Turner (Ed.), *The ritual process: Structure and anti-structure* (pp. 94–113). Aldine Publishing.

Treaty on the Functioning of the European Union, 13 December 2007, 2008/C 115/01. United Nations Human Rights. (2013). Threatening the rights of LGBT persons in Eastern Europe. Retrieved December 19, 2022, from https://www.ohchr.org/en/stories/2013/08/threatening-rights-lgbt-persons-eastern-europe

Vieten, U. M., & Poynting, S. (2016). Contemporary far-right racist populism in Europe. *Journal of Intercultural Studies, 37*(6), 533–540.

Von der Leyen, U. (2020, September 17). *State of the Union Address by President von der Leyen at the European Parliament Plenary.* Retrieved December 19, 2022, from https://ec.europa.eu/commission/presscorner/detail/en/SPEECH_20_1655

Wesolowsky, T. (2021). The worrying regression of LGBT rights in Eastern Europe. Retrieved December 19, 2022, from https://www.rferl.org/a/lgbt-rights-eastern-europe-backsliding/31622890.html

Winiewski, M., Świder, M., Bulska, D., Górska, P., Malinowska, K., Matera, J., Mulak, A., Skowrońska, M., Soral, W., & Poniat, R. (2021). *Sytuacja społeczna osób LGBTA w Polsce. Raport za lata 2019–2020*. Kampania Przeciw Homofobii. Retrieved December 19, 2022, from https://kph.org.pl/wp-content/uploads/2021/12/Rapot_Duzy_Digital-1.pdf

Wolpe, H. (1975). The theory of internal colonization: the South African case. In *Collected seminar papers* (Vol. 18, pp. 105–120). Institute of Commonwealth Studies.

Zaccaria, F. (2015). Catholic church, young people, and human rights in Italy. In H. Ziebertz & G. Črpić (Eds.), *Religion and human rights: An international perspective* (pp. 93–102). Springer.

Zeldin, W. (2014). *Slovak republic: Marriage defined as between one man and one woman* [Web page]. Library of Congress.

Zielińska, K. (2015). The roman catholic church and human rights in Poland. In G. Črpić & H. Ziebertz (Eds.), *Religion and human rights: An international perspective* (pp. 137–149). Springer.

Zimmerman, A. (2013). German sociology and empire from internal colonization to overseas colonization and back again. In G. Steinmetz (Ed.), *Sociology and empire: The imperial entanglements of a discipline* (pp. 166–187). Duke University Press.

Žižek, S. (2009). *Violence: Six sideways reflections*. Picador.

Żuk, P., & Żuk, P. (2019). Dangerous liaisons between the Catholic Church and state: The religious and political alliance of the nationalist right with the conservative church in Poland. *Journal of Contemporary Central and Eastern Europe., 27*(2–3), 191–212.

3

Exclusion and Ignorance: International Legal Recognition and Criminalisation Responses to Transgender Communities in the Context of Political Economy

Noel Cross

Introduction

When considering legal responses to transgender communities, it is important to consider the data that suggest that transgender and gender non-conforming people are the frequent targets of verbal, physical, and sexual violence motivated by bias against their gender identity or expression, in countries across the world (Woods & Herman, 2018). This type of activity is currently defined by the Association of Chief Police Officers (ACPO) as a hate crime in the UK (Hall, 2013), as well as being a breach of the Human Rights Act 1998, specifically Articles 8 (right to respect for private and family life) and 14 (right to freedom from discrimination) of the European Convention on Human Rights. Other rights frameworks,

N. Cross (✉)
School of Justice Studies, Criminal Justice, Liverpool John Moores University, Liverpool, UK
e-mail: N.Cross@ljmu.ac.uk

H. Panter and A. Dwyer (eds.), *Transgender People and Criminal Justice*, Critical Criminological Perspectives, https://doi.org/10.1007/978-3-031-29893-6_3

such as the African Charter on People's and Human Rights, include very similar provisions.

Such data would seem to justify legal intervention to protect transgender communities, through legal recognition of their status as well as the introduction of specific criminal offences against hate crime. In fact, this chapter will argue not only that such legal protection of transgender communities across the world is inadequate, but also that it is common for States[1] to proactively criminalise transgender communities in various ways, making their very existence a crime. Any analysis of State responses to transgender communities must therefore consider legal frameworks which discriminate against this social group, as well as legal frameworks which aim to protect them.

Such analysis must also accept the social construction of both crime and the response to crime across different States. Crime in general is not an objective entity, but a product of socially created definitions and human evaluation (Young, 1999). As such, each society selects a suitable amount of crime based on the State's social and political needs at the time (Christie, 2004). Of course, social elites, through political decision-making and judicial action in criminal courts, hold most of the power in terms of which types of behaviour are criminalised at any given point in time. Similarly, there will always be variations in any transgender-focused recognition and criminalisation framework between the 'law in the books' and the 'law in action' (Packer, 1968), in terms of how laws both support and criminalise transgender communities in criminal justice practice. Nonetheless, it is important to consider a range of social, economic, and political factors when examining individual States' legal responses to transgender community activities. Such a holistic analysis will be the focus of this chapter.

The structure of the chapter will be as follows. The first section will define key terms to be used in the chapter, as well as developing a theoretical framework to be used in analysis later. Following this, patterns in legal recognition and criminalisation of transgender communities will be contextualised within available data on wider social, economic, and

[1] Within the context of this chapter, 'State' is defined as a nation or territory representing an organised political community under one government.

political frameworks in operation in a range of countries in Africa, Asia, Europe, and North America, focusing on legal definitions which support transgender communities, and legal definitions which socially exclude and criminalise them. Analysis of countries which do not have specific laws criminalising transgender communities, but which do use other less specific laws to criminalise them in practice, will also be included. Such analysis is exploratory, due to the limitations of transgender-specific data and variations in the definition of crime in different areas of the world. Taking such limitations into account, it is argued that comparative legal analysis is an important step forward in understanding the full extent of States' failure to protect transgender communities across the world.

Definitions and Theoretical Frameworks

Before commencing comparative analysis, it is important to define key terms being used in this chapter and the theoretical framework which will be used for subsequent analysis. 'Transgender' is defined as referring to people who do not appear to conform to heteronormative gender norms by presenting and living genders that were not assigned to them at birth, or by presenting and living genders in ways that may not be readily intelligible in terms of more traditional conceptions. This definition may or may not be used to include 'transsexual', meaning people who use hormonal and/or surgical technologies to alter their body in ways that may be construed as at odds with the sex assignment at birth, or which may not be readily intelligible in terms of traditional conceptions of sexed bodies (Bettcher, 2007, cited in Chakraborti & Garland, 2009).

The theoretical framework used in this chapter draws upon the work of Cavadino and Dignan (2006a, 2006b). Cavadino and Dignan (2006a, 2006b) link different States' responses to crime to the conditions of political economy prevalent in a particular state. More specifically, they compare levels of legal punitiveness against a range of social, economic, and political factors. The results of their analysis are shown in Table 3.1 (Cavadino & Dignan, 2006b).

Table 3.1 Comparison of socio-economic and political conditions and criminal justice responses

Socio-economic and penal indices	Regime types: Neo-liberalism	Conservative corporatism	Social democratic corporatism	Oriental corporatism
Economic and social policy organisation	Free market, minimal welfare State	Status-related, moderately generous welfare State	Universalistic, generous welfare State	Private sector-based 'welfare corporatism': bureaucratic, paternalistic
Income differentials	Extreme	Pronounced but not extreme	Relatively limited	Very limited
Status differentials	Formally egalitarian	Moderately hierarchical, based on traditional occupational rankings	Broadly egalitarian, only limited occupation status differentials	Markedly hierarchical, based on traditional patriarchal ranking
Citizen-State relations	Individualised, atomised, limited social rights	Conditional, moderate social rights	Relatively unconditional and generous social rights	Quasi-feudal corporatism; strong sense of duty
Social inclusivity/exclusivity	Clear tendency towards social exclusion	Some exclusion relating to participation in civil society	Very limited tendency towards social exclusion	Alienation of 'outsiders', otherwise little social exclusion
Political orientation	Right-wing	Centrist	Left-wing	Centre-right
Dominant penal ideology	'Law and order'	Rehabilitation	Rights-based	Apology-based restoration and rehabilitation
Mode of punishment	Exclusionary	Mixed	Inclusionary	Inclusionary

	Regime types			
Socio-economic and penal indices	Neo-liberalism	Conservative corporatism	Social democratic corporatism	Oriental corporatism
Examples	USA, England and Wales, Australia, New Zealand, South Africa	Germany, France, Italy, The Netherlands	Sweden, Norway, Finland	Japan

Cavadino and Dignan's (2006a, 2006b) approach, while useful in terms of linking legal responses to political economy, has some limitations in terms of its use in this chapter. First, Cavadino and Dignan's (2006a, 2006b) analysis is based around imprisonment rates in different countries when compared to social, political, and economic factors. As such, this chapter's focus is on different States' responses to transgender communities through 'supporting' and 'exclusionary' laws themselves. However, just as Cavadino and Dignan (2006a, 2006b) selected imprisonment rates as a measure because imprisonment data are more objective and easier to access, so it is argued that laws are (or at least should be!) publicly available documents. Second, Cavadino and Dignan's (2006a, 2006b) analysis was not focused on issues relating to gender, as the analysis in this study is.

Third, there are a range of methodological criticisms of Cavadino and Dignan's (2006a, 2006b) work, which are put forward, for example, by Nelken (2009). Nelken (2009) argued that Cavadino and Dignan (2006a, 2006b) overlook the importance of other factors affecting punitiveness, such as general, media, and political culture in a particular state for example. Nelken (2009) also argued that differences in criminal procedure (in terms of process and political independence), and meanings given to tolerance and punitiveness by various actors in each state's criminal process, are the best way to move beyond ethnocentrism and relativism in comparative analysis. While Nelken's (2009) points are valid, they carry less weight in relation to the type of analysis being used here. Nelken's (2009) analysis is based on in-depth knowledge of one state's penal and political economy (Italy). This chapter's analysis covers a wide range of different countries, in a way which precludes the type of deep analysis used by Nelken. As such, it is argued that Nelken's (2009) methodological criticisms are not enough to invalidate the use of Cavadino and Dignan's (2006a, 2006b) model in this chapter.

Fourth and finally, this chapter aims to take as wide-ranging an approach to legal analysis as possible. This includes discussion of legal responses to transgender communities in African States. Cavadino and Dignan (2006a, 2006b) only included South Africa in their comparative analysis and not any other African countries. They characterised South Africa as a neoliberal, exclusionary, right-wing State. However, they did not consider the impact of colonialism on African States, in terms of the limited impact of democracy following independence from European empires, the inheritance of exclusionary laws and cultural practices targeting social 'outsiders', such as transgender communities, from the days of colonial occupation, and the struggle to adapt economic practices to fit dominant globalised marketplaces (Lawrence, 2010).

The chapter therefore adds a fifth model to the four put forward by Cavadino and Dignan (2006a, 2006b). This fifth model is termed *post-colonial*, to reflect social and political trends in African and Asian countries which might help to explain legal attitudes towards transgender communities. The post-colonial model can be applied not only to States which were previously part of the British Empire, but also States which were previously part of other empires, such as those of France or the USSR, as recently as the twentieth century. Such a model shares many of the features of neoliberalism, but adds a tendency towards underdeveloped economies, lack of fair access to global economic markets, and political exclusion into the analysis, alongside the neoliberal features of minimal welfare state, extreme income differentials, cultural conservatism, and exclusionary penal responses.

Using this amended theoretical framework, the chapter attempts to make connections between States' 'supporting' and 'excluding' legal responses to transgender communities and wider political, social, and economic factors, across five broad geographical areas—Africa, Asia, Europe, the Americas, and Oceania.

Africa

A small group of African countries directly criminalise diverse gender expression, including transgender communities, through specific criminal offences. These are Gambia, Malawi, Nigeria, and South Sudan—all situated in the central region of Africa, apart from Malawi in the south-east of the continent. Immediately, a common historical factor emerges, in the sense that all these countries were formerly part of the British Empire at various points during the nineteenth and twentieth centuries, and all but Nigeria's laws date from the time of colonialism (Nigeria's law has its roots in Islamic Sharia law) (ILGA World, 2020). As these States became absorbed into the British Empire, their new colonial rulers imported English sumptuary laws, which regulated permissible types of clothing according to social class and rank. These laws had emerged as part of English law as early as the 1300s and were fully established as legal principles by the 1500s in England (Hall, 2012). Nigeria's use of Sharia law, particularly in the north of the country, has resulted not only in a specific offence criminalising transgender communities, but also in this being a capital offence, with the maximum punishment available death by stoning—although in practice public whipping is the main form of punishment used by Sharia courts (Human Dignity Trust, 2022). In Malawi and South Sudan, the maximum penalty associated with the expression of gender identity or expression by transgender communities is 14 years' imprisonment.

A more common 'excluding' legal approach towards transgender communities in African States is tacit criminalisation through non-specific criminal laws such as offences against public order or public decency (used against transgender communities in Botswana, Gambia, Lesotho, Malawi, Morocco, Namibia, Rwanda, Tunisia, Uganda, Zambia, and Zimbabwe), or through criminal offences against same-sex sexual conduct (evident in Burundi, Cameroon, Gambia, Ghana, Liberia, Malawi, Mauritius, Morocco, Nigeria, Tanzania, Uganda, Zambia, and Zimbabwe) (ILGA World, 2020). There is also evidence of a range of African countries criminalising transgender people based on discriminatory discourse characterised by perceived and fictitious transgender lifestyle factors, such as sex work and substance use, or by misrepresentation and fraud laws transformed by strict cultural norms on gender into weapons against transgender communities (in Zambia, Burundi, and Kenya) (ILGA World, 2020). Finally, search, arrest, and detention of transgender people without any legal basis are common in Zimbabwe, Burundi, and Mauritius (ILGA World, 2020).

Overall, of a total of 25 African States for which information was available, 20, or 80%, were found to use de facto criminalisation techniques against transgender communities, through a combination of sexual offence laws, drug laws, and vaguely defined public order-related provisions (ILGA World, 2020). A case study from Tanzania illustrates how even relative political and economic stability cannot protect transgender communities from criminalisation-based abuse in practice. Tanzania's constitution includes strong language on non-discrimination, human dignity, and the eradication of all forms of discrimination and injustice, a key reason why Tanzania is the only east African country not to have been seriously affected by political and ethnic violence since its independence. However, persecution of transgender communities persists. For example, Alex N., a transgender man, was sexually assaulted by police in Dar es Salaam in 2009. He was 18 at the time. The manager at the bar where he worked, who accused him of being a lesbian and having a 'bad attitude', turned him in to police. When Alex arrived at the police station, he said, police told him to take off his clothes and touched his breasts and vagina. They beat him on his arms and back with a belt and then forced him to wear women's clothing and clean the police station. He was only released after six days of detention and was too afraid to make a complaint against police (Human Rights Watch, 2013).

In line with the political economy model discussed above, clear patterns can be identified when 'excluding' criminal law use is compared to social, economic, and political indicators. The two countries identified as using all three tools of legal discrimination mentioned above are Gambia and Malawi. Of these, Malawi ranks 157th out of 192 countries in terms of life expectancy, with the Gambia ranking 170th out of 192 (United Nations, Department of Economic and Social Affairs, Population Division, 2019). Both countries rank among the world's least developed countries, with economies heavily dependent on agriculture and highly vulnerable to climate change factors such as drought, and political systems characterised by democracy deficits and authoritarian, corrupt governance (CIA, 2020).

It would be misleading and reductive to characterise all African States in the same social, political, and economic way. However, all of the 29 lowest-ranked countries in the world for life expectancy are currently African countries (United Nations, Department of Economic and Social Affairs, Population Division, 2019). Only one African country (Mauritius) is classed by the Economic Intelligence Unit's Freedom Index as being a full democracy, with the majority of African States classed as 'hybrid regime' or 'authoritarian' on the basis of electoral process, functioning of government, political participation, political culture, and civil liberties (Economic Intelligence Unit, 2021, p. 48). Furthermore, only five African countries (Tunisia, Ghana, Namibia, Botswana, and South Africa) were classed as being 'free' in terms of political freedoms and respect for human rights in 2020 (Freedom House, 2021). In other words, most African countries who criminalise transgender people either directly or indirectly also rank highly in terms of social, economic, and political inequality. The *World Happiness Report* is based on (among other measures) real GDP per capita, social support, healthy life expectancy, and people's perception of their freedom to make life choices, generosity, and perceptions of corruption. This report ranks the African States discussed in this section as among the unhappiest in the world, with seven of the least happy States being African, and only one other State ranked lower for happiness levels than Zimbabwe (Helliwell et al., 2021, pp. 19–21).

Interestingly, within the contexts outlined above, there is also evidence of African courts upholding transgender rights and offering a more supportive legal approach. In 2019, a Zimbabwean transgender woman successfully took legal action against police for unlawful arrest and detention. South Africa and Namibia have legal provisions allowing transgender and gender diverse people to change their gender legally (although such provisions are often inaccessible due to lack of information and surgery pre-requisites). Transgender people in South Africa, Kenya, and Botswana have had their right to change or remove gender markers on identity documents upheld by the courts (ILGA World, 2020, p. 18). The legal picture for protection of transgender communities in Africa is therefore not entirely bleak, with some evidence of the judiciary intervening to support transgender human rights. It is still evident, though, that there are clear links between the neoliberal and post-colonial models discussed above and the legal responses to transgender communities across Africa, with widespread disregard of human rights. In other words, the law in African States excludes and punishes transgender communities far more than it supports and recognises them, and high levels of religiosity and post-colonial social, economic, and political structures are key explanatory factors for this situation.

Asia

ILGA World (2020) points out that evidence of laws recognising and supporting transgender communities in Asia has been very limited, beyond a law passed in Pakistan in 2017 allowing gender marker change to occur without discrimination. By contrast, in Kazakhstan, current proposals to change the law would mean that transgender people would have to wait until the age of 21 to obtain gender recognition and other human rights, a move which is likely to trigger further discrimination against transgender communities.

As is the case with African States, a small number of Asian States have specific laws criminalising transgender lives. These are mainly States in the Arabian Peninsula and States in the far East. In Saudi Arabia, Brunei, and the United Arab Emirates, transgender identity and expression is a capital offence, punishable by death by stoning in Saudi Arabia. Of the other Asian countries who have specifically transphobic criminal legislation (Lebanon, Jordan, Kuwait, Oman, Sri Lanka, Myanmar, Indonesia, and Malaysia), maximum sentences range from three years' imprisonment in Oman to 20 years' imprisonment and whipping in Malaysia. All these countries have high levels of religiosity (Islam in all cases except Myanmar, where most of the population are Theravada Buddhist), involving religions which traditionally exclude transgender identity and expression.

In Turkmenistan and Uzbekistan, the same type of conflation of gender identity with sexual orientation often present in African States (see above) results in transgender people being arrested under laws which criminalise male same-sex sexual conduct (ILGA World, 2020). Of the 32 countries for which information was available, nine used de facto criminalisation against transgender communities, using the same mixture of public order offences against 'decency' or similar and sexual offences evident in the discussion of African States above (ILGA World, 2020).

In addition to 'excluding' de jure and de facto criminalisation, the existence of 'supporting' legislation, where it exists, is limited. A group of Asian States, such as India, Japan, Mongolia, Nepal, and Singapore, are in the process of making transgender recognition more difficult, by requiring surgical reassignment, or even sterilisation (in the case of

Japan). The approach of China is typical in this respect—allowing transgender people to change their names and genders on identity documents in principle, but then attaching so many conditions to doing so (full surgical reassignment, reaching 20 years of age, and notary-confirmed letters of consent from family members) that it is almost impossible to do so in practice (Luhur et al., 2021).

Finally, there is widespread evidence of state-supported violence used by police against transgender people and then legitimised by courts who validate such violence, in Iran, Kuwait, and Lebanon for example. Such practices increase in frequency in areas where Sharia law is applied. For example, in the Aceh region of Indonesia, which has a Sharia criminal code, it was reported that in 2018, police officers raided several beauty salons, detained around 12 transgender employees, and forced some of them to cut their hair, wear traditionally male clothes, and speak in 'masculine' voices while in custody for several days (United States Department of State, 2019, p. 29). Such humiliation points not only to a dominant discourse in the law in Asian States of exclusion and punitiveness in relation to transgender communities, but also to the kind of brutalising and inhumane treatment at the hands of criminal justice agencies in practice that signifies de facto criminalisation.

Applying socio-political analysis to the Asian States discussed in the previous paragraph reveals significant disparity between different States. Some of the countries discussed above spent extended periods of their history as part of a European colonial empire, with Myanmar, Sri Lanka, Brunei, India, and Singapore formerly being part of the British empire, and Turkmenistan and Uzbekistan being part of the USSR empire as recently as the early 1990s. There is significant variation in political terms. The Economic Intelligence Unit now classifies Japan as being fully democratic, Singapore, India, Indonesia, Malaysia, Sri Lanka, and Mongolia as 'flawed democracies', Nepal and Lebanon as hybrid regimes, and Iran, Saudi Arabia, United Arab Emirates, China, Oman, Myanmar, Kuwait, Turkmenistan, and Uzbekistan as authoritarian States (Economic Intelligence Unit, 2021). Freedom House (2021) only classes Japan and Mongolia as being free in democratic terms, India, Sri Lanka, Indonesia, and Malaysia as partially free, and all other Asian States discussed in this section being classed as not free. The World Happiness Report ranked no Asian State discussed in this section higher than 25th and 26th out of 149 in terms of happiness between 2018 and 2020 (the United Arab Emirates and Saudi Arabia, respectively), with the other States ranked much lower (Helliwell et al., 2021).

Relating this discussion back to the models of political economy outlined at the start of the chapter, it is significant that Cavadino and Dignan (2006a, 2006b) characterised Japan as being socially paternalistic and hierarchical, with exclusion of those seen as being outsiders in the social sense. This oriental corporatism model, applied uniquely to Japan by Cavadino and Dignan (2006a, 2006b), could also be used to explain why, despite Japan's economic power, limited income differentials, and high levels of political democracy, its policy towards transgender communities remains largely exclusionary. A second group of Asian countries, such as Saudi Arabia, Brunei, and the United Arab Emirates, could not be described as post-colonial due to their economic wealth, but do display political authoritarianism and cultural conservatism based on religious beliefs, particularly Sharia law. On this basis, these States fit more closely with Cavadino and Dignan's (2006a, 2006b) neoliberal model, albeit with less political freedom and democracy than the neoliberal States used as examples by them (such as the United Kingdom and the USA). A third group of Asian countries who criminalise transgender communities in either a de jure or de facto manner (or both) fit more closely into the post-colonial model. Their politically authoritarian tendencies join together with under-developed economies and predominantly conservative cultures as potential explanations for these States' continued exclusion and punitiveness towards transgender communities, in terms of both the law itself and how the law is enforced in practice.

Europe

As with Africa and Asia, Europe is a socio-economically, politically, and geographically complex area. Nonetheless, some trends can still be identified in relation to legal recognition and exclusion of transgender communities.

In terms of legal recognition, under the influence of European Court of Human Rights jurisprudence, several countries (including Belgium, Portugal, France, Greece, and Luxembourg) have recently introduced legal transgender recognition which does not require sterilisation or surgical reassignment as a precondition for recognition as a transgender person (ILGA World, 2020). In some European countries, such as Denmark and Norway, name and gender changes are simple administrative procedures that require no court-based process to enact.

While these more progressive moves characterise some European countries, progress towards a rights-based approach has not been consistent. There are still some European countries (Bulgaria, Cyprus, Lithuania, Latvia, and Romania) with no legislative provision for gender reassignment (European Commission Directorate General for Justice and Consumers, 2020). In addition, of the countries who do recognise the right to change gender, a significant group require proof of medical procedure (such as sterilisation, gender reassignment surgery, or hormone treatment). This group of States, which includes the UK as well as Slovakia, Czechia, Poland, Finland, Austria, Estonia, Spain, and Italy (European Commission Directorate General for Justice and Consumers, 2020), has made the process of transgender recognition considerably more difficult and expensive. In the UK, for example, the government has refused to update the 2004 Gender Recognition Act. This is the case despite most transgender people who were surveyed saying they found the process of applying for gender change recognition bureaucratic, time-consuming, and expensive (King et al., 2020). Under the 2004 Act, the UK legal recognition process involves paying to obtain a gender recognition certificate which can only be granted following a medical declaration of gender dysphoria and following proof of engagement with medical treatment on the part of the applicant.

There are also a range of other European States which still require medical procedures (such as sterilisation, surgery, or hormone treatment) before gender recognition can be legally approved. States in this category include Spain, Italy, Poland, and Finland. Finally, there are also European States which require diagnosis or supervision by a medical body (European Commission Directorate General for Justice and Consumers, 2020). States in this category are Slovenia, Germany,

Hungary, Croatia, Sweden, and The Netherlands (European Commission Directorate General for Justice and Consumers, 2020). Therefore, despite the upholding of transgender rights by the European Court on Human Rights and evidence of 'supporting' legislation for transgender communities in Europe, the journey towards full equality for transgender communities in the eyes of the law in Europe is far from complete.

Turning to 'excluding' legislation which criminalises transgender expression and identity, on the surface, Europe appears to be a role model for other parts of the world to follow. No European country has any legislation which specifically criminalises transgender people in this way, unlike either Africa or Asia (Human Dignity Trust, 2022). However, such a view is misleading and again emphasises the importance of analysing criminalisation in criminal justice practice as well as criminalisation within the law itself. When analysis looks beyond specific anti-transgender laws to include laws of other types used to target transgender communities in practice, the European picture becomes quite different. Of the 49 European countries for which information on criminalisation is available, eight have legislation which is used to criminalise transgender expression and identity—Albania, Armenia, Azerbaijan, Georgia, Russia, Serbia, Turkey, and Ukraine (ILGA World, 2020). What is particularly striking here is how transgender lived experiences are equated with prostitution (as in Armenia, Serbia, and Russia), seen as threats to public order and safety in the shape of 'hooliganism' or 'disorderly conduct' (as in Azerbaijan and Georgia), or have both approaches used against them (as in Turkey and the Ukraine) (ILGA World, 2020).

Even in European States which do not show any obvious signs of de jure or de facto criminalisation, discrimination can still emerge, through judicial common law decisions for example. In England, in the case of *McNally* [2013] EWCA Crim 1051, the defendant, using the name 'Scott Hill', formed a relationship with the complaint, a female, who apparently believed that the defendant was a cisgender man. This relationship resulted in the defendant digitally and orally penetrating the complainant. The complainant then discovered that McNally was not cisgender male and contacted police. The defendant was then charged with six counts of sexual assault by penetration and sentenced to three years' custody in a young offender's institution. The Court of Appeal dismissed the defendant's appeal against conviction, stating that there was evidence of 'active deception' on the defendant's part, which removed the complainant's consent to the sexual activity that took place between them. Sharpe (2017) argues that such an approach wrongly assumes that gender identity must be static to be authentic. Sharpe (2017) goes on to argue that McNally genuinely believed they were male at the time of the sexual contact, and that it is highly unlikely that the complainant believed that McNally was male, given that McNally had a voice in the female range, breasts, and had not benefited from the masculinising effects of male hormones. Sharpe (2017) therefore concluded not only that *McNally* was wrongly decided, but also that the decision represents clear and potentially dangerous discrimination against transgender communities in terms of their risk of being criminalised.

Focusing political economy analysis on European countries which use de facto statutory legislation against transgender communities, it is evident that most of these States were either formerly part of the Soviet empire (Armenia, Azerbaijan, Georgia, Russia, and the Ukraine) or formerly part of the 'Eastern Bloc' of countries which were directly under the political, economic, and social influence of the USSR from the end of the Second World War until the early 1990s (Albania and Serbia). Of these States, none are classed at a higher level than 'flawed democracy' (Albania and Serbia) by the Economic Intelligence Unit, while Ukraine, Georgia, and Turkey are classed as 'hybrid regimes', and Russia and Azerbaijan fall into the 'authoritarian' category in political terms (Economic Intelligence Unit, 2021). Freedom House (2021) similarly classes all these States as either 'partly free' or 'not free' in terms of political freedom and civil liberties. The World Happiness Report, which is based on (among other measures) real GDP per capita, social support, healthy life expectancy and people's perception of their freedom to make life choices, generosity, and perceptions of corruption, tells a similar story. None of the States mentioned in this paragraph are ranked any higher than 43rd out of 149 (Serbia), with Albania and Turkey ranked much lower at 93 and 104, respectively (Helliwell et al., 2021).

It could therefore be argued that most of the States using de facto 'excluding' criminalisation against transgender communities could be described as post-colonial in political and economic terms. It is noticeable, however, that when restrictions to 'supporting' legislation, such as medical treatment or surgery requirements, are taken into account, the States involved go beyond Cavadino and Dignan's (2006a, 2006b) neoliberal category (where such an approach might be expected). They therefore include States using the more politically moderate conservative corporatist model (such as Germany and Italy) and even States generally using the more progressive social democratic corporatist model, such as Sweden and Finland. Full compliance with the Yogyakarta Principles of 2007 is rare in Europe given they are not binding on European States, but do reflect the latest state of international human rights standards in relation to sexual orientation and gender identity (European Commission Directorate General for Justice and Consumers, 2020). This is despite the progressive work done by the European Court of Human Rights in upholding the rights of transgender people.

The Americas

Discussion in this section will cover States in North America, the Caribbean, Central America, and South America. In terms of 'supporting' legislation, in North America, recent progress has been made. In Canada, 10 of the 13 provinces and territories now offer more than male or female options on at least some identification documents, and most areas have also removed surgical requirements for legal gender marker changes, although many provinces still require a letter by a healthcare professional confirming that the gender change is appropriate, making the process of changing gender more expensive (ILGA World, 2020). Meanwhile, in the USA, although most States now allow people to change their gender on identity documents (such as driving licences) without proof of a surgical procedure, only 22 of the 50 federal States allow changing of the gender marker on a birth certificate without showing proof of sex reassignment surgery. This means that a majority of US States still require such proof, and in addition, only 16 States will allow a name change without making a public announcement (ILGA

World, 2020). This slows the process of gender recognition down as well as threatening privacy.

In Central and South America, 'supporting' legislation in terms of allowing name change is common (with only Belize, Grenada, Dominica, and Nicaragua not granting this right), but allowing change of the gender marker on identity documents is less common, and not allowed in Antigua and Barbuda, Bahamas, Barbados, Belize, Dominica, Grenada, Guatemala, Haiti, Honduras, Jamaica, Nicaragua, Paraguay, and Saint Lucia (ILGA World, 2020). It is only possible to change gender markers without surgical or sterilisation requirements in Argentina, Bolivia, Brazil, Chile, Colombia, Ecuador, Mexico, Panama, Peru, and Uruguay (ILGA World, 2020). Therefore, 'supporting' legislation to uphold the human rights of transgender communities has had limited impact in all parts of the Americas.

Turning now to 'excluding' legislation which criminalises transgender lives, no countries in the Americas have criminal offences which specifically target transgender communities in this way (Human Dignity Trust, 2022). However, a range of countries exercise de facto criminalisation by using other offences to target transgender people. A total of 12 countries in the Americas use de facto criminalisation in this way, through a mixture of drugs offences, sex worker offences, and offences against public decency or morality which are often broadly defined and offer significant discretion to police to use their powers against transgender people without any substantive legal basis for doing so. These 12 countries cover Central and South America (Argentina, Bolivia, Chile, Colombia, Cuba, Dominica, Ecuador, El Salvador, Honduras, Peru, Uruguay, and Venezuela) (ILGA World, 2020).

Turning to broader measures of social and political freedom in the Americas, most countries in the Americas can be classed as either 'flawed democracies' or 'hybrid regimes'. Only Chile and Costa Rica are fully democratic, while Venezuela is classed as 'authoritarian' on one analytical measure (Economic Intelligence Unit, 2021). Freedom House only considers Venezuela, Nicaragua, and Cuba to be 'not free' in political and democratic terms, with all other American countries judged to be at least partially free (Freedom House, 2021). Meanwhile, according to the United Nations Human Development Index, which measures economic inequality in States across the world, no American country was ranked higher than 43rd for equality apart from Canada and the USA (16th and 17th, respectively) (United Nations Development Programme, 2020). The World Happiness Report tells a similar story. In 2020, beyond the USA and Canada (ranked 14th and 15th, respectively for happiness), the next highest ranked American countries were mid-table: Chile at 38, Argentina at 47, Colombia at 55, and others lower (Helliwell et al., 2021).

It is therefore apparent that while overt criminalisation of transgender communities is less common in the Americas than in Africa or Asia, legislation upholding transgender human rights on issues such as name and gender recognition is limited. It is also apparent that exclusionary treatment cuts across different types of social and political models as defined in Cavadino and Dignan's (2006a, 2006b) work (although it should be added that they did not include any Central and South American States in their political economy analysis of punitiveness). This points to the importance of dominant cultural beliefs in different States in explaining the predominantly exclusionary treatment given to transgender people.

Oceania

For the purposes of this section of the chapter, Oceania includes Australia, Aotearoa New Zealand, and the various Pacific Island States in the Melanesia, Polynesia, and Micronesia areas. In terms of 'supporting' legislation, only Australia and Aotearoa New Zealand have options for legal gender change recognition. It is important to note, however, that the presence of such 'supporting' legislation tells us more about how transgender people's rights in these States have been recorded than about the happiness, health, and safety of people who are transgender, gender diverse, or have indigenous gender identities in Australia and Aotearoa New Zealand (ILGA World, 2020). Evidenced strongly is how those indicators have skewed away from understandings of quality of life among indigenous communities in particular. Indeed, in Aotearoa New Zealand, birth certificate gender markers can only be changed through a judicial process which may require medical interventions, and which has no third gender option (ILGA World, 2020). Elsewhere in Oceania, name changes are only possible in American Samoa, Kiribati, Marshall Islands, and Tonga if a mistake in name registration can be proved, while in the Cook Islands, Fiji, and Samoa, name changes are available without proof of error (ILGA World, 2020). As in other parts of the world, then, 'supporting' legislation protecting the rights of transgender communities is limited in a range of political economies in Oceania. In terms of 'excluding' legislation, of the States for which information is available, Tonga is the only Oceanic state which criminalises transgender lives in law, through a criminal offence prohibiting male sex workers from impersonating females while 'soliciting in a public place for an immoral purpose'. There is no record of recent enforcement of this criminal offence, nor of de facto criminalisation of transgender communities anywhere else in Oceania. However, the mere fact of this offence's existence as part of Tongan criminal law—as with the numerous obstacles to recognition of transgender status in other States in Oceania—points to the hidden cultural and moral ideologies serving to exclude transgender communities from everyday life.

Again, as discussed in earlier sections of this chapter, it is striking that there are no clear correlations between democracy levels, political freedom, and legal tolerance towards transgender communities in Oceania. For example, Australia and Aotearoa New Zealand are two of the most democratic States in the world, with very high standards of civil liberties generally (Economic Intelligence Unit, 2021, Freedom House, 2021), and high levels of societal happiness, ranked between 2018 and 2020 as the 9th (Aotearoa New Zealand) and 11th happiest countries in the world (Helliwell et al., 2021). Australia and Aotearoa New Zealand also have the most developed and wealthy economies in the Oceania region. However, while both States have options for legal gender change recognition, only five of the eight Australian territories and States have clear legislation confirming that no sex reassignment surgery is required before a gender marker change can take place on official documents (ILGA World, 2020). Meanwhile, in Aotearoa New Zealand, gender marker change on birth certificates is subject to a test specific to the person, based on medical evidence and advice, to show commitment to gender change. This process could involve sex reassignment surgery in some cases, but not in others (ILGA World, 2020). The uncertainty inherent in this process of gender recognition is likely, it is argued, to increase levels of stress and resentment among transgender people who wish to have their gender change legally recognised on official documents.

Conclusion and Future Research Recommendations

This chapter examined the differences in de jure and de facto criminalisation of transgender communities in different regions of the world, by comparing criminalisation in different States to the type of social, political, and economic factors used to explain criminal punishment more generally by Cavadino and Dignan (2006a, 2006b). Cavadino and Dignan's (2006a, 2006b) models were only able to explain differences in 'protecting' and 'excluding' legislation across different geographical areas of the world to a limited extent. It is argued that Cavadino and Dignan's (2006a, 2006b) political economy models were of limited usage for three key reasons.

First, Cavadino and Dignan's (2006a, 2006b) model analysed criminal punishment in a general sense, using prison rates in different States as a measure of punitiveness. On the other hand, this chapter has focused more specifically on legal responses to transgender communities, in two different contexts: the extent to which legislation protects transgender communities by upholding their human rights (by allowing gender marker changes on official documentation to be made without gender reassignment surgery or other medical procedures for example) and the extent to which legislation excludes transgender communities, either through specific criminal offences or through use of other criminal offences to target transgender communities. This chapter has therefore attempted to use evidence of legislative content and criminal justice practice to measure punitiveness, rather than prison rates as Cavadino and Dignan (2006a, 2006b) did. As such, the analysis in this chapter also differs from studies which have correlated imprisonment rates in particular States with the amount of GDP spent on welfare (Downes & Hansen, 2006), or which have compared imprisonment rates with levels of relative income equality in different States (Wilkinson & Pickett, 2007).

Second, Cavadino and Dignan's (2006a, 2006b) analysis did not cover some geographical areas. They only discussed South Africa among African States, for example, and only discussed Japan among Asian States, as well as not including any South or Central American countries in their analysis. This chapter, while subject to limitations in available information on legislation and its enforcement from some geographical areas of the world, was able to include analysis of a range of States in Africa, Asia, the Americas, and Oceania, as well as analysis of the States in Europe and North America that Cavadino and Dignan (2006a, 2006b) included in their work. The extension of Cavadino and Dignan's (2006a, 2006b) political economy analysis of punitiveness in this chapter also necessitated the tentative development of a new socio-economic model, the post-colonial model, to add to the neoliberalist, conservative corporatist, social democratic corporatist, and oriental corporatist models developed by Cavadino and Dignan (2006a, 2006b).

Third, Cavadino and Dignan's (2006a, 2006b) existing models and approach could not explain legal attitudes towards transgender communities and their lifestyles in detail. For example, even some social democratic corporatist States identified by Cavadino and Dignan (2006a, 2006b) as being tolerant and lenient in terms of general approach to criminal punishment, such as Sweden and Finland, imposed punitive restrictions on transgender people who wished to change their gender marker on official documents. Countries who were politically free and highly democratic, such as Australia, also placed similar restrictions on supporting transgender rights. Such widespread intolerance points to a wide range of mediating variables through which political economy can shape punitive and intolerant attitudes, such as crime levels, general culture, media culture, political culture, and political institutions—as Cavadino and Dignan themselves have advocated in other work (Cavadino & Dignan, 2008, cited in Nelken, 2009). Dominant cultural and moral ideologies would seem to be particularly important in understanding why States with a range of differing political economies shared the same exclusionary values in relation to transgender people.

In terms of more general conclusions, it was found that negative legal attitudes towards transgender communities were common across the world. This was true both in terms of ostensibly 'protecting' legislation which on closer analysis carried with it often intrusive, time-consuming, expensive, and stressful obstacles faced by transgender people who wished to enforce their human rights to recognition, and in terms of the extent of criminalisation of transgender lives. While relatively few States used legislation which specifically criminalised transgender communities, a much wider range of States used other types of criminal offence against these communities or took criminal justice action against them without any specific legal basis for doing so. There was evidence that very few States took a consistently proactive approach to upholding transgender rights and avoided criminalising transgender lifestyles.

This chapter has provided an exploratory approach to linking social, political, economic, and cultural factors to legal attitudes towards transgender communities in different parts of the world. It is noticeable, however, that much of the data used as an evidential base for analysis in the chapter is quantitative in nature and consists of large-scale numerical data. Next steps for research into recognition and criminalisation of transgender communities should focus on obtaining deeper, richer data from transgender communities themselves, in terms of how they view the law's treatment of them in the state they live in. Research has tried to capture the voices of transgender people (e.g. European Commission Directorate General for Justice and Consumers, 2020) but has attempted to do so through the methodological means of quantitative surveys. Future research should use more qualitative techniques to capture the lived experiences of transgender people, and their relationships with the law, both positive and negative. Future research should also focus on capturing hegemonic cultural and moral conditions in different States and linking these to legal and criminal justice responses in those areas, as these factors seemed to show promise in explaining positive and negative legal attitudes towards transgender communities in different parts of the world. Finally, it should do more to obtain the perspectives of those working within criminal processing systems in different areas, to understand their perspectives on how the law does and should approach transgender people, echoing the argument made more generally about comparative criminal justice by Nelken (2009). Given the considerable challenges transgender communities continue to face in expressing themselves and their chosen identities freely and without interference from the law and those who put the law into action, such further research is required urgently as a means of bringing social justice closer for transgender communities.

References

Cavadino, M., & Dignan, J. (2006a). *Penal systems: A comparative approach.* Sage.

Cavadino, M., & Dignan, J. (2006b). Penal policy and political economy. *Criminology and Criminal Justice, 6*(4), 435–456.

Chakraborti, N., & Garland, J. (2009). *Hate crime: Impact, causes and responses.* Sage.

Christie, N. (2004). *A suitable amount of crime*. Routledge.

CIA. (2020). *The World Factbook.* Retrieved October 23, 2020, from https://www.cia.gov/library/publications/resources/the-world-factbook/

Downes, D., & Hansen, K. (2006). *Welfare and punishment: The relationship between welfare spending and imprisonment.* Centre for Crime and Justice Studies. Retrieved February 22, 2022, from https://www.crimeandjustice.org.uk/publications/welfare-and-punishment-relationship-between-welfare-spending-and-imprisonment

Economic Intelligence Unit. (2021). *Democracy Index 2020.* Retrieved January 25, 2022, from https://www.eiu.com/n/campaigns/democracy-index-2020/

European Commission Directorate-General for Justice and Consumers. (2020). *Legal gender recognition in the EU: The journeys of trans people towards full equality*. Publications Office of the European Union. Retrieved February 3, 2022, from https://data.europa.eu/doi/10.2838/085419

Freedom House. (2021). *Global freedom status map.* Retrieved January 25, 2022, from https://freedomhouse.org/explore-the-map?type=fiw&year=2021

Hall, N. (2013). *Hate crime* (2nd ed.). Routledge.

Hall, S. (2012). *Theorizing crime and deviance*. Sage.
Helliwell, J. F., Layard, R., Sachs, J. D., De Neve, J.-E., Aknin, L. B., & Wang, S. (2021). *World Happiness Report 2021*. Retrieved February 22, 2022, from https://worldhappiness.report/ed/2021/#appendices-and-data
Human Dignity Trust. (2022). *Map of countries that criminalise the gender identity/expression of trans people*. Retrieved February 3, 2022, from https://www.humandignitytrust.org/lgbt-the-law/map-ofcriminalisation/?type_filter=crim_gender_exp
Human Rights Watch. (2013). *"Treat us like human beings": Discrimination against sex workers, sexual and gender minorities, and people who use drugs in Tanzania*. Human Rights Watch. Retrieved February 4, 2022, from https://www.hrw.org/report/2013/06/18/treat-us-human-beings/discrimination-against-sex-workers-sexual-and-gender#_ftnref129
ILGA World: Chiam, Z., Duffy, S., Gonzalez Gil, M., Goodwin, L., & Patel, N. T. M. (2020). *Trans legal mapping report 2019: Recognition before the law*. ILGA World.
King, D., Paechter, C., & Ridgway, M. (2020). *Gender recognition act: Analysis of consultation responses*. Government Equalities Office. Retrieved January 28, 2022, from https://assets.publishing.service.gov.uk/government/uploads/system/uploads/attachment_data/file/919890/Analysis_of_responses_Gender_Recognition_Act.pdf
Lawrence, P. (2010). The African tragedy: International and national roots. In V. Padayachee (Ed.), *The political economy of Africa*. Routledge.
Luhur, W., Brown, T. N. T., Liu, M., & Shaw, A. (2021). *Public opinion of transgender rights in China*. UCLA School of Law Williams Institute. Retrieved January 28, 2022, from https://williamsinstitute.law.ucla.edu/wp-content/uploads/Public-Opinion-Trans-China-English-Jun-2021.pdf
Nelken, D. (2009). Comparative criminal justice. *European Journal of Criminology, 6*(4), 291–312.
Packer, H. (1968). *The limits of the criminal sanction*. Stanford University Press.
Sharpe, A. (2017). Queering judgment: The case of gender identity fraud. *The Journal of Criminal Law, 81*(5), 417–435.
United Nations, Department of Economic and Social Affairs, Population Division. (2019). *World Population Prospects 2019*. Retrieved February 3, 2022, from https://www.un.org/development/desa/pd/
United Nations Development Programme. (2020). *Inequality-Adjusted Human Development Index*. Retrieved February 9, 2022, from https://hdr.undp.org/en/composite/IHDI

United States Department of State. (2019). *Indonesia 2018 Human Rights Report.* United States Department of State, Bureau of Democracy, Human Rights and Labour. Retrieved February 3, 2022, from https://www.State.gov/wp-content/uploads/2019/03/INDONESIA-2018.pdf

Wilkinson, R., & Pickett, K. (2007). The problems of relative deprivation: Why some societies do better than others. *Social Sciences and Medicine, 65*, 1965–1978.

Woods, J. B., & Herman, J. L. (2018). Anti-transgender hate crime. In N. Hall, A. Corb, P. Giannasi, & J. G. D. Grieve (Eds.), *The Routledge international handbook on hate crime.* Routledge.

Young, J. (1999). *The exclusive society*. Sage.

Case List

McNally [2013] EWCA Crim 1051.

4

Transgender and Gender Non-conforming Young People and the School-To-Prison Pipeline: Too Crucial to Ignore

DeShaun LaChance and Angela Dwyer

Introduction

Identity is arguably the most important core aspect of a person. As Grossman and D'Augelli (2006) point out, developing and integrating a positive identity is a developmental task for all young people. For transgender young people, however, there is the "additional challenge of integrating a complex gender identity, with their cultural and ethnic backgrounds, personal characteristics, and family circumstances" (Grossman & D'Augelli, 2006, p. 113). Many young people spanning across the globe self-identify as being transgender, nonbinary, gender

D. LaChance
Illinois Department of Human Rights, Chicago, IL, USA

A. Dwyer (✉)
School of Social Sciences, Tasmanian Institute of Law Enforcement Studies, University of Tasmania, Glen Waverley, VIC, Australia
e-mail: angela.dwyer@utas.edu.au

H. Panter and A. Dwyer (eds.), *Transgender People and Criminal Justice*, Critical Criminological Perspectives, https://doi.org/10.1007/978-3-031-29893-6_4

non-conforming, or gender diverse. Most have shared a common internal struggle with their sense of their true gender identity from early on.

Young people, whose gender identity contrasts with their biological sex, are often questioned about their gender expression, which may feel like an affront (Snapp et al., 2015, p. 67). The reason for challenging young people about their gender identity, particularly young people that identify as transgender, nonbinary, gender non-conforming, and gender diverse, emerges out of social and cultural expectations about how gender should be displayed in cisnormative ways (where the gender displayed should align with their sex assigned at birth), and about how sexuality should align with heteronormative heterosexuality. These social and cultural expectations are powerfully policed by the general population, particularly in public spaces and institutions like schools and workplaces. These forms of informal policing of gender and sexuality diversity are most often manifested acutely in the form of hate crimes. For example, while LGBTQ+ communities comprise approximately 4.5% of the US population, they are disproportionately targeted for hate and violence. According to the FBI, 1,445 people were the victim of a hate crime due to sexuality in 2018, while another 215 were targeted based on their gender identity (Hinduja & Patchin, 2020, p. 1). These forms of hate violence stem directly from these social and cultural expectations.

Due to the predominantly global shared binary view of gender, transgender and gender non-conforming (herein TGD) young people are faced with greater hardships than any other minority group. When they are school age, they often experience detrimental bullying and violence, perpetrated by their cisgender peers and quite often, school staff, which often leads to transgender and gender non-conforming young people dropping out of school. This is compounded when many young people are also rejected by their families, which leads to homelessness. These experiences therefore lead to surviving on their own on the streets, something which most often leads to transgender and gender non-conforming young people being quickly introduced to police harassment and violence. This is especially true for transgender and nonbinary young people of color, with significant racial disparities between students of color—Indigenous, Black, Latinx,[1] and Māori,[2] and students of European descent—White and Pakeha.[3]

This chapter argues that experiences of TGD young people described above lead them to be overrepresented in what is now called the school-to-prison pipeline. According to the ACLU (2015, as cited in Glickman, 2016, p. 275), the school-to-prison pipeline is a term developed to explain the relationship between the policies that push at-risk young people "out of classrooms and into juvenile and criminal justice systems. The pipeline is composed of policies which can be arranged into three main categories: achievement, discipline, and safety" (Glickman, 2016, p. 276). The lack of resources in certain school districts, mounted with pressures imposed by test-driven accountability, creates incentives for schools to actively push the neediest children out of their schools (Kim et al., 2010). Civil rights' advocates call this process "the school-to-prison pipeline" (Nelson & Lind, 2015) precisely because of how these policies are designed to push certain children out of school and into criminal processing systems, where prison is the end of the road. Such policies most often rely on zero-tolerance policy measures where slight disciplinary infractions from TGD young people, often characteristically acts of self-protection, are met with harsh discipline, and can lead to suspensions, detentions, and expulsions as a pathway out of school (Snapp et al., 2015, p. 70).

While there is a growing body of research describing how race impacts the school-to-prison pipeline, far less is known about the school discipline experiences of TGD young people as compared with other young people within the pipeline population (Snapp et al., 2015, p. 58). The lack of research shows young transgender people have largely been overlooked in the growing body of scholarship related to the school-to-prison pipeline (Rosentel et al., 2021, p. 482). Drawing on data from the United States, Australia, New Zealand, the United Kingdom, and Brazil, this chapter outlines forms of abuse and violence present in school spaces and suggests ways to stop transgender and gender non-conforming

[1] Pronounced "La-teen-ex," includes the numerous people of Latin American descent whose gender identities are on a spectrum.

[2] Indigenous New Zealanders.

[3] Pakeha is a term used to refer to a New Zealander of white, anglo-saxon descent.

young people, particularly young people of color, from ending up in the school-to-prison pipeline. First, the chapter discusses the history of policing gender. Second, it provides a global overview of the detrimental effects of discrimination and violence in schools. Third, it describes how transgender, and gender non-conforming young people come to be incarcerated. The chapter concludes with some policy suggestions that might be helpful in reducing the number transgender and gender non-conforming young people that are incarcerated, as well as suggestions that may help transgender and gender non-conforming students finish their education.

Histories of Policing Gender

People who contradicted social expectations of what was considered typical for men or for women have existed since the earliest days of colonial settlement in what is now the United States (Stryker, 2017, p. 45). What is now known as the state of Massachusetts, first passed laws against cross-dressing in the 1690s (Stryker, 2017, p. 45). How people display their gender identity has been the subject of informal and formal policing and governance for some time. Starting in the 1850s, several US cities began passing municipal ordinances that made it illegal for people to appear in public in a dress not belonging to his or her sex (Stryker, 2017, p. 46). One of several anti-cross-dressing laws passed in the middle of the nineteenth century, the ordinance was enacted in 1863, reading in part as follows: "If any person shall appear in a public place in a dress not belonging to his or her sex, he should be guilty of a misdemeanor, and on conviction, shall pay a fine not exceeding five hundred dollars" (Stryker, 2017, p. 47).

American public schools as we know them came into existence in the late nineteenth and early twentieth centuries, and along with them came gendered dress codes that reflected the gendered separation of society large (Glickman, 2016, p. 267). Until just a few decades ago, police officers enforced what were known as "sumptuary laws," laws which required people to wear "gender appropriate" clothing (INCITE!, 2015). In this sense, what gender appropriate clothing referred to implied those assigned male sex at birth to wear "masculine" attire only, and for those assigned female sex at birth, to only wear garments that would be considered feminine. Those who did not comply were subjected to arrest for "impersonating another gender" (INCITE!, 2015, p. 5). Police would demand identification which, for trans people whose appearance might not match the name or gender designation on their IDs, often led to arrest on suspicion of prostitution, vagrancy, loitering, or many other so-called nuisance crimes (Stryker, 2017, p. 77). Grbach (2012) states that "gendered dress codes are a specific point of entry for the school to prison pipeline because clothing choices is an integral part of gender identity and expression" (as cited in Glickman, 2016, p. 276).

While it might be easy to dismiss these ideas and practices as historical, thinking about TGD people as criminal or medically abnormal continues to heavily influence how people think about TGD people in contemporary times. More importantly, practices focused on policing gender persist today, but in different forms. For instance, when police officers request identification from transgender or gender non-conforming people, and it does not match the person's assumed gender based upon their appearance, police often make presumptions that "transgender people are fraudulent, deceitful, or inherently suspicious" which can in turn lead to "verbal abuse, harassment, and physical abuse" (INCITE!, 2015, p. 5).

How TGD Young People Experience Bullying and Violence in Schools

Bullying and violence experienced by TGD young people in schools is widespread and well documented, with research suggesting that schools are a dangerous place for them (Singh, 2012, p. 691). Thus, while most people would agree that proper education is essential for a productive future, educational settings are among the least affirming environments for gender variant young people (Mallon, 2009). These experiences often start with bullying. Bullying incorporates a range of different behaviors, including direct actions, such as hitting or pushing, and indirect actions, "such as repeatedly teasing, spreading harmful rumors and social exclusion" (Education Review Office, 2019, p. 7). It is peer victimization, occurring repeatedly over time, and involving an imbalance of power between the bully and victim (Collier et al., 2013). Bullying is characterized by three criteria: "intentionality, repeatability and imbalance of power" (de Oliveira et al., 2015, p. 276). Bullying occurs when individuals or groups seek to harm, intimidate, or coerce someone who is perceived to be vulnerable. Furthermore, it can be a form of discrimination, particularly if it is based on a child's gender identity or sexuality (NSPCC, 2021). It is important to note that bullying is an expansive term: it incorporates a range of different types of behaviors, and often surveys of bullying in schools will incorporate measures of physical and sexual assault as forms of bullying.

Bullying that specifically targets young people based on their gender identity and/or expression has been a problem for decades (Hinduja & Patchin, 2020). For TGD students, one of the ultimate verbal harassments is being called by their birth name, after indicating that a chosen name was preferable (Grossman & D'Augelli, 2006). Clements (2018) describes deadnaming as when someone, intentionally or not, refers to a person who's TGD by the name they used before they affirmed their gender (medically or not). One might also hear it described as referring to someone by their "birth name" or their "given name", which can occur anywhere in a trans person's life: from personal relationships to the classroom, through to workplaces (Clements, 2018, para. 3).

TGD students are especially impacted by bullying according to research showing that, "even after accounting for protective school factors, hearing peers make negative comments or use slurs based on gender identity and expression was correlated with lower perceptions of school safety" (Collier et al., 2013, p. 8). In Australia, those who identify as "LGBTI, gender diverse or living with an intersex variation, suffer from negative experiences and are bullied more than their non-LGBTI peers" (Victoria Safe Schools, 2022, p. 2). A health and well-being survey with 8,500 New Zealand secondary school students found nearly one in five transgender students had experienced bullying at school on a weekly basis (Clark et al., 2014). Additionally, more than half of transgender students were afraid someone at school would hurt or bother them (Clark et al., 2014). The national transgender discrimination survey provides the most comprehensive data collection of school bullying experienced by transgender, nonbinary, and gender non-conforming students in the United States (Grant et al., 2011). Those who expressed a transgender identity or gender non-conformity, while in grades K-12, reported alarming rates of harassment (78%), physical assault (35%), and sexual violence (12%) (Grant et al., 2011, p. 33). In the same study, MTF[4] students reported higher rates of physical and sexual assault, while FTM[5] students and gender non-conforming students reported higher rates of harassment and bullying (Grant et al., 2011).

A key concern in recent years has been the growth of cyberbullying: children and young people using digital technologies, and especially social media, to inflict psychological harm on others. Cyberbullying presents a particular challenge to schools, as it can be more difficult to detect, and can continue outside of school time and off-site (Educational Review Office, 2019, p. 7). A child can be bullied online when they are alone, in their bedroom trying to relax or do homework, so it can feel like there is no escape (NSPCC, 2016). According to Abreu (2018), studies show that gender expansive adolescents are disproportionally more often victims of cyberbullying than their cisgender counterparts (as cited in Hinduja & Patchin, 2020). As a result, some transgender and gender non-conforming young people engage in self-harm behavior, such as cutting, as a coping mechanism (Collier et al. 2013).

It would be erroneous to assume that bullying and violence like this was only perpetrated by students against TGD young people. Teachers and staff members whose job in part includes ensuring student safety, were too often the perpetrators of harassment and violence in K-12 schools in the United States (Grant et al., 2011, p. 33). For example, "[t]hirty-one percent (31%) of the sample reported harassment by teachers or staff, 5% reported physical assault by teachers or staff and 3% reported sexual assault by teachers or staff" (Grant et al., 2011, p. 33). These experiences are especially common for young TGD people of

4 Male to female.

5 Female to male.

color. The National Transgender Discrimination survey (2008) showed that Black queer young people who attended school reported alarming rates of harassment, physical assault, and sexual assault at school. The same research showed that Latinx and multiracial respondents reported the highest levels of harassment and bullying by their teachers at 35% and 42% respectively (Grant et al., 2011, p. 38). Furthermore, multiracial and American Indian students experienced the highest levels of physical assault by teachers and staff by 6% (Grant et al., 2011). Black students experienced much higher rates of sexual assault by teachers (7%), relative to their peers of any race (Grant et al., 2011).

Bullying and violence perpetrated against TGD young people in schools has significant impacts. There are several intersecting factors that sometimes contribute to their pathways out of school, such as compromised mental health (sometimes because of school experiences), learning challenges, and family problems, or homelessness (Snapp et al., 2015). According to a recent study conducted by The Trevor Project (2020), a high percentage of transgender and nonbinary young people reported symptoms of major depressive disorders and generalized anxiety disorders. They had also engaged in self-harming behaviors, and many had seriously considered suicide, with some even attempting suicide. Sadly, 46% of LGBTQ+ young people in this study reported that they wanted psychological or emotional counseling from a mental health professional but were unable to receive it (The Trevor Project, 2020).

All adults involved in education, including teachers, teacher educators, administrators, counselors, and school psychologist, are necessarily (un)knowing participants who actively contribute to TGD youth suicide. This is why the everyday experiences with sociocultural norms and values, and the daily aggressions students encounter at school, have been referred to as the school-to-coffin pipeline (Wozolek et al., 2017, p. 394). The complexity of the schooling context for TGD young people is best demonstrated by case studies of students that have experienced this. "Pat Doe", a young trans girl, designated male at birth and at that time, diagnosed with having gender identity disorder, was prohibited from enrolling in the eighth grade if she wore "girls" clothing or accessories to school (Flynn, 2009, p. 487). It should be noted that Pat expressed her gender identity through wearing skirts, jewelry, and other accessories deemed feminine (Flynn, 2009, p. 491).

Another infamous case demonstrates how significant the outcomes can be for TGD young people. In 2008, Lawrence "Larry" King, an American 15-year-old teenager, who was openly gay and gender non-conforming, was shot and killed by a classmate while at his California school. Since King was Latinx, short for his age, and known for his effeminacy, this "made him a prime target for homophobic bullying" (Perkiss, 2013, p. 785). Though homophobic bullying is different than transphobic bullying, Larry was nonetheless targeted not just because he was gay, but also because of his appearance, behavior, and physical traits that transgressed cisnormative expectations in the schooling environment (Family Lives, 2021). King's killer, a 14-year-old male student at the time, "had previously been tried for a charge of murder with a hate crime enhancement, however a deadlocked jury could not reach a verdict" (Tala, 2011, para. 4). Yet the day before the killing, the student reportedly told at least one of his classmates they should "[s]ay goodbye to Larry because [you aren't] going to see him again" (Perkiss, 2013, p. 782).

Lesser-known facts about the case of Larry King are that, although King had a family, at the time of his death he was living in a foster care facility for abused and neglected children (Cathcart, 2008). This fact reflects the harsh reality that many TGD young people often lack a strong family support unit, with young people often estranged from their families because they do not support them because they are TGD. The lack of these family networks can lead to very serious victimization and fatal violence for these young people, even in the supposedly safe environment of school grounds. Most importantly, though, the lack of these family support networks can mean that young people victimized in these serious ways can end up having contact with police in public spaces, especially if they are exiled from the family and are experiencing housing insecurity. Time on the street and homelessness place immeasurable burdens on young people to fend for themselves to survive: "they are vulnerable to arrest whether or not they are engaged in illicit activities" (Snapp et al., 2015, p. 75). This is the point at which TGD young people can most easily move through into the school-to-prison pipeline.

How TGD Young People Enter the School-To-Prison Pipeline

In response to sometimes irrational fears of school violence, school administrators have developed a variety of overzealous discipline policies, which includes mandatory zero-tolerance policies (NAACP, 2018, p. 3). Harsh school discipline policies disproportionately affect students who identify as transgender (Anti-Defamation League, 2015). Zero-tolerance policies are set up to quickly suspend, expel, and even arrest young people, for committing the slightest infraction (NAACP, 2018). Examples includes pushing other students, throwing food, cursing, or disobeying a teacher (NAACP, 2018, p. 4). Even more problematically, these types of behaviors can manifest when TGD young people respond to bullying by fighting back, and when this happens, "they are often blamed and punished for their own victimization" (Snapp et al., 2015, p. 69). Such "push-outs" for non-disciplinary measures include disenrolling truant young people from high school, or counselors encouraging struggling students to enroll in GED programs (Kim et al., 2010). These more minor concerns often escalate to even more serious exclusions in schooling settings, including increased frequency of being suspended, being expelled from school, and being arrested at school (Kim et al., 2010). Such things increase the risks of juvenile and, eventually, adult incarceration (Hemphill et al., 2017). Given this drastic outcome, the school-to-prison pipeline is one of the most urgent challenges in education today (NAACP, 2018, pp. 2–3).

In the United States, the school-to-prison pipeline works in a way that suggests the public school system tends to neglect and expel students who need extra educational and social support (Deckert, 2015), and this is how TGD young people would flow into this pipeline. One of the ways zero-tolerance policies are implemented at public schools is that school districts often hire police officers to work onsite. In some schools, they are referred to as "School Resource Officers (SRO)'s and [they] have the power to arrest students at schools" (Nelson & Lind, 2015). This is said to offer an added measure of security, but this can be extremely detrimental to students, because "behavior that might once have led to detention, suspension, or expulsion can result instead in jail time and a criminal record" (Behne, 2017, p. 102). According to the Anti-Defamation League, as many as 3.3 million young people are suspended or expelled from school each year in the United States, approximately double the rate of the 1970s, with about 92,000 students arrested in school during the 2011–2012 school year (ADL, 2015, p. 11). This number is overwhelmingly high, especially since many of these arrests are for non-violent behavioral infractions. When children attend schools that "place a greater value on discipline and security than on knowledge and intellectual development, they are attending prep schools for prison" (Davis, 2003, p. 40). Research clearly indicates that multiple systems of support fail when TGD young people are engaging in schooling environments, which subsequently make it difficult to successfully complete school and excel (Snapp et al., 2015).

Among the most troubling aspects of how TGD young people enter the school-to-prison pipeline are the grave disparities which provoke unnecessary law enforcement referrals for certain identifiable subgroups who are marginalized and vulnerable. This is especially apparent with transgender young people of color (Kim et al., 2010) and transgender young people who are exiled from their family of origin and end up homeless (Grant et al., 2011).

TGD Young People of Color and the School-To-Prison Pipeline

In the United States, there is no surprise that the pipeline disproportionately affects children of African-American and Hispanic descent (Deckert, 2015), with racial profiling typically targeting African-Americans as well as other young people of color (Behne, 2017). At every stage of the juvenile legal system, young Black people are treated more harshly than young white people (Henning, 2021, p. 471). In part, these disparities are the result of the longstanding racist stereotype that African-Americans, especially men and boys, are dangerous and predatory (NAACP, 2018). According to Arkles (2009, as cited in Green, 2017, p. 43), TGD young people of color are disproportionally exposed to incarceration as they are often more likely to engage in survival crimes like prostitution and the selling and consumption of illegal drugs.

These experiences of young people of color are not unique to the United States, with similar patterns documented in other contexts where colonization and dispossession impacted the lives of Indigenous people showing "that colonization is not just a historic event of the past but continues its repressive operations in social, political, economic and cultural processes" (Deckert, 2015). While there is a lack of specific statistics for TGD young people in these contexts, statistics around schooling are very revealing around racial bias. Trans kids are to be found in *every* population, whether they make themselves visible or not (Zaman et al., 2021, p. 39). In New Zealand, racial disparities exist between Māori students and Pakeha students. Deckert (2015) reports that in New Zealand, Child Youth Families (CYF), disproportionally place Māori children in "out-of-home care" compared to Pakeha children. The children who are placed there are at a "higher risk of further abuse, suffer from educational underachievement, depression, and drug and alcohol abuse and are more likely to be incarcerated" (Deckert, 2015). CYF's racially biased placement practices guarantee that it is predominantly Māori children who are being fed through "the social services to prison pipeline" (Deckert, 2015). In Queensland, Australia, Indigenous young people accounted for just 7% of young people between ages 10 and 17 years. However, they also comprised 55% of those under youth justice supervision Indigenous young people are subjected to school exclusion disciplinary actions for fighting, "which they said is often in defense against unaddressed bullying and racism in schools" (Graham et al., 2022, p. 189).

School climate can influence how TGD young people are pushed out of schooling environments. Holmes and Cahill (2004) emphasize that young people are coming out earlier as transgender, but many school administrators and teachers are not keeping up with this cultural change. Behne (2017) mentions that children of color are more likely than white children to be suspended or expelled from school and to live in poor neighborhoods with high police presence. Higher rates of victimization like this, combined with higher rates of suspension, means that the chances that TGD young people will have an interaction with police is exponentially increased. As Hemphill et al. (2017) points out, "for those students who are already uninterested in attending school, suspension could be seen as a reward" (p. 17). This in turn can lead to students engaging in potentially negative behaviors, such as, "participating in illegal activity, possibly, just to make up for lost time that they would be in school" (Hemphill et al., 2017, p. 17). Significant time spent unsupervised outside the school environment may allow young people greater opportunity to associate with antisocial peers (Hemphill et al., 2017, p. 9). Both anti-trans school expulsion/denial of enrollment and denial of gender appropriate facilities at school were associated with being more likely to experience anti-trans mistreatment by police (Rosentel et al., 2021). Furthermore, suspended students may begin to develop an "outsider" mentality, internalizing their self-identity as "a bad student", and become alienated and detached from the school community (Hemphill et al., 2017).

Compounding even further the issues discussed above is how schools that TGD young people attend are all too often under-resourced public schools (Kim et al., 2010). In 2000, African-Americans represented only 17% of public school enrollment nationwide, but accounted for 34% of suspensions. Likewise, in 2003 African-American young people comprised only 16% of the nation's overall population of young people but accounted for 45% of juvenile arrests. TGD young people of color are overrepresented in nearly every prominent pathway into the juvenile justice system (Perry and Green, 2014). A range of key factors influence these pathways, particularly living in poverty, housing insecurity, drug use, antisocial behaviors, gang membership, being a victim of bullying, and experiencing mental health issues (Perry and Green, 2014). These types of experiences demonstrate clearly how TGD young people are pushed out onto the streets because of schools zero-tolerance policies, global systemic racism, and school dropout due to constant bullying.

TGD Young People, Family Exile, Housing Insecurity, and the School-To-Prison Pipeline

Although families are slowly becoming more accepting of young people who are sexuality and/or gender diverse, there is no doubt that families not accepting these young people leads to their exile from their family of origin (Asquith et al., 2017). Where family violence occurs against TGD young people in families of origin, research has found "a strong apparent link to homelessness" (Grant et al., 2011, p. 102). Once on the streets, transgender young people experience longer periods of homelessness than other young people (Choi et al., 2015, p. 13), and therefore face a much higher risk of being introduced into the criminal legal system. The U.S. Department of Education suggests that annually, over eight hundred thousand children experience homelessness (Kim et al., 2010), and even though they only comprise about 5–8% of the total youth population (Wodda & Panfil, 2020), an estimated 40% of these young people identify as LGBTQ+ (Fraser et al., 2019).

Trying to survive on their own on the streets, often leads TGD young people to engage in risky behavior they may not typically engage with. Young people who engage in what is sometimes called "survival sex" are often homeless. Research shows that higher percentages of LGBTQ+ young people exchange sex to meet needs such as food, clothing, and shelter, than their non-LGBTQ+ peers (Wodda & Panfil, 2020). This puts TGD young people at a heightened risk of entering the school-to-prison pipeline (Hunt & Moodie-Mills, 2020). Hunt and Moodie-Mills (2020, p. 3) point out that, often out of despair and a need for survival, homeless transgender young people are more likely to resort to criminal behaviors, such as "selling drugs or theft, which puts them at risk of arrest and detainment". Unfortunately, young people are also at a greater risk of being detained for committing crimes related to homelessness in general, such as violating youth curfew laws and sleeping in public spaces (Hunt & Moodie-Mills, 2020). "When neither schools nor families claim youth, they may be held for longer than necessary and end up in detention centers" (Snapp et al., 2015, p. 74). While research also shows these young people can be offered "unexpected opportunities for fostering resilience" (Alessi et al., 2020, p. 11249), it is abundantly clear that the risks and harm involved might often outweigh these positives. Since "transgender people are often directly impacted by police suspicion" (Wodda & Panfil, 2020, p. 50), there is little to no chance of successfully living on the street, without winding up in the juvenile and later adult legal system.

There are numerous stories of family abuse and exile of TGD young people around the world. The story of Jane Doe is a prime example of transgender people experiencing mistreatment at home before being exiled from the family of origin and ending up and homeless and engaged with the criminal legal system. Since she was eight years old, Jane Doe had been beaten and raped by various people (including relatives) for wearing dresses and presenting herself as a female as opposed to the male sex she was assigned at birth (Bauer, 2014, para. 4). By the time she was 12 years old, the Connecticut Department of Children and Families (DCF) became her legal guardian (Bauer, 2014, para. 5). On January 28, 2014, Jane Doe allegedly assaulted a staff worker at a juvenile facility in Massachusetts (Bauer, 2014, para. 6). According to Jane Doe's lawyer Aaron Romano, the most recent incident was sparked when a male staffer at the Massachusetts facility put Doe in a bear hug restraint from behind (Bauer, 2014, para. 7). Romano stated that this is a girl who has been sexually abused; she is inclined to interpret actions with that view (Bauer, 2014, para. 7). DCF cited an obscure statute, which allows a child to be held in adult facility, if it is deemed in their best interest (Bauer, 2014, para. 8). Initially, the state wanted to place Jane Doe in an adult male facility, but after her lawyer objected, she was sent to a women's facility (Bauer, 2014, para. 8). Federal law prohibits juveniles to be housed with adults, Jane Doe was housed in solitary confinement (Bauer, 2014, para. 8).

How to Stop TGD Young People from Entering the School-To-Prison Pipeline

As the abuse experienced by TGD young people on the streets is even more pervasive in detention and correctional settings, it is urgent that school and criminal processing practitioners attempt to slow the trickle of TGD young people into the school-to-prison pipeline (The Annie E. Casey Foundation, 2015). Schooling practitioners can engage a range of different strategies for beginning this work, particularly those aimed at reducing the rejection of TGD young people by families, and promoting supportive, accepting family responses when TGD young people disclose their identities. These must be funded and implemented in a range of educational settings (Mountz, 2020).

First, TGD students should feel safe attending school and a range of things need to be implemented to make school cultures as safe as possible. Curriculum should teach about the histories of discrimination against TGD people, as well as about the existence of TGD people, to ensure school students (and teachers!) have cultural awareness of these issues. Changes in school and school curriculum should be swift and done with genuine care, beginning with "high quality preschools" (Kim et al., 2010, p. 17) and moving through every level of educational systems. School staff need adequate training about the unique issues impacting the lives of TGD young people, and this includes administrative and teaching staff—not teaching staff alone. There is also a dire need for access to competent guidance counselors and school psychologists (Kim et al., 2010). School managers and teachers need to be carefully screened to ensure they are supportive of TGD young people and do not hold transphobic attitudes, and racial and ethnic classroom dynamics between teachers and students must be addressed starting with pre-employment screening of teachers and other staff in terms of racist attitudes.

Second, a range of changes can be made to the structures and processes of schools to ensure TGD young people are being supported. Schools should have policies that support TGD students seeking to affirm their gender while they are still attending school. TGD students should be allowed access to whichever bathroom and locker room spaces they feel the safest and most gender affirming, and public and independent schools should move moving toward all bathrooms being "gender neutral" or "all gender" (National Association of Independent Schools, n.d., p. 11), something already being considered for widespread implementation in independent schools internationally. Providing non-stigmatized options for any student who needs them establishes conditions that meet the needs of every child (National Association of Independent Schools, n.d.). To address intersecting experiences of vulnerability for TGD young people, well-trained specialist educators are needed to support TGD students who may have learning disabilities.

Third, there is also a need for "resources that specifically target the students at greatest risk of failing school and becoming court involved" (Kim et al., 2010, p. 18). Programs need to be developed and introduced that are "designed to reduce the use of suspensions, expulsions, and school-based arrests and toward improving rates of graduation for students, including those who have been incarcerated or educated in alternative schools" (Kim et al., 2010, p. 10). These programs can be implemented in schooling environments, but they can also be implemented in after-school contexts, and youth and other community services away from schooling environments. These types of initiatives will not only benefit TGD students, but also other LGBTQ+ identified, poor, homeless, and students of color who require additional support to maintain engagement with education.

Fourth, practitioners need to prioritize the creation of affirming and welcoming before- and after-school programs that will support TGD young people with free food, finding adequate shelter if needed, and to connect with other TGD young people and support staff in ways that develop a sense of safety and belonging. This could include the development of gender affirming educational programs, with free tutoring, and provision of ESL/ELL programs for TGD young people whose first language may not be English (Deckert, 2015). Creating affirming TGD drop-in centers, outreach programs, after-school activities, and sport teams will provide safe spaces for TGD young people to go and have fellowship with one another, in a safe environment. TGD young people can be supported to finish and further their education and/or provide them with skills for career development, and not have to result to crime to take care of themselves. To ensure success, it is vital to hire diverse, unbiased staff who believe in protecting and supporting the safety and fairness of all young people.

Fifth, and something that costs nothing to start, and can be quickly implemented everywhere, is allowing TGD young people to be called by their chosen names and correct pronouns while at school and in contact with service providers organizations. When transgender and nonbinary young people report having their pronouns respected by all or most of the people in their lives, they attempt suicide at half the rate of those who did not have their pronouns respected (Trevor Project, 2020).

Finally, some consideration might be given to the implementation of a new program in New Zealand that focuses on racial and ethnic classroom dynamics, but which may be reworked to target TGD students worldwide. They plan to provide "culturally responsive classroom management" consisting of five essential components. The first component is the recognition of one's own ethnocentrism because "a culturally responsive Pakeha teacher needs to understand what it means to be Pakeha in New Zealand society" (Savage, 2010, p. 38). The second component is knowledge of students' cultural backgrounds "to develop the skills for cross-cultural interaction and to show support for Māori cultural aspirations" (Savage, 2010, p. 39). The third component consists of "developing an understanding of the broader social, economic, and political context in order for teachers to understand the pursuit of social justice and the need for culturally responsive classrooms" (Savage, 2010, p. 39). This includes a focus on "a strength-perspective, where teachers must be aware of the wider social, economic, and political environments that have in the past contributed to the inequity in New Zealand society" (Savage, 2010, p. 39). The fourth component is "the ability and willingness to use culturally appropriate behaviour management strategies" that are sensitive to "culturally specific behavioural norms" (Savage, 2010, p. 39). The fifth component is "commitment to building caring classrooms" where "both school managers and teachers need to have knowledge and respect of Māori culture and protocols and an ability and willingness to use culturally appropriate management strategies" (Savage, 2010, p. 40).

Reflecting the structure of the New Zealand program above, a similar program of work may be developed and implemented around TGD young people. The program would be revised and would be focused on intensive training of staff so they are trained: to recognize their privileges in different forms; to support the aspirations of TGD young people; to understand the intersections of different vulnerabilities with gender diversity; to understand and implement behavior management strategies informed by knowledge of TGD issues (for instance, using discretion where a TGD young person is retaliating against discrimination/harassment from other students/teachers); and to interact with TGD young people from a position of respect and dignity to promote a caring, supportive classroom environment. These training programs could be implemented in conjunction with community-based restorative programs that direct TGD young people who do get into trouble away from criminal processing systems altogether, and into more supportive restorative programs focused on community reintegration (Tyminski, 2021). Authentic social change in the lives of TGD young people might also be supported by getting social workers to collaborate with young transgender activist groups that exist nationally and internationally and begin the process of having TGD young people document their own histories, in addition to creating their own support networks within their own communities (Mountz, 2020), to produce true change for TGD people. All these strategies would go some way to improving schooling climates for TGD young people so they might be better retained and engaged to finish their schooling.

Conclusion

This chapter demonstrates there is an abundance of research that has been done, and continues to be done, which shows that school bullying, racism, transphobia, and the effects thereof, such as homelessness and family exile, are all contributing factors to the global effects of the school-to-prison pipeline. Given that attending school can be one of the most traumatic aspects of growing up as a TGD young person, this is incredibly problematic considering how many TGD young people are currently flowing into the school-to-prison pipelines around the world (Grossman & D'Augelli, 2006). Schooling and criminal processing practitioners therefore need to work together to create more inclusive, safer spaces to ensure that TGD young people can succeed in school and live well equipped to becoming self-sufficient, productive people in society. For social change to support all trans kids, social movements must build powerful coalitions with other marginalized communities (Zaman et al.,

2021, p. 39). It is not enough to assume that all teachers care for all students, especially in school settings where the person teaching may not share the same background as the students being taught.

References

Abreu, R. L., & Kenny, M. C. (2018). Cyberbullying and LGBTQ youth: A systematic literature review and recommendations for prevention and intervention. *Journal of Child & Adolescent Trauma, 11*, 81–97.

Alessi, J., Greenfield, B., Manning, D., & Dank, M. (2020). Victimization and resilience among sexual and gender minority homeless youth engaging in survival sex. *Journal of Interpersonal Violence, 36*(23–24), 11236–11259.

Anti-Defamation League. (2015). www.adl.org/education-outreach

Asquith, N., Dwyer, A., & Simpson, P. (2017). A queer criminal career. *Current Issues in Criminal Justice, 29*(2), 167–180.

Bauer, S. (2014). *Why is Connecticut holding a transgender teen in solitary?* https://www.motherjones.com/politics/2014/05/transgender-16-year-old-solitary-cell-adult-prison/

Behne, A. M. (2017). *Racial profiling: Everyday inequality.* Twenty-First Century Books.

Cathcart, R. (2008). Boy killing, labeled hate crime, stuns a town. *The New York Times*. Retrieved December 20, 2022, from http://www.nytimes.com/2008/02/23/us/23oxnard.html?_r=1&

Choi, S. K., Wilson, B. D., Shelton, J., & Gates, G. J. (2015). *Serving our youth 2015: The needs and experiences of lesbian, gay, bisexual, transgender, and questioning youth experiencing homelessness*. Williams Institute. Retrieved December 20, 2022, from https://escholarship.org/uc/item/1pd9886n

Clark, T. C., Lucassen, M. F. G., Bullen, P., Denny, S. J., Fleming, T. M., Robinson, E. M., & Rossen, F. V. (2014). The health and well-being of transgender high school students: Results from the New Zealand adolescent health survey (Youth'12). *Journal of Adolescent Health, 55*, 93–99.

Clements, K. C. (2018). *What is deadnaming?* Healthline. Retrieved December 20, 2022, from https://www.healthline.com/health/transgender/deadnaming

Collier, K. L., Van Beusekom, G., Bos, H. M., & Sandfort, T. G. (2013). Sexual orientation and gender identity/expression related peer victimization in adolescence: A systematic review of associated psychosocial and health outcomes. *Journal of Sex Research, 50*(3–4), 299–317.

Davis, A. (2003). *Are prisons obsolete?* Seven Stories Press.

Deckert, A. (2015, November 12). *The social services to prison pipeline*. The Indigenous Criminologist. Retrieved December 20, 2022, from https://juantauri.blogspot.com/2015/11/the-social-services-to-prison-pipeline.html

de Oliveira, W. A., Silva, M. A., de Mello, F. C., Porto, D. L., Yoshinaga, A. C., & Malta, D. C. (2015). The causes of bullying: Results from the National survey of school health (PeNSE). *Revista latino-americana de enfermagem, 23*(2), 275–282.

Education Review Office. (2019). *Bullying and prevention and response in New Zealand schools*. Retrieved December 20, 2022, from https://ero.govt.nz/our-research/bullying-prevention-and-response-in-new-zealand-schools-may-2019

Family Lives. (2021). *Bullying UK: What is homophobic bullying*. Retrieved December 20, 2022, from https://www.bullying.co.uk/general-advice/what-is-homophobic-bullying/

Flynn, T. (2009). Instant (gender) messaging: Expression-based challenges to state enforcement of gender norms. *Temple Political & Civil Rights Law Review, 18*, 465.

Fraser, B., Pierse, N., Chisholm, E., & Cook, H. (2019). LGBTIQ+ homelessness: A review of the literature. *International journal of environmental research and public health, 16*(15), 2677.

Glickman, D. J. (2016). Fashioning children: Gender restrictive dress codes as an entry point for the trans school to prison pipeline. *American University Journal of Gender, Social Policy & the Law, 24*(2), 263–284.

Graham, L. J., Killingly, C., Laurens, K. R., & Sweller, N. (2022). Over-representation of Indigenous students in school suspension, exclusion, and enrolment cancellation in Queensland: Is there a case for systemic inclusive school reform? *The Australian Educational Researcher*, 1–35.

Grant, J. M., Mottet, L. A., Tanis, J., Harrison, J., Herman, J. L., & Keisling, M. (2011). *Injustice at every turn: A report of the national transgender discrimination survey.* National Center for Transgender Equality and National Gay and Lesbian Task Force.

Grbach, L. (2012). Transgender student dress: Free speech and protected expression in public schools. *Temp. Pol. & Civ. Rts. L. Rev., 22*, 526.

Green, M. (2017). LGBTQ+ youth of color in the school-to-prison pipeline: Freedom, liberation, and resistance. *Aleph, UCLA Undergraduate Research Journal for the Humanities and Social Sciences, 14*, 37–54.

Grossman, A. H., & D'Augelli, A. R. (2006). Transgender youth: Invisible and vulnerable. *Journal of Homosexuality, 51*(1), 111–128.
Hemphill, S., Broderick, D., & Heerde, J. (2017). *Positive associations between school suspension and student problem behaviour: Recent Australian findings.* Australian Institute of Criminology.
Henning, K. (2021). *Rage of innocence: How America criminalizes black youth.* Pantheon Books.
Hinduja, S., & Patchin, J. W. (2020). *Bullying, cyberbullying, and sexual orientation/gender identity.* Cyberbullying Research Center. cyberbullying.org
Holmes, E. S., & Cahill, S. (2004). School experiences of gay, lesbian, bisexual and transgender youth. *Journal of Gay & Lesbian Issues in Education, 1*(3), 53–66.
Hunt, J., & Moodie-Mills. C. A. (2020). *The unfair criminalization of gay and transgender youth: An overview of the experiences of LGBT youth and the juvenile justice system.* Center for American Progress. Retrieved December 20, 2022, from https://www.americanprogress.org/article/the-unfair-criminalization-of-gay-and-transgender-youth/
INCITE! (2015). *Policing gender*. Retrieved December 20, 2022, from https://incite-national.org/policing-gender/
Kim, C. Y., Hewitt, D. T., & Losen, D. J. (2010). *The-school-to-prison pipeline: Structuring legal reform.* New York Press.
Mallon, P. G. (2009). *Social work practice with transgender and gender variant youth* (2nd ed.). Routledge.
Mountz, S. (2020). Remapping pipelines and pathways: Listening to queer and transgender youth of color's trajectories through girls' juvenile justice facilities. *Journal of Women and Social Work, 35*(2), 177–199.
NAACP Legal Defense and Educational Fund, Inc. (2018). *Dismantling the school-to-prison pipeline: Racial segregation.* Retrieved December 20, 2022, from https://www.naacpldf.org/our-thinking/issue-report/criminal-justice/dismantling-the-school-to-prison-pipeline/
National Association of Independent Schools (NAIS) & Gender Spectrum. (n.d.). *Transgender students and school bathrooms.* Retrieved December 20, 2022, from https://www.nais.org/media/MemberDocuments/Legal/NAIS_GenderSpectrum_Transgender_Students_School_Bathrooms.pdf
Nelson, L., & Lind, D. (2015). The school-to-prison pipeline, explained: Police officers in classrooms are just the tip of the iceberg. Retrieved December 20, 2022, from https://www.vox.com/2015/2/24/8101289/school-discipline-race

NSPCC (2016). What children are telling us about bullying: Childline bullying report 2015/16. [London]: NSPCC.

NSPCC Learning. (2021). *Protecting children from bullying and cyber bullying*. Retrieved December 20, 2022, from https://learning.nspcc.org.uk/child-abuse-and-neglect/bullying#heading-top

Perkiss, A. D. (2013). A new strategy for neutralizing the gay panic defense at trial: Lessons from the Lawrence King case. *UCLA Law Review, 60*, 778–824.

Perry, J. R. & Green, E. R. (2014). *Safe & Respected: Policy, Best Practices & Guidance for Serving Transgender & Gender Non-Conforming Children and Youth Involved in the Child Welfare, Detention, and Juvenile Justice Systems*. New York City, New York City's Administration for Children's Services.

Rosentel, K., Lopez-Martinez, I., Crosby, R. A., Salazar, L. F., & Hill, B. J. (2021). Black transgender women and the school-to-prison pipeline: Exploring the relationship between anti-trans experiences in school and adverse criminal-legal system outcomes. *Sexuality Research and Social Policy, 18*, 481–494.

Savage, C. (2010). Culturally responsive classroom management in New Zealand. In V. Green & S. Cherrington (Eds.), *Delving into diversity: An international exploration of issues of diversity* (pp. 35–44). New Sciences Publishers Inc.

Singh, A. A. (2012). Transgender youth of color and resilience: Negotiating oppression and finding support. *Sex Roles, 68*, 690–702.

Snapp, S. D., Hoenig, J. M., Fields, A., & Russell, S. T. (2015). Messy, butch, and queer: LGBTQ+ youth and the school-to-prison pipeline. *Journal of Adolescent Research, 30*(1), 57–82.

Stryker, S. (2017). *Transgender history: The roots of today's revolution* (2nd ed.). Seal Press.

Tala, A. (2011). *Teen gets 21 years for murder of gay classmate*. Medical Daily. Retrieved December 20, 2022, from https://www.medicaldaily.com/teen-gets-21-years-murder-gay-classmate-238753

The Annie E. Casey Foundation. (2015). A guide to juvenile detention reform. In *Lesbian, gay, bisexual and transgender youth in the juvenile justice system*. Shannan Wilber. Retrieved December 20, 2022, from https://www.aecf.org/resources/lesbian-gay-bisexual-and-transgender-youth-in-the-juvenile-justice-system

The Trevor Project. (2020). *2020 national survey on LGBTQ+ youth mental health*. Retrieved December 20, 2022, from https://www.thetrevorproject.org/survey-2020/

Tyminski, M. (2021). *The roles of the zealous advocate: Implementing LGBTQ+IA+ conscious ethics in juvenile criminal defense to combat the school-to-prison pipeline*. Scholarly Commons at Hofstra Law. Hofstra Law Student Works. Retrieved December 20, 2022, from https://scholarlycommons.law.hofstra.edu/cgi/viewcontent.cgi?article=1019&context=hofstra_law_student_works

Victoria State Government. (2022). *Safe schools: Guide to making your school safe and inclusive for LGBTI students*. Victoria State Government, Education and Training. Retrieved December 20, 2022, from https://www.education.vic.gov.au/Documents/about/programs/health/safeschoolsguide.pdf

Wodda, A., & Panfil, V. R. (2020). *Sex-positive criminology* (1st ed.). Routledge.

Wozolek, B., Wootton, L., & Demlow, A. (2017). The school-to-coffin pipeline: Queer youth, suicide, and living the in-between. *Cultural Studies ↔ Critical Methodologies, 17*(5) 392–398.

Zaman, H., Chen, S., Zhu, X., & Habib, S. (Eds.). (2021). *Gender, diversity, and inclusion: International workshop proceedings.*

5

Policing Transgender People

Angela Dwyer and Jace Valcore

Introduction

A transgender woman of colour is physically attacked by a stranger she passed on the street and defends herself with a pair of scissors from her purse. The attacker dies as a result, and she is arrested by police charged with manslaughter. A transgender woman of colour is walking down the street and police stop her and ask her questions, search her, and arrest her when they find condoms in her handbag. A transgender woman of colour is murdered and police misgender her in the media conference about the killing. A transgender woman engaged in sex work has her mugshot

A. Dwyer (✉)
School of Social Sciences, Tasmanian Institute of Law Enforcement Studies, University of Tasmania, Glen Waverley, VIC, Australia
e-mail: angela.dwyer@utas.edu.au

J. Valcore
College of Public Service, Criminal Justice, University of Houston Downtown, Houston, TX, USA

H. Panter and A. Dwyer (eds.), *Transgender People and Criminal Justice*, Critical Criminological Perspectives, https://doi.org/10.1007/978-3-031-29893-6_5

uploaded onto a police website along with her deadname and her sex assigned at birth. A transgender woman of colour is arrested outside a beauty store after a dispute with someone at the store, and she called 911 for assistance, and when she resists arrest, police officers slam her face into the concrete, punch her, and knee her in the face, torso, and ribs.

All of these are lived experiences of transgender people when encountering police officers, typically in public spaces, where often violent experiences with police unfold. Police profile transgender people as sex workers, misgender them, use excessive force on them, and arrest and charge them with crimes when they defend themselves. These experiences mean transgender people, and particularly transgender people of colour, have considerably negative outcomes from police. As such, this chapter examines these issues in Australia and in the United States through reference examples. First, we detail exactly what practices comprise policing with transgender people. Second, we show how these practices have emerged out of a specific context of historical colonisation. Third, we argue that the colonising violence, made possible by historical laws, continues into the twenty-first century, and is manifested through policing practices with transgender people. Fourth, we examine the different suggestions for improving police relationships with transgender people, and our fifth point contextualises this as we overview the different challenges to doing this improvement work with police organisations. Sixth, and finally, we examine how any improvement work with policing is ultimately still investing in carceral systems designed to punish transgender people, and we outline various case study examples of strategies that transgender people have implemented to divest in policing as a carceral practice.

Context and Definitions

The policing of transgender people involves all ways in which social institutions, governments, and individuals attempt to control, regulate, criminalise, and punish human behaviour and expression which fails to conform to ahistorical, essentialist definitions of sex and gender. In countries and societies around the globe, social systems and government institutions have been organised according to the mistaken belief that human beings can be easily and readily categorised into two groups: male and female, terms which are often used interchangeably with man and woman (see Spade, 2015). These biological classifications have limited use, even to physicians, who now contend that the most important determinant is not the sex listed on a person's birth certificate, but their gender identity (Adkins, 2016; American Medical Association, 2021). There is an infinite number of ways in which human beings may describe or define their gender, but those who identify outside of the male = man and female = woman binary, can be widely defined as transgender or nonbinary. Transgender and nonbinary people are perceived by some to be a threat to the social order because they do not conform to stereotypical ideas about sex or gender. Rather, they challenge existing norms around gender presentation and expression, and defy long-held beliefs about physical sex characteristics as the sole determinant of gender identity (see e.g., Spade, 2015; Stryker, 2017).

Transgender and nonbinary people consistently have their gender expression and identity policed in social settings and contexts, including in school, the workplace, public accommodations, and social media. There are several ways in which gender non-conformity is socially policed, ranging from verbal abuse to homicide. For example, in family, school, and childcare settings, children are often pushed to play with gender-specific toys, are discouraged from play-acting as characters of the "opposite sex", and are teased or bullied for violating the expectations of their assigned sex around clothing, mannerisms, and other preferences (Meadow, 2018). This policing of gender expression comes from parents, teachers, and peers alike (Meadow, 2018; see also James et al., 2016). As adults, transgender people report numerous forms of discrimination and harassment, including but not limited to familial rejection, denial of health care, loss or denial of employment, physical assault, and sexual harassment because of their transgender identity (James et al., 2016).

The most extreme forms of gender policing include physical and sexual assault and homicide. Transgender women of colour especially experience disproportionately high rates of assault, interpersonal violence, and homicide because they are trans. A report by Flores et al.

(2021) found that transgender people experience criminal victimisation at a rate four times higher than that of cisgender people. Studies have found (see: Guadalupe-Diaz, 2019; King et al., 2021) that transgender people suffer high rates of intimate partner violence, including psychological and physical abuse, stalking, and sexual assault. Transgender women are the victims of homicide at disproportionately high rates, as well, and are too frequently killed by heterosexual men whose sense of masculinity is threatened by their attraction to a trans woman (Lee & Kar Yu Kwan, 2014; Wodda & Panfil, 2015).

The social policing of trans people is bolstered by laws and criminal processing systems that codify anti-trans attitudes and heteronormative gender expectations. Police are the gatekeepers to criminal processing systems and are empowered with the discretion to enforce criminal laws. There are varying forms of legislation that target and criminalise the bodies and lives of trans people around the world. For instance, for decades cross-dressing ordinances in the US cities gave police permission to invade LGBTQ+ bars and harass and physically search people, primarily pants-wearing lesbians and drag queens, for wearing clothing of the "opposite sex". It took several years for Houston advocates including psychiatrist Dr. Jay C. Maxwell and attorney Phyllis Frye to convince the courts and the Houston City Council to repeal its cross-dressing ordinance in 1980 (*Houston Chronicle*, 1980, 2015). More recently, several US states have debated and attempted to pass legislation making it illegal for transgender people, especially young people, to receive affirming health care, participate in sports, or access sex-segregated public facilities (see: National Center for Transgender Equality, 2022). These laws once again provide legal justification for police—and other agents of social control—to harass and assault transgender and nonbinary people.

These types of laws and police practices are not a modern phenomenon, or even just a conservative backlash to the increasing visibility and acceptance of gender diversity. They have emerged from processes of colonisation where legislative frameworks from other imperialist nations have been overlaid onto the lives and spaces of the colonised, and through which transgender people are consistently a key target for control and domination.

The History of Colonisation and Gender Policing

For centuries, the patriarchal gender norms of European countries and colonists, supported largely by rigid religious belief systems, have been forced upon the world (Mogul et al., 2011). There is historical and anthropological evidence that, prior to colonisation, indigenous and native cultures across the globe recognised, accepted, and in some cases, even celebrated and honoured, diverse gender identities and presentations (Hill, 1935; PBS, 2015). On nearly every continent and throughout history, there have been people who held a third gender or dual gender status. In many Native American tribes, they were/are known as "two-spirit people", denoting the combination of masculine and feminine spirits they possess (Lang, 2016).

English and Spanish colonisers came from countries where sodomy and buggery were punishable by death. They believed the gender diversity and same-sex relations they observed in indigenous cultures to be immoral and abnormal (Mogul et al., 2011). In the Americas, the Spanish pointed to it as a reason to exterminate thousands of native peoples, colonise their lands, and force them to convert to Christianity (Lang, 2016). The violence perpetrated against Native and Indigenous people because of perceived sex and gender role violations has since been termed gendercide (Warren, 1985). Possibly the first recorded incident of gendercide[1] occurred in 1513 when Spanish conquistador Vasco Nunez de Balboa encountered the Indigenous people of Quaraca (in what is now Panama). He saw what he perceived to be forty men "dressed as women" engaging in sexual relations with each other and ordered them to be dismembered by being thrown to his dogs (Mogul et al., 2011). This type of violent punishment continued for centuries and was also perpetrated or directed by Christian clergy, military and government agents, and judges.

[1] Gendercide is defined as "the deliberate extermination of persons of a particular sex" (Grech 2015, p. 851). A particularly powerful commentary about the impact of this process on the lives of transgender women is provided by Brown (2022).

In the British colonies, there was a history of regulating dress to prevent people from disguising themselves as a race, social rank, or profession to which they did not belong. Several laws and city ordinances, the first in Massachusetts in 1690, were passed across the American colonies and later US cities that explicitly punished cross-dressing, or "… appearing in public in dress not belonging to his or her sex" (Stryker, 2017, p. 47). As previously noted, during the twentieth century masculine-presenting lesbians, drag queens, and transgender women were regularly harassed and arrested by police enforcing laws which required them to be wearing at least three articles of clothing that corresponded with their assigned sex (Calhoun, 2017).

In the nineteenth and twentieth centuries, medical scientists and psychologists provided evidence that sex and gender diversity were innately human and natural. For example, in 1864–1865 Austrian Karl Heinrich Ulrichs anonymously published a theory of biology developed to describe those who have a soul opposite from the sex of their physical body. German doctor Magnus Hirschfield believed that the unique combination of genetics, secondary sex characteristics, psychological inclinations, sexual preferences, and culturally acquired habits and traits present in each person meant that there were more than 43 million different kinds of genders, or humans (Stryker, 2017). Hirschfield established the Institute for Sexual Science in 1919, helped to coordinate care for the first male-to-female surgical procedure for Dorchen Richter in 1931 (and also Lilli Elbe), and worked with Berlin police to end the harassment and arrest of transgender people. Hitler personally labelled Hirschfield as "…the most dangerous Jew in Germany…" (Stryker, 2017, p. 56) forcing him to flee the country; in 1933 the Institute and its library were ransacked and burned.

Unfortunately, advances in medical and psychological science during the twentieth century did not bring an end to violence and discrimination against trans people. For several decades, in North America, for instance, Indigenous peoples were subjected to forced migration, relocation, and removal. Thousands of Native children were taken from their homes and sent to Christian boarding schools and/or given to White families for adoption. Many of them were assaulted, emotionally abused, and given a substandard education. All of them were severed from their culture, including the proud history of two-spirit people and traditions of gender diversity (Lang, 2016). These moves by colonial police forces substantially shaped how transgender people of colour interact with police today.

In the United States in the 1950s and '60s, police raids of queer recreational establishments were common, as were the beating and raping of drag queens. Popular history points to resistance and uprisings against police brutality, specifically Compton's Cafeteria in 1966 and Stonewall Inn in 1969 uprisings, as significant turning points in LGBTQ+ history and the fight for civil rights. These were some of the first documented cases of resistance to police actions, and they were largely instigated and led by drag queens and trans women such as Sylvia Rivera and Marsha P. Johnson (Stryker, 2017). The uprisings shone a light not only on police abuses, but also on broader economic and structural forces working against LGBTQ+ communities and led to the formation of several gay and transgender activist groups and organisations. In the following decades, however, strong political and social backlash resulted in continued arrests, broken alliances, and forceful attempts to strengthen heteronormative and genderist institutions through policing and the growth of explicitly trans-exclusive groups (Stryker, 2017).

The 1993 case of Brandon Teena exemplifies the blaming and shaming that transgender people often experience when interacting with law enforcement. Brandon was a young trans man without access to hormones or any gender-affirming care who dated cisgender women. When two of his friends, Tom Nissen and John Lotter, found out about Brandon's "gender identity crisis", they confronted him, depantsed him, showed his genitalia to his girlfriend, then beat him, shoved him in a car, drove to a remote location, and raped and beat him some more (Jones, 2017). Brandon was interviewed about his assault by Sheriff Charles Laux, who interrogated every detail of the incident, including Brandon's professed virginity, the depth of the forced penetration, the fact that Tom "couldn't get it in you?", and much else (Jones, 1996, p. 225). A recording of the interrogation can be found on YouTube and is partially transcribed in Jones (1996, 2017). Laux questioned Brandon about his gender and sexual orientation (Jones, 1996):

> "Why do you run around with girls instead of guys, being you are a girl yourself? Why do you make girls think you are a guy?"
>
> "I haven't the slightest idea."
>
> "You haven't the slightest idea," Laux mocked. "You go around kissing on girls?"
>
> "The ones that know about me."
>
> "The ones, the girls that don't know about you, thinks you are a guy, do you kiss them?"
>
> "I don't know what this has to do with what happened last night". (p. 226)

The Sheriff continued to press Brandon about his relationships and behaviour with girls, to which Brandon replied that he had a "sexual identity crisis" but could not explain further. The final few minutes of the interview were erased, so it is unknown what else Brandon reported or was forced to explain (Jones, 1996). The Sheriff's line of questioning suggested that he did not believe Brandon's story and did not take his assault seriously, which is unfortunately common for victims of sexual assault, especially those that are perceived to be blameworthy (Worthen, 2016). Despite the existence of rape-kit evidence, Nissen and Lotter were not arrested, only questioned about the incident. A few days later they murdered Brandon in retaliation for the police report, along with Philip Devine and Lisa Lambert, with whom Brandon was staying (Jones, 1996).

Policing Transgender People in the Twenty-First Century

It would be erroneous to assume that serious forms of police mistreatment perpetrated against transgender people, like that experienced by Brandon Teena, have faded into irrelevance in contemporary, presumably more progressive times. Law enforcement continue to over-police, surveil, and even raid queer leisure spaces, such as bars and clubs. Lambda Legal (2015a) filed suit for a 2009 incident in which the Atlanta Police Department aggressively conducted an illegal raid on a queer night spot and harassed patrons, though none were charged with crimes. While these types of police actions impact the lives of queer people generally, there is ample evidence suggesting that they especially impact the lives of transgender people. A primary influencing factor appears to be the workings of cisnormativity: that is, the social expectation that a person is cisgender, that their sex assigned at birth (e.g., female) aligns with their gender identity (e.g., feminine). For instance, Amnesty International (2005) reported how police officers across the United States consistently interact with people whose appearance deviates from normative expectations of gender, and how this greatly impacted "the quality of police interactions" (p. 18). Police officers often stop, question, and search transgender people simply on the observation that their appearance does not seem to align with their sex assigned at birth or the sex listed on their identification documentation. Worse still, police searches often involve groping the genitals of the transgender person (Mogul et al., 2011) as a way of "genital checking", either to satisfy their own curiosity or "for the purpose of identifying the gender of the person being addressed" (Greenberg, 2020, p. 236).

Police interactions with transgender people often come about through the mundane policing interactions produced by "quality of life (QOL) policing [through which] police target typically noncriminal activities or summary offenses, such as sleeping in public or urinating in public" (Greenberg, 2020, p. 226). Many, if not most, of these interactions are brought about simply because police officers are out in public where transgender people are. Recent research projects around the United States have documented many examples of these types of interactions and the harms they lead to for the transgender people involved. Although involvement in sex work was the key focus of one Urban Institute study, only 9% of LGBTQ+ young people reported that trading sex was the reason for being stopped by police (Dank et al., 2015). Many interactions between police and trans young people happened because they were walking around in "known strolls", places where people were known to trade sex (Dank et al., 2015). A transgender Latina woman in a study in New York recounts her experience with police when she was buying tacos (Make the Road New York, 2012):

> They grabbed me and handcuffed me. They found condoms in my bra and said I was doing sex work. After handcuffing me they asked me to kneel down and they took my wig off. They arrested me and took me away. (p. 4)

As evidenced above, mundane everyday undertakings of transgender people lead to very harmful interactions and outcomes with police. At the more serious end of the scale, a survey of trans people in Atlanta (SNaP Co, 2016) reports that 8% of trans women had been coerced into sexual activity by police officers in their interactions with them, an abuse of power that was also reported by trans women in the 2015 US Trans Survey (James et al., 2016).

An apparent theme emerging out of existing research is how cisnormative assumptions drive the interactions that police officers have with transgender people and how this can often lead to violence and other forms of police misconduct. Substantial police misconduct has been reported in recent research (Mallory et al., 2015). Analysing incident reports collected by the National Coalition of Anti-Violence Programs, one study found that over 30% of reports "involved a police officer as the primary aggressor in an instance of hate violence" (Farr, 2016, p. 15). In a study by Lambda Legal (2015a), transgender people (18%) were twice as likely as cisgender people (9%) to be searched by police, and this jumped to 25% when considering transgender people of colour, and even higher for transgender women of colour (36%). Thirty-six per cent of transgender respondents noted that police officers had accused them of a crime that they did not commit, 72% reported hostile attitudes from police in their interactions with them, and 16% of transgender women of colour reported being subjected to sexual harassment when they interacted with police (Lambda Legal, 2015a). Twenty-two per cent of US Trans Survey respondents who had interacted with police in the previous year firmly believed they had been arrested simply because they were transgender (James et al., 2016). Of those same respondents who had interacted with police in the previous year, 49% stated that police misgendered them, 20% said they were verbally harassed, 19% were asked inappropriate questions about medical transition, 11% were assumed to be sex workers, 4% were attacked physically, 3% were assaulted sexually, and 1% were forced to engage in sex to avoid being arrested (James et al., 2016). With these types of police responses to transgender people documented in research, there is little wonder that transgender people do not trust police (Greenberg, 2020) and do not feel comfortable seeking their help (James et al., 2016).

Transgender people who are victimised are typically reluctant to seek assistance from police, even when the victimisation is as serious as intimate partner violence (Greenberg, 2020). Further violence from police is their central fear in these types of situations, as the comments of a transgender woman of colour highlight (Guadalupe-Dias & Jasinski, 2017):

> I mean I was in mid transition…I am still a man on record and my ID and stuff and I'm black. I'm black in [southern state]. It's like first they're going to see I'm this black dude that got beat up by a white man, think that we're gay, then see that I'm trans and that I'm in mid transition and it would be a disaster having to explain all of that and you know the police have a certain way of looking at trans people. (p. 786)

Police violence is also experienced by transgender people when they are the victims of hate-motivated violence from members of the public. When transgender people survive violent, hate-motivated attacks, police contribute to the criminalisation of transgender people by charging them with assault, and sometimes murder, even when the transgender person was acting in self-defence. The New Jersey 7, a group of lesbian, gender non-conforming women, were physically assaulted and threatened with rape by strangers on the street, and when they defended themselves, they were charged with "gang assault" and sentenced to 11 years in prison (African American Policy Forum, 2015). An activist campaign gained an acquittal, retrials, and shorter sentences (African American Policy Forum, 2015).

Another famous case is that involving Cece McDonald, who experienced transphobic harassment from a group of people that escalated to physical violence. When a male in the group ran at Cece to assault her, she pulled out a set of hairdressing scissors; he impaled himself on the scissors and died. Even though the scissors were clearly being used in self-defence, police charged Cece with two counts of second-degree murder. She accepted a plea bargain of two counts of second-degree manslaughter grounded in criminal negligence rather than murder. She was sentenced to 41 months in prison (Avery, 2012). While these examples might seem like outliers, many interactions with transgender people like these unfold every day around the world. Police officers working at the frontline of these interactions have the discretion not to arrest, and prosecutors have the legal authority not to charge or prosecute, a transgender person that is defending themselves against a hate-motivated attack. So, bias-motivated decisions, injustices, and other forms of discrimination make all transgender people, and particularly transgender women of colour, feel profoundly unsafe in public and in the presence of police officers.

As noted in the research outlined above (e.g., James et al., 2016), one of the core policing issues impacting the lives of transgender women currently is the police profiling of trans women as sex workers. Academics and commentators have noted that transgender women, and particularly those of colour, are disproportionately profiled by police as sex workers when they are in public spaces. They are often stopped, searched, and arrested for having condoms on their person—possessing condoms is interpreted by police as being engaged in sex work, even when this is not the case. This process has been dubbed "walking while trans", and advocates note that it is not just the highly discriminatory policing practices that are harmful (Carpenter & Barrett Marshall, 2017). For instance, some trans women have reported that police asked them to remove their pants or skirts to satisfy police curiosity about what genitals they have under their clothing (Hansenns et al., 2014). While this is degrading enough, their sexual health suffers over the long term when they restrict their use of condoms simply because they do not carry condoms with them for fear of arrest. Policing experiences are even worse for transgender people that rely on sex work for income. Transgender people are often denied full-time work and, therefore, often end up working in "underground" occupations related to drug and sex work economies, including the selling of black-market hormones (Rodgers et al., 2017). This means that some transgender people have even more problematic experiences with police because they engage with sex work to survive, including being mocked, threatened, and demeaned by police officers, in addition to being subject to significant violence (Lambda Legal, 2015b).

Even more disturbing is how often police are involved in the killing of transgender people around the world. After seeking asylum in the United States for anti-transgender violence she experienced in El Salvador, and subsequently having her asylum claim rejected by a court in the United States, Camila Diaz was murdered by three El Salvadoran police officers. These officers arrested Diaz for public nuisance and intoxication and then proceeded to kidnap and beat her, and threw her out of a moving vehicle, leading to critical injuries. Although she was treated in hospital, she died three days after the attack. The two police officers involved were charged and convicted of 20 years in prison for her murder (Human Rights Watch, 2020).

Although the officers involved were convicted of the murder of Diaz (Human Rights Watch, 2020), this is not always the outcome of incidents involving police crime and abuses. Typically, these cases are characterised by substantial complexities involving alcohol and mental health issues, missing evidence, falsified police statements that contradict witness statements, and most commonly, a lack of disciplinary or criminal outcomes for police officers. In 2008, Duanna Johnson was subjected to a savage beating by two police officers who were subsequently fired, but not charged with criminal assault (Brown, 2008). In another case, Nizah Morris accepted a courtesy ride provided from a police officer due to intoxication and was then found on the road with fatal head injuries. Witnesses stated they saw Nizah in police custody, yet the officer that attended the scene said that a crime had not occurred. As such, even though the medical examiner ruled her death a homicide, there was no initial police investigation into her death, meaning important evidence went missing and no further police investigation was possible (Richardson, 2015); her homicide remains unsolved (African American Policy Forum, 2015). Kayla Morris was experiencing a psychotic episode in 2013 when her roommate called police and eight officers attended the scene. Police then used multiple forms of restraint on her, and after 10 minutes of being restrained face down, she died (Veklerov, 2014). Although the family requested an investigation, the circumstances of her death have never been examined in court. In each of these cases, police have not been subject to any criminal justice outcome, and each of the victims were transgender women of colour.

Besides police abuse, transgender people are murdered by members of the public at alarming rates. For example, the latest discussion about these crimes suggests that a transgender person is killed once every three days by members of the public (Stoltzer, 2017). Staggeringly, though, this is just an estimate—there exists no process by which the numbers of transgender people killed are officially recorded (Stoltzer, 2017). Adding to this horrid situation is the frequent misgendering of the victims in the media by police officers investigating the murders (DeJong et al., 2021), and this is often just one harm done in what are often gross mishandlings of the investigations into the deaths of transgender people around the world (Waldron & Schwencke, 2018). Misgendering has far-reaching consequences as it means transgender people are not recognised as they identify: for instance, a transgender woman misgendered by police will be recognised and recorded as the death of a male. This means our knowledge of the murders of transgender people is inaccurate because police lack understanding, and sometimes refuse to recognise and record the deceased person as a transgender person.

Ignorance leading to the misrecognition, and therefore lack of recording, of the murders of transgender people is situated firmly within policing processes (such as police custody) that are typically organised around binary notions of sex. As DeJong et al. (2021, p. 143) concluded in their research on the reporting of transgender murders in the media, "police practice…reliance on gender binaries can have deleterious effects on the clearance of these cases and represents a commitment to an impractical and ineffective method of victim identification, which ultimately can delay offender apprehension". More commonly, however, it means dehumanising and unsafe experiences for transgender people when they are arrested and processed for police custody. For example, transgender women will be searched by male police officers at the point of custody because police policy may stipulate that people with male sex characteristics are searched by officers with male sex characteristics. A transgender woman may be held in a custody cell with other men because her gender identity as a transgender woman is overridden by policy stating that people with male sex characteristics need to be housed with other people with male sex characteristics. This is a profoundly unsafe practice because transgender people can experience sexual assault in custody settings far more frequently than cisgender people (Jenness, 2010). These harmful practices clearly indicate a dire need for significant policing reforms.

Improving Police–Transgender Relations

The research discussed above shows that the experiences of transgender people with police are, typically, profoundly negative, and substantially harmful. Some police organisations have recently taken steps towards trying to build more positive relationships with queer communities generally (see: Tomsen, 2009). A range of different initiatives exist that seek to improve the relationships between queer communities and police generally, like the 21st Century Policing report (Copple & Dunn, 2017) that provides specific guidance on the different ways that police organisations can explicitly support LGBTQ+ people, including sample policies (Copple & Dunn, 2017). As with other marginalised communities, however, police organisations have approached building relationships with LGBTQ+ communities in terms of a homogeneous "silo" group (Bartkowiak-Theron et al., 2017). For instance, the 21st Century Policing report fails to articulate the specific issues and experiences of transgender and gender diverse people whose experiences can be quite different from gay, lesbian, and bisexual people. A good example of this is LGBTQ+ police liaison programmes, which have been one of the most common ways that Australian police organisations have sought to produce better outcomes for queer communities in their interactions with police. These programmes comprise specially trained police officers who take up a volunteer role and make themselves available to provide support and advice to queer communities when they are having contact with police, in addition to supporting other police officers internally when they are interacting with queer communities. Programmes like this have had some useful outcomes, but they are also subject to a range of influencing factors which shape queer people's access to the liaison officers (Dwyer & Ball, 2020; Dwyer et al., 2020, 2022a). Most importantly, though, these programmes can elide the explicit experiences of transgender and gender diverse people simply because their issues are substantively different to those with diverse sexualities.

There are police organisations attempting to break down the "silo" of LGBTQ+ experiences and focus specifically on policies to support transgender and gender diverse people (Greenberg, 2020). For example, The New South Wales Police Force in Australia has an overarching *Strategy on Sexuality, Gender Diversity and Intersex 2019–2022* (NSW Police Force, 2019) that parses out more explicitly how transgender and gender diverse people might be supported by police. However, other police organisations have developed more specific policies focused only on supporting transgender and gender diverse people. The Queensland Police Service (2020) developed the *Good Practice Guide for Interaction with Transgender Clients*, as referenced in their Operational Management manual (QLD Police Service, 2021). Similarly, the U.S. Department of Justice Community Relations Service provides guidance around *Supporting Communities Struggling with Conflict and Tension Based on Gender Identity* (DOJ, n.d.), as well as specific training for officers about how to respectfully communicate and interact with transgender people (DOJ, 2016). These types of resources provide explicit information to officers about transgender and gender diverse people, the issues that impact their lives, and how best to interact with them so they feel supported and respected, particularly around preferred names and pronoun use.

The most comprehensive outline of how police organisations can best support transgender people in their practice is provided by Greenberg (2020, p. 246) who outlines a list of "concrete best practices that police can use to foster trust between themselves and transgender communities". While best practice policing with transgender people may be challenging for some agencies to implement (Dwyer, 2019), Greenberg's (2020) suggestions provide an outstanding starting point for any organisation seeking to better support, and criminalise less, transgender people experiencing police contact. Topping this list is a set of guidelines specifically addressing transgender–police interactions. Oversight boards comprising members of the public and transgender people should also be a priority, in addition to the appointment of a LGBTQ+ liaison with whom transgender people can discuss issues. To improve levels of trust between vulnerable communities, and particular transgender people of colour, and police, the common practice of pat down searches must cease. This should be supported with further trust-building activities with transgender people, including acknowledging past problematic policing. Police competency training about transgender people needs to be more than just "one-and-done" style and needs to "go beyond basic transgender competency around terms and pronouns [to also] address the use of stereotypes and their impact on police activities" (Greenberg, 2020, p. 247). Training should also include discussions of, and develop information (on websites, flyers) about, intimate partner violence that is inclusive of transgender people. Mandatory arrest policies should be avoided as "antithetical to increasing trust between transgender communities and the police", policing services should be "victim directed", and police officers should actively "pursue alternatives to arrest and punishment" (Greenberg, 2020, p. 247).

The Challenges of Improving Police–Transgender Interactions

There is no doubt these forms of policies constitute a positive step towards better outcomes for transgender people. However, the key issue with such initiatives is that the extent to which they are positively influencing how police interact with transgender people is unknown at this stage. Research is yet to take a targeted approach to evaluating these forms of policies and initiatives and we have some evidence suggesting that "policy change does not necessarily lead to change on the ground" (Copple & Dunn, 2017, p. 11). More importantly, audits that have been conducted of police policies supporting transgender people around the United States have found wide variance around the "existence and scope of policies governing interactions with LGBTQ+ people" (Ritchie & Jones-Brown, 2017, p. 36) and concluded that there is "a strong need for strengthening policies and training across the board" (National Center for Transgender Equality, 2019, p. 103)—as no police department audited met the criteria required to protect and serve transgender people

(National Center for Transgender Equality, 2019). Furthermore, research reviewing police policies that exist in the United States demonstrates that some still use "problematic and essentialist" language which can lead to harmful experiences (Greenberg, 2020, p. 236). This indicates that police organisations, in the United States at least, have additional work to do to better support transgender people.

Being able to document whether these initiatives produce better outcomes for transgender people is a challenging task. Many factors broadly influence the resourcing and fiscal landscape of policing at the best of times, but it appears that how police organisations are structured and administered can be a more significant hurdle for the effectiveness of police service enhancement programmes. In Australian research conducted by Dwyer (2020), the administration of police organisations was found to significantly thwart access to, and effectiveness of, police service enhancement programmes designed to build relationships between police and LGBTIQ+ people generally. Decision-making by police administrators, the structures of administrative processes (such as recording hate-motivated violence), police rostering, and police policy (such as restrictive uniform policies and police tenure policies), were all highlighted as elements that stopped police organisations from supporting LGBTQ+ people. Other research by Dwyer et al. (2020) documented similar issues with services provided by LGBTQ+ police liaison programmes, noting substantial barriers stopping LGBTQ+ people from being supported by liaison officers. For instance, while one police organisation had a LGBTQ+ police liaison programme, liaison officers who were part of these programmes often spoke about how high-level police managers did not demonstrate investment in these programmes and this manifested as an apparent lack of support for the liaison officers and what they were doing in that role (Dwyer et al., 2020). All these issues were raised just in research around LGBTQ+ police liaison programmes that are not solely focused on transgender people. Nonetheless, these issues show how fraught the policing landscape is when police organisations are attempting to implement any policy designed to better support LGBTQ+ people, let alone transgender people specifically.

A more significant challenge that may thwart the effectiveness of policies designed by police organisations to support transgender people is police culture. There is a clear need to implement training to bolster the success of policy implementation (Burke et al., 2015). However, research has shown this can be incredibly challenging and complex precisely because police are highly resistant to changes in policy and procedure that require them to treat transgender people with respect (Israel et al., 2017). Cisnormative and heteronormative institutions, like schools (Ferfolja, 2007) and police (Israel et al., 2017), sustain anti-transgender attitudes and practices. Policies and training seeking to enculturate police officers towards supporting transgender people fundamentally challenge ingrained cisnormative and heteronormative ideas. This was made evident in Australian research by Dwyer et al. (2022b) who interviewed a police officer that identified as gender-neutral and was undergoing hormonal gender affirmation processes. This officer refused to disclose this in their workplace because they so commonly heard derogatory comments about transgender women using women's bathrooms in their workplace, and this was at a police organisation that had done extensive work to support LGBTQ+ police officers (Dwyer et al., 2022b).

Further evidence challenging the effectiveness of policy implementation emerges out of research demonstrating that the attitudes of police officers themselves can be a significant barrier. In their study of LGBTQ+ competency training more broadly, Israel et al. (2017) found a range of different forms of police resistance and beliefs that undermined the effectiveness of this training. Police officers undergoing training had deeply held beliefs about LGBTQ+ people, including: "LGBTQ+ people allege discrimination to get out of trouble"; "LGBTQ+ people want special treatment"; "LGBTQ+ concerns are no longer as much of an issue because there is greater acceptance"; and "LGBTQ+ people should not take language so seriously" (Israel et al., 2017). Israel et al. (2017) also noted non-verbal embodied forms of resistance, such as negative facial expressions and a closed posture, during training that manifested resistance to this training. An Australian observational study of police competency training about transgender people documented police officers making comments and interacting with one another in ways that reinforced stereotypes about transgender people (Miles-Johnson, 2016). Derogatory comments made by officers during the training were common, and the lesbian and gay police officers facilitating the training did not challenge these comments (Miles-Johnson, 2016), a stark demonstration of how "without proper supervision, these policies may not be adhered to" (Greenberg, 2020, p. 237). These are the types of cultural issues that prevent policies and training implemented by police organisations from having the desired effect.

What Trans People Do to Protect Themselves from Policing

In a landscape where anti-discrimination and hate crime laws are insufficient for keeping transgender people safe or improving their well-being (Ashley, 2018), police organisations will need sustained investment in a variety of measures to support transgender people. Activities like hiring liaison officers to create safe place partnerships, local spaces, and businesses (BPD, n.d.), increasing the number of transgender police officers (BPD, 2013), or implementing guidelines to support transgender victims of sexual assault (OVC, 2014), might seem useful, but they ultimately work through the assumption that policing can (and should) be reformed to improve policing experiences for transgender people. These activities still invest in policing as a worthy, legitimate part of a criminal processing system (Mogul et al., 2011), a system structured in inherently undemocratic ways, such as denying police discretion by mandating daily quotas to demonstrate police accountability (Vitale, 2017). There is little space for options focused on more transformative forms of justice that "prioritise the needs of the survivor and help them recover from their trauma" (Greenberg, 2020, p. 245). Policing as an institution and profession is focused on enforcing and upholding "the goal of the carceral state [which] is to punish and lock up offenders" (Greenberg, 2020, p. 245).

Recent discussions have called for defunding or divesting from police organisations and reinvesting into community care programmes and basic services (Cunneen, 2020), but these are not brand-new ideas (IC,

2020a). There are two movements specifically working to protect transgender people in their interactions with police. The first is focused on teaching transgender people how to protect themselves in situations where they are likely to encounter police. For instance, the *Sylvia Rivera Law Project* collaborated with the National Center for Transgender Equality to develop a comprehensive toolkit for transgender people when they are participating in direct actions (e.g., protests, civil disobedience) (SRLP & NCTE, 2011). There are also toolkits developed by lesbian, gay, bisexual, two-spirit, trans, and gender non-conforming people of colour providing explicit advice about how to safely negotiate police contact (SOS, 2022). These toolkits produced by and for transgender people sit alongside other resources seeking to support vulnerable, marginalised communities generally to stop and intervene on violence in their communities in ways that do not involve police (Creative Interventions, 2021), in addition to resolving community conflicts before they escalate to violence (Restorative Response Baltimore, 2017).

The second movement is attempting to disconnect and decentre the reliance on police as first responders to better protect vulnerable people in communities (Abt Associates, 2020; Beck et al., 2022), and particularly transgender people and people of colour (IC 2020b). Some of these initiatives work from a co-responder model, where police are still involved, but they partner and respond with mental health/other professionals to call outs from vulnerable people in crisis (Krider et al., 2020). There are many recent successful examples of these programmes that have been undertaken (Krider et al., 2020). Other initiatives, however, entirely exclude police involvement and instead use organised community response teams for vulnerable, marginalised people experiencing a crisis. Police are not part of these response teams, and many recent successful examples of these programmes also exist (Butler & Sheriff, 2020). While some of these response initiatives are in their infancy, research has found initial evidence of their effectiveness. The central effectiveness of these programmes is evidenced by a significant reduction in reports of less serious crimes and no detectable impact on the number of serious crimes being reported (Dee & Pyne, 2022). Researchers reporting on these outcomes note that the reduction of reporting of less serious crimes is indicative of the absence of police in the response because "health-focused first responders are less likely to report individuals they serve as criminal offenders" (Dee & Pyne, 2022, p. 1).

Conclusion

The circumstances by which transgender people interact with police are complex, informed by colonial laws, attitudes of police and transgender people, and other intersecting forms of marginalisation and vulnerability. There is no doubt these interactions cause significant harms and lead to long-term consequences for, and sometimes deaths of, transgender people. Outcomes like this cannot be ignored in contemporary landscapes where quality-of-life policing initiatives are driving the over-policing of daily mundane activities that comprise the lives of transgender people. In the context of such harm, there are community-organised first response initiatives that are taking the responsibility of first response away from police to ensure that harm is lessened in the lives of transgender people. These community initiatives might be some of the more powerful examples of how we move forward in spaces without police intervention. They represent significant possibilities for supporting transgender people in ways that do not involve police, and may avoid harming, and prevent deaths of, transgender women of colour like Nizah and Kayla precisely because police are not being called to respond when they are experiencing a crisis involving intoxication or mental health issues.

References

Abt Associates. (2020). *A guidebook to reimagining America's crisis response systems: A decision-making framework for responding to vulnerable populations in crisis*. Retrieved December 21, 2022, from https://www.abtassociates.com/files/Projects/PDFs/2020/reimagining-crisis-response_20200911-final.pdf

Adkins, D. (2016). Expert declaration of Deanna Adkins, M.D., *Carcano v. McCrory*, No. 1:16 cv-00236, 2016 WL 4256691 (May 16, 2016), *injunction granted*, 203 F. Supp. 3d 61 (M.D.N.C. 2016).

African American Policy Forum. (2015). *Say her name: Resisting police brutality against black women. July 2015 Update.* Center for Intersectionality and Social Policy Studies.

American Medical Association. (2021). *Removing the sex designation from the public portion of the birth certificate (Resolution 5-I-19).* Report of the Board of Trustees. Retrieved June 15, 2021, from https://www.ama-assn.org/system/files/2021-05/j21-handbook-addendum-ref-cmte-d.pdf

Amnesty International. (2005). *Stonewalled: Police abuse and misconduct against lesbian, gay, bisexual and transgender people in the U.S.* Amnesty International British Section.

Ashley, F. (2018). Don't be so hateful: The insufficiency of antidiscrimination and hate crime laws in improving trans well-being. *University of Toronto Law Journal, 68*(1), 1–36.

Avery, D. (2012). *Trans woman Chrishaun "CeCe" McDonald sentenced to 41 months for slaying attacker*. Queerty. Retrieved December 21, 2022, from https://www.queerty.com/trans-woman-chrishaun-cece-mcdonald-sentenced-to-41-months-for-slaying-attacker-20120604

Baltimore Police Department (BPD). (2013). *GLBT recruitment*. Youtube. Retrieved December 21, 2022, from https://www.youtube.com/watch?v=tOvfJAy4MbQ&t=433s

Baltimore Police Department (BPD). (n.d.). *Safe place initiative: What is safe place BPD?* Retrieved December 21, 2022, from https://www.baltimorepolice.org/community/safe-place-initiative

Bartkowiak-Theron, I., Asquith, N. L., & Roberts, K. A. (2017). Vulnerability as a contemporary challenge for policing. In N. L. Asquith, I. Bartkowiak-Theron, & K. A. Roberts (Eds.), *Policing encounters with vulnerability*. Palgrave.

Beck, J., Stagoo-Belfort, A., & Tan de Bibiana, J. (2022). *Civilian crisis response: A toolkit for equitable alternatives to police*. Retrieved December 21, 2022, from https://www.vera.org/civilian-crisis-response-toolkit

Brown, H. M. (2022). The forgotten murders: Gendercide in the twenty-first century and the destruction of the transgender body. In J. Cox, A. Khoury, & S. Minslow (Eds.), *Denial: The final stage of genocide?* (pp. 184–195). Routledge.

Brown, R. (2008). Murder of transgender woman revives scrutiny. *The New York Times*. Retrieved December 21, 2022, from https://www.nytimes.com/2008/11/18/us/18memphis.html
Burke, T. W., Owen, S. S., & Few-Demo, A. (2015). *Law enforcement and transgender communities*. FBI Law Enforcement Bulletin. Retrieved December 21, 2022, from https://leb.fbi.gov/articles/featured-articles/law-enforcement-and-transgender-communities
Butler, S., & Sheriff, N. (2020). *Innovative solutions to address the mental health crisis: Shifting away from police as first responders*. The Brookings Institution. Retrieved December 21, 2022, from https://www.brookings.edu/research/innovative-solutions-to-address-the-mental-health-crisis-shifting-away-from-police-as-first-responders/
Calhoun, C. (2017). 'Bullseye on their back': Police profiling and abuse of trans and gender non-conforming individuals and solutions beyond the Department of Justice guidelines. *Alabama Civil Rights and Civil Liberties Review, 8*(1), 127–144.
Carpenter, L. F., & Barrett Marshall, R. (2017). Walking while trans: Profiling of transgender women by law enforcement, and the problem of proof. *William and Mary Journal of Race, Gender, and Social Justice, 24*(1), 5–38.
Copple, J. E., & Dunn, P. M. (2017). *Gender, sexuality, and 21st Century Policing: Protecting the rights of the LGBTQ+ community*. Office of Community Oriented Policing Services.
Creative Interventions. (2021). *Creative interventions toolkit: A practical guide to stop interpersonal violence*. Retrieved December 21, 2022, from https://www.creative-interventions.org/wp-content/uploads/2020/10/CI-Toolkit-Final-ENTIRE-Aug-2020-new-cover.pdf
Cunneen, C. (2020, June 10). *Defunding the police could bring positive change in Australia. These communities are showing the way*. The Conversation. Retrieved December 21, 2022, from https://theconversation.com/defunding-the-police-could-bring-positive-change-in-australia-these-communities-are-showing-the-way-140333
Dank, M., Yahner, J., Madden, K., Banuelos, I., Yu, L., Ritchie, A., Mora, M., & Conner, B. (2015). *Surviving the streets of New York: Experiences of LGBTQ+ youth, YMSM, and YWSW engaged in survival sex*. Urban Institute.
Dee, T. S., & Pyne, J. (2022). A community response approach to mental health and substance abuse crises reduced crime. *Science Advances, 8*, 1–9. https://www.science.org/doi/pdf/10.1126/sciadv.abm2106

DeJong, C., Holt, K., Helm, B., & Morgan, S. (2021). "A human being like other victims": The media framing of trans homicide in the United States. *Critical Criminology, 29*, 131–149.

The Department of Justice (DOJ). (2016). *Respecting identity: Law enforcement training and the transgender community*. Community Relations Service. Retrieved December 21, 2022, from https://www.justice.gov/crs/video/respecting-identity-law-enforcement-training-and-transgender-community

The Department of Justice (DOJ). (n.d.). *Supporting communities struggling with conflict and tension based on gender identity*. Community Relations Service. Retrieved December 21, 2022, from https://www.justice.gov/crs/our-focus/gender-identity

Dwyer, A. (2019). Queering policing: What is best practice with LGBTQ+ communities? *Current Issues in Criminal Justice, 31*(3), 396–411.

Dwyer, A. (2020). Queering police administration: How policing administration complicates LGBTIQ-police relations. *Administrative Theory and Praxis, 42*(2), 172–190.

Dwyer, A., & Ball, M. (2020). "You'd just cop flak from every other dickhead under the sun": Navigating the tensions of (in)visibility and hypervisibility in LGBTI police liaison programs in three Australian states. *Journal of Contemporary Criminal Justice, 36*(2), 274–292.

Dwyer, A., Ball, M., Bond, C., Lee, M., & Crofts, T. (2022a). Support provided by LGBTI police liaison services: An analysis of a survey of LGBTIQ people in Australia. *Police Quarterly, 25*(1), 33–58.

Dwyer, A., Asquith, N., Mason, R., and Rodgers, J. (2022b). LGBTIQ Tasmanians and Tasmania Police. Tasmanian Institute of Law Enforcement Studies (TILES), Contract Report.

Dwyer, A., Ball, M., Lee, M., Crofts, T., & Bond, C. (2020). Barriers stopping LGBTI people from accessing LGBTI police liaison officers: Analysing interviews with community and police. *Journal of Contemporary Criminal Justice, 33*(3), 256–275.

Farr, P. (2016). *Queer victims: Reports of violence by LGBTQ+I survivors result in violent assaults by police* (Masters Dissertation). Arizona State University.

Ferfolja, T. (2007). Schooling cultures: Institutionalizing heteronormativity and heterosexism. *International Journal of Inclusive Education, 11*(2), 147–162.

Flores, A. R., Meyer, I. H., Langton, L., & Herman, J. L. (2021). Gender identity disparities in criminal victimization: National crime victimization survey, 2017–2018, *American Journal of Public Health*. https://ajph.aphapublications.org/doi/epub/10.2105/AJPH.2020.306099

Grech, V. (2015). Gendercide and femineglect. *Early Human Development, 91*(12), 851–854.

Greenberg, K. (2020). Best practices in policing. In A. M. Messinger & X. L. Guadalupe-Diaz (Eds.), *Transgender intimate partner violence: A comprehensive introduction* (pp. 224–257). New York University Press.

Guadalupe-Diaz, X. L. (2019). *Transgressed: Intimate partner violence in transgender lives*. New York University Press.

Guadalupe-Diaz, X. L., & Jasinski, J. (2017). "I wasn't a priority, I wasn't a victim": Challenges in help seeking for transgender survivors of intimate partner violence. *Violence Against Women, 23*(6), 772–792.

Hansenns, C., Moodie-Mills, A. C., Ritchie, A. J., Spade, D., & Vaid, U. (2014). *A roadmap for change: Federal policy recommendations for addressing the criminalization of LGBT people and people living with HIV.* Center for Gender & Sexuality Law at Columbia Law School.

Hill, W. W. (1935). The status of the hermaphrodite and transvestite in Navaho culture. *American Anthropologist, 37*(2), 273–279.

Houston Chronicle. (1980, April 14). Court upsets cross dressing ban applying to transsexuals. *Houston Chronicle*, p. 4.

Houston Chronicle. (2015, September 3). Unsung hero—Transgender judge should be celebrated as someone who led a social revolution. *Houston Chronicle*.

Human Rights Watch. (2020, July 31). *El Salvador: Police officers convicted for transgender murder; further efforts needed to prevent, prosecute hate crimes.* Retrieved December 21, 2022, from https://www.hrw.org/news/2020/07/31/el-salvador-police-officers-convicted-transgender-murder

Interrupting Criminalization (IC). (2020a). *The demand is still #Defundthepolice #Fundthepeople #Defendblacklives: Lessons from 2020.* Retrieved December 21, 2022, from https://defundpolice.org/wp-content/uploads/2020/12/DefundThePoliceUpdate-1.pdf

Interrupting Criminalization (IC). (2020b). *What's next: Safer and more justice communities without policing*. Retrieved December 21, 2022, from https://static1.squarespace.com/static/5ee39ec764dbd7179cf1243c/t/5f85c390635cac03f35913d5/1602601934251/What%27s+Next+Report+.pdf

Israel, R., Bettergarcia, J. N., Delucio, K., Avellar, T. R., Harkness, A., & Goodman, J. A. (2017). Reactions of law enforcement to LGBTQ+ diversity training. *Qualitative Study, 28*(2), 197–226.

James, S. E., Herman, J. L., Rankin, S., Keisling, M., Mottet, L., & Anafi, M. (2016). *The report of the 2015 U.S. transgender survey.* National Center for Transgender Equality.

Jenness, V. (2010). From policy to prisoners to people: A 'soft mixed methods' approach to studying transgender prisoners. *Journal of Contemporary Ethnography, 39*(5), 517–553.

Jones, A. (1996). *All she wanted: A true story of sexual deception and murder in America's heartland*. Pocket Books.

Jones, A. (2017). *All he wanted: "Brandon Teena" the transgender boy who paid the ultimate price.* Aphrodite Jones Books.

King, W. M., Restar, A., & Operario, D. (2021). Exploring multiple forms of intimate partner violence in a gender and racially/ethnically diverse sample of transgender adults. *Journal of interpersonal violence, 36* (19-20).

Krider, A., Huerter, R., Gaherty, K., & Moore, A. (2020). *Responding to individual in behavioral health crisis via co-responder models: The roles of cities, counties, law enforcement, and providers.* Policy Research, Inc. and National League of Cities. Retrieved December 21, 2022, from https://www.theiacp.org/sites/default/files/SJCResponding%20to%20Individuals.pdf

Lambda Legal. (2015a). *Protected and served?* Retrieved December 21, 2022, from https://www.lambdalegal.org/protected-and-served

Lambda Legal. (2015b). *Protected and served? Police.* Retrieved December 21, 2022, from https://www.lambdalegal.org/node/30531

Lang, S. (2016). Native American men-women, lesbians, two-spirits: Contemporary and historical perspectives. *Journal of Lesbian Studies, 20*(3/4), 299–323.

Lee, C., & Kar Yu Kwan, P. (2014). The trans panic defense: Heteronormativity, and the murder of transgender women. *Hastings Law Journal, 66*, 77–132.

Make the Road New York. (2012). *Transgressive policing: Police abuse of LGBTQ+ communities of color in Jackson Heights.* Retrieved December 21, 2022, from https://nyf.issuelab.org/resource/transgressive-policing-police-abuse-of-LGBTQ+-communities-of-color-in-jackson-heights-queens.html

Mallory, C., Hasenbush, A., & Sears, B. (2014/2015). Addressing harassment and discrimination by law enforcement against LGBT police officers and community members to improve effective policing. *LGBTQ+ Policy Journal, 5*, 79–87.

Meadows, E. (2018). Sexual health equity in schools: Inclusive sexuality and relationship education for gender and sexual minority students. *American Journal of Sexuality Education, 13*(3), 297–309.

Miles-Johnson, T. (2016). Policing diversity: Examining police resistance to training reforms for transgender people in Australia. *Journal of Homosexuality, 63*(1), 103–136.

Mogul, J. L., Ritchie, A. J., & Whitlock, K. (2011). *Queer (in)justice: The criminalization of LGBT people in the United States*. Beacon Press.
National Center for Transgender Equality. (2019). *Failing to protect and serve: Police department policies towards transgender people*. Washington, DC.
National Center for Transgender Equality. (2022). *2021 State Action Center*. Retrieved December 21, 2022, from https://transequality.org/2021-state-action-center
New South Wales (NSW) Police Force. (2019). *Strategy on sexuality, gender diversity and intersex 2019–2022*. Retrieved December 21, 2022, from https://www.police.nsw.gov.au/__data/assets/pdf_file/0012/478794/13346_Policy_on_Sexuality_and_Gender_Diversity_110419_Online.pdf
Office for Victims of Crime (OVC). (2014). *Responding to transgender victims of sexual assault*. Office of Justice Programs, Washington. Retrieved December 21, 2022, from https://ovc.ojp.gov/sites/g/files/xyckuh226/files/pubs/forge/about_why.html
PBS. (2015). *A map of gender-diverse cultures*. PBS Independent Lens. Retrieved December 21, 2022, from https://www.pbs.org/independentlens/content/two-spirits_map-html/
Queensland (QLD) Police Service. (2019). *Chapter 1: Operational management*. OPM Issue 84.2 Public Edition. Retrieved December 21, 2022, from https://www.police.qld.gov.au/sites/default/files/2021-11/OPM%20-%20Chapter%201%20-%20Operational%20Management.pdf
Queensland Police Service (2021). Operational Management Manual. Queensland, Australia: Queensland Police Service. https://www.police.qld.gov.au
Restorative Response Baltimore. (2017). *An introduction to Restorative Response Baltimore*. Retrieved December 21, 2022, from https://www.restorativeresponse.org/
Richardson, M. (2015). *Killed outright or left to die: Black (trans)women and the police state*. Society for Cultural Anthropology. Retrieved December 21, 2022, from https://culanth.org/fieldsights/killed-outright-or-left-to-die-black-transwomen-and-the-police-state
Ritchie, A. J., & Jones-Brown, D. (2017). Policing race, gender, and sex: A review of law enforcement policies. *Women & Criminal Justice, 27*(1), 21–50.
Rodgers, J., Asquith, N. L., & Dwyer, A. (2017). Cisnormativity, criminalisation, vulnerability: Transgender people in prisons. *Tasmanian Institute of Law Enforcement Studies Briefing Paper, 12*, 1–13.

Safe OUTside the System Collective (SOS). (2022). *Violence intervention safety tips for survivors and bystanders*. The Audre Lorde Project. Retrieved December 21, 2022, from https://alp.org/files/Safety_Tips.doc.pdf

Solutions Not Punishment Coalition (SNap Co). (2016). *"The most dangerous thing out here is the police": Trans voices on police abuse and profiling in Atlanta: A report by the Solutions Not Punishment Coalition*. Atlanta, GA.

Spade, D. (2015). *Normal life: Administrative violence, critical trans politics, and the limits of law*. Duke University Press.

Stoltzer, R. L. (2017). Data sources hinder our understanding of transgender murders. *American Journal of Public Health, 107*(9), 1362–1363.

Stryker, S. (2017). *Transgender history* (2nd ed.). Seal Press.

Sylvia Rivera Law Project (SRLP) & National Center for Transgender Equality (NCTE). (2011). *Participating in direct actions: A guide for transgender people*. Retrieved December 21, 2022, from https://transequality.org/sites/default/files/docs/resources/DirectAction_Nov2011_FINAL-1.pdf

Tomsen, S. (2009). *Violence, prejudice, and sexuality*. Routledge.

Veklerov, K. (2014, May 7). Leaked documents shed new light on Kayla Moore's in-custody death. *Daily Californian*. Retrieved December 21, 2022, from https://www.dailycal.org/2014/05/07/leaked-documents-shed-new-light-kayla-moore-death/

Vitale, A. (2017). The end of policing.

Waldron, L., & Schwencke, K. (2018, August 10). *Deadnamed: The way cops in Jacksonville and other jurisdictions investigate the murders of transgender women adds insult to injury and may be delaying justice*. ProPublica. Retrieved December 21, 2022, from https://www.propublica.org/article/deadnamed-transgender-black-women-murders-jacksonville-police-investigation

Warren, M. A. (1985). *Gendercide: The implications of sex selection*. Rowman & Allanheld.

Wodda, A., & Panfil, V. R. (2015). "Don't talk to me about deception": The necessary erosion of the trans* panic defense. *Albany Law Review, 78*(3), 927–971.

Worthen, M. G. F. (2016). *Sexual deviance and society: A sociological examination*. Routledge.

6

US Transgender Homicides (2013–2020): Exploring Homicide Characteristics and Police Disclosure During Criminal Investigations

Heather Panter

Introduction: Transgender Homicide Victimology and Social Portrayals

Previous researchers (see: Edelman, 2014; Grant et al., 2011) have highlighted social factors that impact transgender bias and victimology. Compared to the general population, a transgender person is four times more likely to live in extreme poverty and is twice as likely as their cisgender (i.e., non-transgender identity) counterparts to be unemployed or homeless (see Grant et al., 2011). Grant et al. (2011) found that 47% of their sample (n = 6,450 transgender and gender non-conforming identities) experienced economic discrimination through discrimination in hiring, firing, and promotion. Grant et al. (2011) found that over 25% of their respondents lost a job due to discrimination based on their

H. Panter (✉)
School of Justice Studies, Liverpool Centre for Advanced Policing Studies, Liverpool John Moores University, Liverpool, UK
e-mail: h.a.panter@ljmu.ac.uk

H. Panter and A. Dwyer (eds.), *Transgender People and Criminal Justice*, Critical Criminological Perspectives, https://doi.org/10.1007/978-3-031-29893-6_6

gender identity. Specifically, Dinno (2017) found that US Black and "Latino/Latina/Latine" transgender women face higher homicide rates than US Black and "Latino/Latina/Latine" cisgender identities overall.

Notably because of different intersectional social and economic issues, some transgender women may have to rely upon illegal means to financially support themselves. Rodrıguez-Madera et al. (2017) found that 56% of their transgender sample (*n* = 59) engaged in sex work, drug sales, and other illegal activities for income. Sevelius (2013) found Black transgender women are especially subject to intersectional institutionalised forms of racism, genderism, and transphobia, and therefore black transgender identities may be forced to rely upon sex work as a necessary means of survival. Sex work inherently involves extreme heightened levels of exposure to violence for transgender identities specifically (see Ganju & Saggurti, 2017). Further, previous research (see Platt & Bolland, 2017) has highlighted how transgender identities (even those outside of sex work) are often fetishised and objectified within society. Ganju and Saggurti (2017) stated that transgender women in general are portrayed "easy game to be sexually exploited" (p. 910) and victimised identities are "disposable and insignificant" (p. 13) within society.

Notably to date, some studies (see Buss et al., 2021; DeJong et al., 2021; Momen & Dilks, 2021; Osborn, 2022; Seely, 2021; Wood et al., 2019) have examined how transgender victimology was presented in media coverage. For example, Wood et al. (2019) used content analysis of media coverage of 23 Black and Hispanic transgender women murdered in 2016. Wood et al. (2019) found five major themes during the analysis of these murders: brutality of the murders; the trivialisation of the murders; misgendering the victims; the emotional toll on significant others; and resiliency among transgender communities. Wood et al. (2019) further stated that black transgender women are often viewed as "disposable" (p. 12) and misgendering/deadnaming occurs in these cases because they are "delegitimized" (see Booth, 2015). Previous researchers have stated that transgender identities are often socially perceived as criminals (Sloop, 2000), sexualised (see MacKenzie & Marcel, 2000), fetishised (see Platt & Bolland, 2017), and viewed by police as being sexually deviant gender betrayers (see Panter, 2018). Further, Wood et al. (2019) theorised that misgendering in the media occurs because of "structural ideological paradigms of cis-genderism and transphobia" (p. 12).

Other studies have highlighted the differences in the ways that transgender homicide victims are presented to the media compared to cis homicide victims, namely being portrayed as "less than" others or inhuman and disposable (see Barker-Plummer, 2013; Billard, 2016). Notably, Black and Hispanic transgender women are more likely to be portrayed as deviant people while being blamed for their own deaths through "risky lifestyles" (e.g., sex work, drug usage, etc.) (DeJong et al., 2021). Often media stories use booking photos, mug shots, crime scene photos, etc., of transgender victims in what June (2017) describes as "over-use of police sourcing". This action can further stigmatise the victim during the process of victim-blaming while solely fitting police narratives (see: DeJong et al., 2021; June, 2017).

Further, Williams (2009) highlighted how the delegitimisation of transgender homicide victims can exist though the presented notion of a "deceiver" type identity which precipitates the homicide through the concealment of their biological sex from homicide suspect(s). Presenting the victim as a "deceiver" essentially "frames" the victim in the media as being responsible for the motives of homicide suspect(s) (i.e., victim-blaming) (DeJong et al., 2021). Williams (2009) found that "Latino/Latina/Latine" transgender homicide victims are often specifically labelled as "deceivers" more than their White counterparts in analysed media reports. Further, Wood et al. (2019) pointed out that Black transgender women who are homicide victims are much more likely to be described as sex workers than other transgender homicide victims.

DeJong et al. (2021) found that in a mixed-method study of 26 transgender homicides in 2018, there existed both positive and negative narratives surrounding victims. Uniquely, this study found that there are increasing stories of more victim portrayal positivity, particularly in LGBTQ+ news sources where victims were much more likely to be identified through their chosen name/identity, less likely to be victim-blamed, and less likely to be deadnamed (DeJong et al., 2021). Out of 218 news articles examined, DeJong et al. (2021) found that deadnaming of the victim was more likely to occur in local new sources (36.4%) comparatively to LGBTQ+ new sources (2.7%) with 75.3% of local news sources (compared to 97.3% of LGBTQ+ news sources) using a victim's chosen name. Optimistically, Dejong et al. (2021, p. 143) through both quantitative and qualitative findings found evidence of media stories "supporting the victim", "humanizing victims", "understanding the issues", and identifying the "growing epidemic" of transgender homicides. Yet, DeJong et al. (2021, p. 143) stressed on-going concerns that deadnaming and misgendering of transgender victims by both police and media may have "deleterious effects on the clearance" rates of transgender homicide cases.

Therefore, answering researchers (see DeJong et al., 2021; June, 2017; Wood et al., 2019) calls for larger sample sizes to be examined regarding victim portrayals in homicide investigations, this study specifically is a multi-year examination of the interaction between the media/police and how transgender homicide victims are portrayed as a victim and how their background of their cases are presented. Namely, this study centres on how these portrayals may impact investigative police practice while highlighting victimological themes present (e.g., ethnicity/race of the victims, frequency of antemortem injuries, disclosed motives, circumstantial details surrounding their deaths, etc.) in American transgender cold cases.

In accordance with other researchers and previous research (see Dwyer, 2019; Erich et al., 2010; Miles-Johnson, 2013, 2015, 2019), the term "transgender" encompassed the following for this study: those who have had gender reassignment surgery to change one sex to the other; those in any process of gender transition; those taking hormones and other medications to help their physical body transition from one to another; those who dress as the gender opposite of their sex because they do not identify with said identity; those who privately and/or publicly dress outside their binary gender identity; those who do not identify with any socialised binary identities; and those who may identify with both socialised binary identities (i.e., gender fluid, gender non-conforming, or femandrogyne).

Theoretical Considerations in Transgender Homicide Investigations

Historically, police interactions and social relationships with members of LGBTQ+ communities have been strained with accusations of negative conduct and anti-LGBTQ+ bias (see Burke, 1994; Colvin, 2009, 2012; Jones & Williams, 2015; Panter, 2018). Further, previous research (see Dworkin & Yi, 2003; Herek, 2002) has suggested that sexual minorities are subjected to enacted stigmas in the form of prejudice and harassment, stereotyped as deviants, and are targets of victimisation and discrimination because of their perceived nonconformity with heterosexual binary gender systems (Leppel, 2016; Thomas et al., 2016). Additional literature (see Rief & Clinkinbeard, 2020; Seymour, 2022; Silvestri, 2017) has highlighted how policing reinforces traditional masculine norms while upholding binary assumptions about gender. Panter (2018) argued that American policing still has ideological issues with perceptions of non-binary gendered identities and elements of transphobic bias still exist within policing. Further cisnormative expectations, influenced by socialised hegemonic masculinity, are constantly reinforced through existing heteronormative ideologies, which are pervasive in policing and society (see Panter, 2018). This concept is upheld by socialised perceptions of acceptable visual representation, acceptable psychological representation, and acceptable emotional representation that rigidly rest within cisnormative perceptions of gender within society and within policing (see Panter, 2018). Therefore, questions arise if, and if present, how these socialised perceptions have an influence upon solvability in transgender homicides specifically.

Understanding Homicide Case Closures and Cold Cases

Talusan (2016) pointed out that when examining transgender homicide trends in 2010, the unsolved rate for transgender homicides was 44% versus an average of 37% for cisgender homicides. Research pertaining to transgender homicide victimisation have previously outlined that Black and Hispanic transgender women are disproportionately affected by violence (see Dinno, 2017; Ijoma, 2018; Teal, 2015; Waters et al., 2018). Wood et al. (2019) found that Black transgender women are more likely to have their identity trivialised and are more likely to be victim-blamed than other transgender identities. In respect to criminal case outcomes, Momen and Dilks (2021) found that while Black transgender victims make up a majority of transgender homicides between 2010 and 2016, their cases were much more likely to not receive a guilty verdict comparatively to their counterparts. Momen and Dilks (2021, p. 70) have encouraged more intersectional research to examine "transgender victim blameworthiness or social value" in respect to homicide trial case outcomes. Notably, a significant aspect in homicide case outcomes relies upon how such investigations are carried out during case closure before they reach prosecution.

Regarding case closure, the FBI's Uniform Crime Reporting (UCR) programme classifies a crime clearance as "closed" in two ways: by arrest or by exceptional means (FBI, 2019). For a case to be cleared by arrest, or "solved", there must be an arrest, a person is charged with the offence, and the case has been turned over for prosecution (FBI, 2019). For example, out of 1,147,991 reported violent crimes, nationally in 2018 there were 14,786 reported cases of murder and non-negligent manslaughter with a 62.3% clearance rate (FBI, 2019).

Previous academic studies have examined factors that have influenced homicide case solvability/closure (see Brookman et al., 2019). For example, Wellford and Cronin (1999) identified 215 independent variables (e.g., drug user/buyer; type of homicidal weapon(s); number of detectives assigned to the case; residence versus a public place; etc.) believed to impact solvability in US homicides. Wellford and Cronin (1999), using multivariate analysis, identified 15 specific variables that related to the probability of closing a case. These were:

> 1) the offender was Black; 2) the offender was Hispanic; 3) a body chart of the victim was prepared; 4) a computer check on the decedent was conducted; 5) a computer check on the suspect was conducted; 6) a computer check on a witness was conducted; 7) a computer check on

> a gun was conducted; 8) the local Criminal Justice Information System (CJIS) was used for computer checks; 9) a witness at the crime scene provided valuable information; 10) friends and acquaintances of the victim were interviewed; 11) neighbours of the victim were interviewed; 12) three or more detectives were assigned to the case; 13) the location of the homicide was private; 14) an eyewitness observed the homicide; 15) the homicide was not drug-related. (Wellford & Cronin, 1999, p. III)

Further, Wellford and Cronin (1999) found that out of 51 characteristics of homicide events and investigative practices, 37 characteristics were solely attributed to police practices. Significantly, Wellford and Cronin (1999) pointed out that police policies and procedures make a significantly important difference in clearing cases.

Brookman et al. (2019) found that even very complex homicide case solvability can be influenced at individual and strategic levels. Namely, police culture and attitudes/perceptions held towards the victim play a main influence upon the quality of how a homicide investigation is carried out (Brookman et al. 2019). Brookman et al. (2019, p. 166) additionally argued that perceptions of detectives held towards certain communities "influence the conduct (and potentially the outcome) of investigations".

In respect to incident characteristics regarding time for case closure, studies have indicated that up to 23% of homicides are cleared by arrest on the day that the homicide occurred (see Puckett & Lundman, 2003; Roberts & Lyons, 2011). Wellford and Cronin (1999) found that over half of their sample of homicide cases involved an arrest within one week. Victim-offender relationship status has also been identified as a strong factor in case solvability. This quick clearance turn-around time is often associated with "domestic homicides". Notably, domestic homicides have the highest clearance rates (see Roberts, 2007; Roberts & Lyons, 2011) compared to "stranger" homicide cases where the offender is unknown to the victim.

Further, there exists research consistency on case clearances rates based on weapon usage. For example, homicides involving firearms have the lowest clearance rates (see Silverman & Kennedy, 1997). This is often due to the physical distance that a firearm gives an offender from the victim (see Alderden & Lavery, 2007; Litwin & Xu, 2007; Regoeczi et al., 2008).

Yet, there exist mixed research findings in respect to identity characteristics of homicide victims. For example, Roberts and Lyons (2011) found that homicides involving US Hispanic cisgender victims were less likely to be solved than cases with White or Black cisgender victims. In contrast, DeCarlo (2016) found that US cases involving young black cis male victims who lived in high poverty areas were prone to remain unsolved. Turner and Kosa (2003) also presented poverty as being a factor when they found that immigrants, homeless, or unidentified victims were overrepresented among cold cases in the United States. Bänziger and Killias (2014) further found that unsolved murders in their Swiss sample involved immigrants (or foreign nationals) and gay men. Brookman et al. (2019) found a nexus between British and American detectives' personal perceptions of "homicides, offenders, victims, witnesses, and communities; their expectations about the solvability of cases and, in turn, the commitment of energy and resources that they and their departments invest into certain kinds of cases" (pp. 167–168). This nexus highlighted how the opinions of detectives towards victims and the culture/attitudes held by detectives can impact case outcomes (Brookman et al., 2019).

Methods

Several steps were involved in the preparation of this study. First, I selected a search period of 1 January 2013–1 July 2020 during which transgender homicides were subjected to heightened media interest due to recent marginally progressive improvements in the social acceptance of transgender identities. Plus, during this time, regulatory policing bodies in the United States began to actively encourage more local agencies to record aspects of transgender victimology. While the Federal Bureau of Investigation (FBI) has included gender identity in annual hate crime statistics since 2015, the Bureau of Justice Statistics posits transgender deaths are 40 times higher than what is contained in said FBI reports (FBI, 2015). Therefore, official statistics regarding transgender homicides are considered conservative estimates as numerous victims are misgendered or deadnamed, which leads to misidentification or misclassification (see Wood et al., 2019).

Therefore, for this study I examined published open-source media reports ($n = 1{,}673$ news articles) of US transgender homicides alongside official data sources (i.e., government reports, police reports, etc.). Official homicide victimisation data came from the FBI's Supplementary Homicide Report (SHR), the most used official data source for homicide data in the United States, alongside yearly Uniformed Crime Reports (UCR). Both FBI's SHR and UCR reports rely upon officers within local or state agencies to submit information about homicide either to a state-level agency or the FBI directly in respect to data collection (Parkin & Gruenewald, 2017). Hence, it should be re-emphasised that current numbers in official statistics should be considered conservative representations. Further, some police departments keep different types of statistical data regarding homicides and there are always continuity issues with classifications of motives/means regarding homicides when looking nationally.

Initial open-media reports were identified through using LexisNexis and NewsBank databases while also searching for all news items published by online and print mainstream news outlets. Further relevant open-source material was initially identified by using a search string that contained the terms "homicide", "murder", and "transgender" alongside the state name/jurisdiction where the reported homicide occurred. This included information on transgender victims from print, news magazines, news, alongside other open-source data from LGBTQ+ research agencies (e.g., *Transgender Europe*'s [TGEU] "Transgender Respect Versus Transgenderphobia Worldwide" Project and "Transgender Murder Monitoring Project"; *Human Right's Campaign*'s [HRC] "Annual Reports of Anti-Transgender Violence" projects) and other advocacy information agencies (e.g., *Transgender Center for Transgender Equality*, *GLAAD*; Anna-Jayne Metcalfe's *Remember Our Dead Project*). This open-source information provided crucial details about the victims, the offenders, and each specific incident not currently recorded in official FBI crime reports or local police reports.

Gruenewald (2012) contended that this open-source research approach works more effectively because reporting on LGBTQ+ homicides are "likely influenced by the relative novelty of these crimes" (p. 3607) and they involve unique circumstances that make them "more likely to become high-profile crimes" (p. 3607). This makes finding data for LGBTQ+ criminal homicides more probable to be found during open-source methods than non-LGBTQ+ homicides. Notably, what classified as *criminal homicide* for this study, like other LGBTQ+ open-sourced homicide studies (see Gruenewald, 2012; Gruenewald & Allison, 2018; Gruenewald & Kelley, 2014; Parkin & Gruenewald, 2017) was any homicide that involved a formal criminal investigation by either local or federal police agencies. This also included homicide investigations where there was no arrest due to self-defence and police use of force deaths as a formal investigation was carried out.

Therefore, a flexible, semi-open coding content analysis procedure was employed (see: Berg, 2004) and all collected data was further thematically analysed. Following previous study guidelines for thematic coding of information from homicides using a blended official data/open-source data approach (see Gray & Parker, 2019; Parkin & Gruenewald, 2017), case information was coded into the following categories: victim's name, victim's self-identified transgender status, victimology concerns (e.g., occupations, risk factors, unique case specifics, etc.), how the media presented the victim's transgender status, how the police presented the victim's transgender status, date/location of the murder, where the body was recovered, date the homicide was discovered/body recovered, type of injury severity during homicide, number of suspects, number of arrest, number of convictions, current status of each case (i.e., solved/unsolved), if hate crime was a motive, motives presented in the media, and the victim's relationship to an offender (if applicable).

After collecting information from all open-sourced materials in combination with official source material, each homicide was attributed to a classification code from each source much like open-source guidelines provided by previous homicide researchers (see Parkin & Gruenewald, 2017). Once this data was accumulated, I measured the frequency of each theme across the whole sample. Additionally, I performed qualitative content analysis on each subsample for a more in-depth analysis by searching for content through the names of victims, including known deadnames for each homicide. By using a combination of open-source qualitative data alongside official sources of homicide data between 01 January 2013 and 01 July 2020, this allowed for this study to identify details that official sources did not provide alone. This quasi mixed-method approach allowed for the creation of a finalised archival spreadsheet (see Mazur, 2010) that highlighted specific case details. This is a similar process used in other homicide research studies (see Hesse-Biber & Griffin, 2013; Patterson et al., 2016).

Notably, if there were missing values on the coded archival spreadsheet, then a further subsequent targeted open-source search was carried out. For this final stage of data collection, the targeted searches had no restrictions on the type of open-sourced material that could be used. This process is similar to Gruenewald's (2012) work on anti-LGBTQ+ homicides, and Gruenewald and Allison's (2018) open-source research on extremist crimes. Parkin and Gruenewald (2017) found this open-source data process alone provides reliable and valid data specifically for homicide studies.

Findings

Descriptions of Victim Identities

When examining US transgender homicides from 01 January 2013 to 01 July 2020 ($n = 166$), there are some notes on victimology and case characteristics that should be considered. In respect to the descriptions of the victims' identity prior to death, 86.74% of victims were identified as transgender women; 4.21% as transgender men; 5.42% as gender fluid, gender non-conforming, or femandrogyne; and 3.61% were identified as cross-dressers. When examining the ethnicity/race of the sample: 78.31% of victims were described as "black" or "mixed"; 12.65% were "white"; 7.83% were "Hispanic" or "Latina"/"Latino"; and 0.60% was identified as Native American in media reports. The mean age of transgender homicide victims in the sample was 30 years of age.

Antemortem Injuries of Victims

When examining disclosed transgender antemortem injuries sustained by the victims, 63.25% received one or multiple gunshot wounds prior to death. In respect to stabbing with various instruments (e.g., knives, screwdrivers, etc.), 16.86% of victim's deaths involved some form of sharp force injury that contributed to death. Seven deaths were reported to involved "strangulation", 11 were "beaten" or received "blunt force injuries", two were "tortured to death", and one was "dismembered". Notably, out of the sample studied 21.68% deaths involved multiple mechanisms of death.

Disclosed Circumstances of Death and Motives

When examining the circumstances of each solved transgender homicide ($n = 166$), sex work or previous arrest for sex work of the victim was disclosed in the media during 26 cases (15.66%). In respect to domestic violence, in 9.64% of cases "domestic violence" was given as a motive for the homicide in open-source media reports. Further, eight cases out of 166 were disclosed in the media by police to be a result of a transgender specific hate crime. Yet, a large majority of disclosed motives were unknown as they were not included in open-source media. Notably, in several cases (namely unsolved ones) surviving family members/friends contend that they believed transgender hate was a motive regardless of preliminary police investigative findings.

Misgendering/Deadnaming Issues in Criminal Investigation

This study found that, during transgender homicide investigations, key themes emerged of how the victim was presented to media outlets. In 67 homicides (59.29% of the sample) in both solved and unsolved homicides, misgendering/deadnaming occurred. At the time of writing, of the 53 transgender homicides unsolved or considered "cold cases", the victim was misgendered/deadnamed during their investigation either by media, police, or both in 28 of these cases (see Case Table 6.1). This finding is unlike DeJong et al. (2021), yet it must be pointed out that the substantial study of DeJong et al. (2021) examined 26 transgender victims over one year—but this chapter examined 166 transgender homicides across 7 years and 6 months total.

During this process of misgendering/deadnaming, there were several cases where police/media used older photos from the victim's deadname identity to seek information on the case from the general public. As a representative example (see Fig. 6.1), when police were seeking information from the general public, they used the identity "David Loera, Hispanic male (D.O.B. 07/31/1972)" to describe the victim. Police also circulated an older driver's licence image that belonged to the victim's deadname identity instead of presenting her current photo as Monica Loera. Notably LGBTQ+ activists specifically criticised Austin Police as it took several days to correct the misinformation provided by police to media outlets (Adams, 2016). Whether or not if this had an impact of case solvability, time is unknown as the case was solved in 10 days and the homicide was deemed as being connected to sex work (refer to Table 6.1).

Another illustrative example of how police can misgender/deadname a victim in the media is the 2018 Celine Walker case in Jacksonville, Florida. It was reported that the Jacksonville Sherriff's Office stated: "an individual was found dead from a gunshot wound". This was after they provided Celine's deadname identity (McKeiver, 2018). McBride (2018), with the Human Rights Campaign, wrote that Walker was not identified as transgender until several days after her death was reported. Roberts (2018) stated that when Jacksonville Sherriff's Office was confronted about the misgendering incident, the sheriff's department stated that they have a "policy that does not refer to victims as transgender". It should be noted that this case took 597 days for an arrest to occur (refer to Table 6.1).

Table 6.1 Individual cases when victims were specifically misgendered/deadnamed by police/media

Victim's name	Transgender identity given by police	Race/ethnicity given	Date of homicide	Location of homicide	Date of arrest reported in media	Time until arrest	Type of homicide and motive given
Doe, Jane (name never released to media)	Transgender woman (described by police as "man who dressed in women's clothes")	Black	Jan 8th, 2013	Sarasota, FL	Jan. 12th, 2013	4 days	Solved (robbery-homicide)
Dove, Cernia "Ce Ce"	Transgender woman (described as "oddly dressed man")	Black	Jan. 8th, 2013	Olmsted Township, OH	May 3rd, 2013	115 days	Solved (killed during suspected sex-work)
Boudreaux, Milan "Mimi"	Transgender woman	Black	Feb. 14th, 2013	Metairie, LA	March 14th, 2013	28 days	Solved (robbery-homicide)
Hartley, Shaun	Transgender woman (described as a witness to "fellow trans-gendervestite prostitute" murder)	Black	Sept. 12th, 2013	Baton Rouge, LA	Sept. 18th, 2013	4 days	Solved (media focused on previous solicitation charges)
Morgan, Eyricka	Transgender woman	Black	Sept. 24th, 2013	New Brunswick, NJ	Sept. 25th, 2013	1 day	Solved (stabbed by housemate)
Hill, Amari	Transgender woman	Black	Nov. 9th, 2013	Richmond, VA			Unsolved
Skinner, Betty	Transgender woman	White	Dec. 5th, 2013	Cleveland, OH			Unsolved

Victim's name	Transgender identity given by police	Race/ethnicity given	Date of homicide	Location of homicide	Date of arrest reported in media	Time until arrest	Type of homicide and motive given
Kidd-Stergis, Brittany-Nicole	Transgender woman	Black	Dec. 6th, 2013	Cleveland, OH	June 5th, 2014	181 days	Solved (unknown motive but prosecutors state "past together")
Edwards, Tiffany	Transgender woman	Black	June 16th, 2014	Walnut Hills, OH	July 2nd, 2014	16 days	Solved (killed during suspected se-work)
Leos, Alejandra	Transgender woman	Latina	Sept. 5th, 2014	Memphis, TN	Sept. 7th, 2014	2 days	Domestic
Sherman, Ashley	Transgender woman	Black	Oct. 27th, 2014	Indianapolis, IN			Unsolved
Fowler, Breana	Transgender woman	Black	Nov. 12th, 2014	Nashville, TN	March 11th, 2015	119 days	Solved (killed after sexual encounter)
Johnson, Keymori Shatoya	Transgender woman	Black	Dec. 6th, 2014	Albany, GA	Dec. 16th, 2015	10 days	Solved (killed during suspected sex-work)
Edwards, Papi	Transgender woman/cross dresser	Black	Jan. 9th, 2015	Louisville, KY	Jan. 28th, 2015	19 days	Solved (killed during sex-work)
Beard, Lamia	transgender woman	Black	Jan. 17th, 2015	Norfolk, VA			Unsolved (media focused on previous prostitution arrests)
Proud, Penny	Transgender woman	Black	Feb. 10th, 2015	Treme (New Orleans), LA			Unsolved
Reinwald, Kristina	Transgender woman	Latina	Feb. 15th, 2015	Miami, FL			Unsolved
Blige, Keyshia	Transgender woman	Black	Mar. 7th, 2015	Montgomery, IL			Unsolved

(continued)

Table 6.1 (continued)

Victim's name	Transgender identity given by police	Race/ethnicity given	Date of homicide	Location of homicide	Date of arrest reported in media	Time until arrest	Type of homicide and motive given
Collins, Jasmine	Transgender woman	Black	June 23rd, 2015	Kansas City, MO	August 24th, 2015	62 days	Solved (killed by acquaintance during argument)
Clarke, India	Transgender woman	Black	July 21st, 2015	Tampa, FL	Oct. 27th, 2015	98 days	Solved (detectives stated "personal relationship")
Haggard, K.C.	Transgender woman	White	July 23rd, 2015	Fresno, CA	Feb 5th, 2018	928 days	Solved (killed during suspected sex work)
Schuler, Shade	Transgender woman	Black	July 29th, 2015	Dallas, TX			Unsolved
Ziona, Zella	Transgender woman	Black	Oct. 15th, 2015	Gaithersburg, MD	Oct. 19th, 2015	4 days	Solved (detectives stated "some degree of friendship")
Loera, Monica	transgender woman	Latina	Jan. 22nd, 2016	North Austin, TX	Feb. 1st, 2016	10 days	Solved ("killed during sex-work")
Sierra, Jasmine	Transgender woman	Latina	Jan. 22nd, 2016	Bakersfield, CA			Unsolved
Clarke, Kayden	Transgender man	White	Feb. 4th, 2016	Mesa, AZ	N/A	N/A	Shot by Police
Young, Maya	Transgender woman	Black	Feb. 20th, 2016	Frankford, PA	March 1st, 2016	10 days	Solved (media focused on previous solicitation arrest despite that not being a motive)
Johnson, Kedarie/Kandicee	Genderfluid	Black	Mar. 2nd, 2016	Burlington, IA	April 12th, 2016	41 days	Solved (sexual-homicide/suspected hate crime)
Thompson, Shante	Transgender woman	Black	April 10th, 2016	Houston, TX	April 21st, 2016	11 days	Solved ("street brawl")

Victim's name	Transgender identity given by police	Race/ethnicity given	Date of homicide	Location of homicide	Date of arrest reported in media	Time until arrest	Type of homicide and motive given
Walker, "Reecey" Tyreece	Transgender woman	Black	May 1st, 2016	Wichita, KS	May 5th, 2016	4 days	Solved (unknown as arrestee was 16)
Successful, Mercedes	Transgender woman (described as "a man who dressed as a woman"/drag queen)	Black	May 15th, 2016	Haines, FL	Oct. 25th, 2017	528 days	Solved ("drug transgenderaction" and "sex work")
Diamond, "Goddess"	Transgender woman	Black	June 5th, 2016	New Orleans, LA			Unsolved
Saffore, T.T.	Transgender woman	Black	Sept. 11th, 2016	Chicago, IL			Unsolved
Alsord, Jazz	Transgender woman	Black	Sept. 23rd, 2016	Birmingham, AL	Oct. 5th, 2016	12 days	Solved (robbery-homicide)
Monroe, India	Transgender woman	Black	Dec. 21st, 2016	Newport News, VA	Dec. 21st, 2016	N/A	Solved (murder-suicide)
Striker, Jojo	Transgender woman	Black	Feb. 8th, 2017	Toledo, OH			Unsolved
Holland, Jacquarrius	Transgender woman	Black	Feb. 19th, 2017	Monroe, LA	Feb. 20th, 2017	1 day	Solved (shot after verbal altercation)
Richmond, Tiara/Collier, Keke	Transgender woman	Black	Feb. 23rd, 2017	Chicago, IL			Unsolved
McElveen, Ciara	Transgender woman	Black	Feb. 27th, 2017	New Orleans, LA			Unsolved

(continued)

Table 6.1 (continued)

Victim's name	Transgender identity given by police	Race/ethnicity given	Date of homicide	Location of homicide	Date of arrest reported in media	Time until arrest	Type of homicide and motive given
Bostick, Kenneth	Transgender man	Black	April 25th, 2017	Manhattan, NY	April 25th, 2017	0 days	Solved
Faulkner, Sherrell	Transgender woman	Black	May 16th, 2017	Charlotte, NC			Unsolved
McFadden, Kenne	Transgender woman	Black	April 9th, 2017	San Antonio, TX	June 7th, 2017	59 days	Solved (trial but suspect found not guilty) pushed into river
Berrios, Josie	Transgender woman	Hispanic	June 13th, 2017	Ithaca, NY	June 15th, 2017	2 days	Solved ("personal relationship")
Morgan, Ebony	Transgender woman	Black	July 2nd, 2017	Lynchburg, VA	July 4th, 2017	2 days	Solved (drug-deal)
Mcglory, Jaylow	Transgender woman	Black	Aug. 4th, 2017	Alexandria, LA	Aug. 4th, 2017	0 days	Solved (Domestic)
Banner, Derricka	Transgender woman	Black	Sept. 12th, 2017	Charlotte, NC	Sept. 13th, 2017	1 day	Solved (acquaintance)
Montez, Stephanie	Transgender woman	Hispanic	Oct. 21st, 2017	Robstown, TX	Nov. 09, 2017	19 days	Solved (known acquaintance/robbery-homicide)
Stevenson, Brooklyn BreYanna	Transgender woman	Black	Nov. 27th, 2017	Oklahoma City, OK	Dec. 22nd, 2017	25 days	Solved (unknown motive)
Seals, Brandi	Transgender woman	Black	Dec. 13th, 2017	Houston, TX			Unsolved (suspected sex-worker)
Walker, Celine	Transgender woman	Black	Feb. 4th, 2018	Jacksonville, FL	Sept. 24th, 2019	597 days	Solved (acquaintance)
Harvey, Tonya	Transgender woman	Black	Feb. 6th, 2018	Buffalo, NY			Unsolved

Victim's name	Transgender identity given by police	Race/ethnicity given	Date of homicide	Location of homicide	Date of arrest reported in media	Time until arrest	Type of homicide and motive given
Fry, Zakaria	Transgender woman	White	Feb. 8th, 2018	Stanley, NM	Feb. 27th, 2018	19 days	Solved (acquaintance)
Wall, Sasha	Transgender woman	Black	April 1st, 2018	Chesterfield County, SC (referred to FBI as sheriff has refused to classify murder as hate crime)			Unsolved
Pierce, Gigi	Transgender woman	Mixed/black	May 21st, 2018	Portland, OR	May 21st, 2018	0 days	Solved (acquaintance)
English, Antash'a	Transgender woman	Black	May 21st, 2018	Jacksonville, FL			Unsolved
Stephens, Diamond	Transgender woman	Black	June 18th, 2018	Meridian, MI			Unsolved
Garden, Sasha	Transgender woman	Black	July 19th, 2018	Orlando, FL			Unsolved (suspected sex- worker)
Moore, London	Transgender woman	Black	Sept. 8th, 2018	North Port, FL			Unsolved
Enriquez, Nikki/Ortiz, Janelle	Transgender woman	Hispanic	Sept. 14th, 2018	Laredo, TX	Sept. 15th, 2018	1 day	Spree killer arrested who was targeting sex-workers (US Border Patrol Supervisor)
Frazier, Ciara	Transgender woman	Black	Oct. 3rd, 2018	Chicago, IL			Unsolved
Martin, Dana	Transgender woman	Black	Jan. 6th, 2019	Montgomery, AL			Unsolved
Scurlock, Chanel	Transgender woman	Black	June 8th, 2019	Lumberton, NC			Unsolved
Cofer, Jordan	Transgender man	White	Aug. 4th, 2019	Dayton, OH	August 4th, 2019	N/A	Mass Shooting (Brother of victim-shot by police at scene)

(continued)

Table 6.1 (continued)

Victim's name	Transgender identity given by police	Race/ethnicity given	Date of homicide	Location of homicide	Date of arrest reported in media	Time until arrest	Type of homicide and motive given
Doe, Pebbles La Dime "Dime"	Transgender woman	Black	Aug. 4th, 2019	Allendale County, SC			Unsolved
Berryman, Jamagio Jamar (Ja'leyah-Jamr)	Gender non-conforming man	Black	Sept. 13th, 2019	Kansas City, KS	Sept. 18th, 2019	5 days	Solved (ex-boyfriend)
Perry, Mia	Transgender woman	Black	Dec. 28th, 2019	Washington, DC			Unsolved (suspected sex-worker)
Milton, Riah	Transgender woman	Black	June 6th, 2020	Liberty Township/Cincinnati, OH			Unsolved (suspected robbery gone bad)

City of Austin
AUSTIN POLICE DEPARTMENT

715 E. 8th St. Austin, Texas 78701 | (512) 974-5017 | austintexas.gov/department/police

IMMEDIATE RELEASE
January 27, 2016
Contact: Public Information Office, 512-974-5017

UPDATE

Murder #1

Case: 16-0220222

Date: Friday, January 22, 2016

Time: 3:01 a.m.

Location: 300 block East Powell Lane

Deceased: David Loera, Hispanic Male (D.O.B. 07/31/1972)

On Friday, January 22, 2016, at approximately 3:01 a.m. Austin Police Officers responded to the 300 block of East Powell Lane in reference to a shooting/stabbing call. Officers arrived and found the victim lying on the ground with apparent trauma. Austin/Travis County EMS transported the victim to the University Medical Center at Brackenridge Hospital where he was later pronounced deceased.

The victim has been identified as David Loera, Hispanic male (D.O.B. 07/31/1972).

An autopsy was performed by the Travis County Medical Examiner's Office and the manner of death was ruled Homicide.

The suspect was described as a White male, in his twenties, 5'11" - 6'0", having a slightly muscular build, last seen wearing a camo hat, brown vest, dark long sleeved undershirt, and dark pants.

The suspect vehicle was described as a newer model, dark, Chevrolet 4-door truck, possibly a 4x4.

On Tuesday January 26, 2016, Homicide detectives identified the suspect in this case as JonCasey William Rowell, White male (D.O.B. 01/10/1987). Rowell was arrested by the Lone Star Fugitive Task Force and has been charged with Murder – 1st Degree, with bond set at $250,000. Rowell is currently in Travis County Jail.

Detectives are asking anyone with any information regarding this incident to call the Homicide Tip Line at 512-477-3588 or Crime Stoppers at 512-472-TIPS or text "Tip 103" + your message to CRIMES.

Fig. 6.1 Representative example of misgendering/deadnaming during Monica Loera's homicide investigation (screenshot)

In cases where there was an arrest made when misgendering/deadnaming occurred, the mean for the sample was 75.34 days between the reported murder and arrest. Notably, there were extreme outliers contained in the sample and this finding should be used with due caution. Yet, it must be acknowledged that by misgendering/deadnaming a victim this can cause a time delay in obtaining investigative information needed. Further cautiously every homicide has different independent variables that cannot be accounted for fully when examining national trends. Regardless a compelling finding in these cases was an analysis of the motive and/or the suspect relationship to the victim present in cases lasting longer than 100 days. Out of the 39 cases solved where misgendering/deadnaming occurred, six cases lasted more than 100 days (15%). In two of those solved[1] cases when the investigation lasted longer than 100 days, the suspect was a known acquaintance of the victim. In the remaining four solved cases when an investigation lasted longer than 100 days, the victim was murdered while engaging in suspected sex work or during a casual sexual encounter with a new acquaintance according to police descriptions.

Theoretical Explanations for Misgendering/Deadnaming of Victims in Homicide Cases

Theoretically, misgendering/deadnaming occurs in both policing and the media for several reasons. First, socialised binary discourses are pervasive through both group cultures and society. There exists a social expectation that identities are heteronormative and adaptive to cisnormative ideologies, thus those who exist outside are non-visible. Wood et al. (2019, p. 12) stated that black transgender lives are "disposable" and lacking value because of these institutionalised and socialised ideologies in both policing and the media. Further, previous studies have highlighted how the media frames transgender identities can serve as a delegitimising

[1] "Solved", means any case where an arrest was made, and the homicide investigation is closed. Notably, an arrest does not mean a successful prosecution.

function through misnaming, misgendering, misusing pronouns, and using deadname identities in news reports (see Barker-Plummer, 2013; Billard, 2016; Buss et al., 2021; DeJong et al., 2021; Osborn, 2022; Seely, 2021; Sloop, 2000; Wood et al., 2019). Thus, by delegitimising (see Booth, 2015) transgender identities and devaluing (see Wood et al., 2019) transgender victimhood in police investigations, in theory a reoccurring cycle of non-personhood and disassociation can continue. If the media and the police present a homicide victim as having disvalued or unrelatable characteristics, then it arguably becomes easier to "other" them (see Tajfel & Turner, 1979) and their identity (re: social identity theory). During this process, police and the media are more apt to detach and present the victim as an object, instead of a person. This can dehumanise the victim further allowing for detachment by police, the media, and the general public in homicide investigations.

Further there are also other secondary explanations for why misgendering/deadnaming occurs during some transgender homicide investigations. Panter (2018) highlighted the lack of police training and police policies regarding understanding transgender identities in both American and British policing. Miles-Johnson (2016) found that during police training, trainers did not challenge negative transgender opinions/comments held by fellow officers. Miles-Johnson (2016) stressed that these negative in-group opinions are upheld cultural within policing resulting in negative out-group perceptions towards transgender people in general. As such, misunderstanding (or in extreme cases police bias) of victim identities/victimology can arguably lead to further estrangement and detachment during transgender homicide investigations. Further, Panter (2018) argued that there have been systematic failures with the integration of transgender identities into policing which contributes to a lack of understanding and empathy towards transgender existence in general. This failure of integration plays a role in effective representation of transgender identities within policing and within society, which arguably is a vital component for cultural changes in cisnormative police cultures and perceptions held by cisgender colleagues towards transgender identities (see Miles-Johnson, 2016, 2019; Miles-Johnson & Death, 2020; Panter, 2018).

Besides socialised bias/misunderstanding of transgender identities, and failures in police training/policies, as previously stated, transgender identities uniquely face systematic and institutional intersectional biases within society. As a result, unfortunately it places (particularly for black transgender women as outlined previously) in higher risk categories due to forced sex work and other illegal means of financial support to overcome intersectional biases. Arguably, because of previous criminality of the victim or how the homicide was carried out (e.g., through sex work, drug deals, etc.), this can further devalue perceptions of gauged "victimhood". Therefore, the way police portray a homicide victim is arguably vital in gaining empathetic public attention and support in investigations when appealing for information in transgender homicides, particularly in cold cases.

Methodological Concerns/Limitations

There are inherent methodological problems when conducting research on transgender homicides, besides methodological issues with open-data sources and the data collection process. Namely, many police departments and the media fail to identify homicide victims as transgender. Also, the transgender victim's identity may still be closeted which may or may not be a factor during identification or during the investigation. The collected sample should be considered a fair, yet cautiously conservative, representation of US transgender homicides during this time frame. Notably, some people may have not been included in the studied sample because their legal name or deadname identity, and their transgender status was not included in media reports, official sources, nor non-profit advocacy blogs.

While years have been spent collecting and coding the sample data set for this research, it should be noted that it would be unfeasible (if not impossible) to ensure 100% accuracy of a homicide victim's transgender identity status. Exact and comprehensive statistics can only be collected from reported cases, and often due to systematic misgendering/deadnaming/non-disclosure this can be very difficult. Further, even when a person identified as transgender in life, family members may deny that they were transgender due to socialised cisnormative bias. For example, in the 2016 India Monroe case, after media and police reports deadnamed her, the news reported that her family buried her under her deadname identity, cut her long hair, and buried her in a man's suit (see Rodriguez, 2017). Arguably, by not acknowledging a murder victim's transgender status, they can be systematically erased and never accounted for within the media, within policing, and within society.

Conclusion

The current study contributes to homicide studies involving transgender victimology. Particularly, this is a multi-year empirical examination of transgender homicide which examined themes present in descriptions of ethnicity/race of the victims, frequency of antemortem injuries, disclosed motives, circumstantial details surrounding their deaths, and other themes present during their investigation. This study found that 78.31% of US homicide victims in the studied sample ($n = 166$) were identified as being "black" or "mixed". Further, this study found that, in respect to transgender identity status, 86.74% of the sample identified as a transgender woman prior to death, with gunshot wounds (63.25%) being the most common antemortem injuries received after stabbing with various instruments (16.86%).

Further, the misgendering/deadnaming of victims was identified as a theme present in 59.29% of US transgender homicide investigations. Wood et al. (2019) theorised that the specific misgendering of black transgender murder victims delegitimised their lives while perpetuating systematic forms of violence and exclusion further marginalising and disenfranchising them. Notably, this could be a concern as this study found that out of 53 unsolved transgender cases spanning from 01 January 2013 to 01 July 2020, 28 victims have been misgendered/deadnamed during their criminal investigation. Within those 28 cases, one victim was identified as a white transgender woman, two were identified as Latina transgender women, and 25 were black transgender women. Therefore, this study found that 89.29% of victims in unsolved transgender homicides were black transgender women.

Arguably more research is warranted in measuring the influence misgendering/deadnaming has upon solvability time and case closures before any claim can be made on the impact it has upon case closures. Yet, the observed theme in 59.29% of sample should not be discredited in this study, with 89.29% of unsolved transgender homicide victims being black transgender women. Notably, future intersectional research should be conducted to determine if misgendering/deadnaming specifically has a direct impact upon solvability times and solvability rates within transgender victimology uniquely, or if other factors like weapon usage, victim circumstances, victim identity, or investigator bias, plays a role in unsolved transgender homicides. Therefore, as this publication is one of the few studies which has used multi-year analysis of investigative themes present in US transgender homicides, I am hopeful that it helps lay additional groundwork for further studies to address this gap in literature.

References

Adams, N. (2016, June 2). *Transgender woman Monica Loera murdered in Austin, Texas and misgendered by the media*. GLAAD. Retrieved July 7, 2015, from https://www.glaad.org/blog/transgender-woman-monica-loera-murdered-austin-texas-and-misgendered-media

Alderden, M., & Lavery, T. (2007). Predicting homicide clearances in Chicago: Investigating disparities in predictors across different types of homicide. *Homicide Studies, 11*, 115–132.

APD Media Distribution List Archives. (2016, January 27). *Austin Police Department Public Information Office*. Austin Police Department. Retrieved January 3, 2020, from https://us5.campaign-archive.com/?u=1861810ce1dca1a4c1673747c&id=a3575c2241

Bänziger, M., & Killias, M. (2014). Unsolved homicides in Switzerland: Patterns and explanations. *European Journal of Criminology, 11*, 619–634.

Barker-Plummer, B. (2013). Fixing Gwen: News and the mediation of (transgender) gender challenges. *Feminist Media Studies, 13*(4), 710–724.

Berg, B. L. (2004). *Qualitative research methods for social sciences* (Vol. 5). Pearson.

Billard, T. J. (2016). Writing in the margins: Mainstream news media representations of transgenderism. *International Journal of Communication, 10*, 4193–4218.
Booth, E. T. (2015). The provisional acknowledgment of identity claims in televised documentary. In J. C. Capuzza & L. G. Spencer (Eds.), *Transgender communication studies: Histories, trends, and trajectories* (pp. 111–126). Lexington Books.
Brookman, F., Maguire, E. R., & Maguire, M. (2019). What factors influence whether homicide cases are solved? Insights from qualitative research with detectives in Great Britain and the United States. *Homicide Studies, 23*(2), 145–174.
Burke, M. (1994). Prejudice and discrimination: The case of the gay police officer. *The Police Journal, 67*(3), 219–229.
Buss, J., Le, H., & Haimson, O. L. (2021). Transgender identity management across social media platforms. *Media, Culture & Society, 44*(1), 1–7.
Colvin, R. (2009). Shared perceptions among lesbian and gay police officers: Barriers and opportunities in the law enforcement work environment. *Police Quarterly, 12*(1), 86–101.
Colvin, R. A. (2012). *Gay and lesbian cops: Diversity and effective policing*. Lynne Rienner Publishers.
DeCarlo, A. (2016). A reason for reasonable doubt in social justice: The weight of poverty, race and gender in lopsided homicide case clearances outcomes. *Contemporary Social Science, 11*, 362–372.
DeJong, C., Holt, K., Helm, B., & Morgan, S. J. (2021). "A human being like other victims": The media framing of transgender homicide in the United States. *Critical Criminology, 29*(1), 131–149.
Dinno, A. (2017). Homicide rates of transgender individuals in the United States: 2010–2014. *American Journal of Public Health, 107*(9), 1441–1447.
Dworkin, S. H., & Yi, H. (2003). LGBT identity, violence, and social justice: The psychological is political. *International Journal for the Advancement of Counselling, 25*(4), 269–279.
Dwyer, A. (2019). Queering policing: What is best practice with LGBTQ+ communities? *Current Issues in Criminal Justice, 31*(3), 396–411.
Edelman, E. A. (2014). Walking while transgender: Necropolitical regulations of transgender feminine bodies of colour in the nation's capital. In J. Haritaworn, A. Kuntsman, & S. Posocco (Eds.), *Queer Necropolitics* (pp. 172–190). Routledge.
Erich, S., Tittsworth, J., & Kersten, A. (2010). An examination and comparison of transgendersexuals of color and their White counterparts regarding

personal well-being and support networks. *Journal of GLBT Family Studies, 6*, 25–39.

Federal Bureau of Investigation. (2015). *About hate crime statistics.* Retrieved December 21, 2022, from https://www.fbi.gov/about-us/cjis/ucr/hate-crime/2014/resource-pages/about-hatecrime

Federal Bureau of Investigation. (2019). *About hate crime statistics.* Retrieved December 21, 2022, from https://www.fbi.gov/about-us/cjis/ucr/hate-crime/2014/resource-pages/about-hatecrime

Ganju, D., & Saggurti, N. (2017). Stigma, violence and HIV vulnerability among transgender persons in sex work in Maharashtra, India. *Culture, Health & Sexuality, 19*, 903–917.

Grant, J., Mottet, L., Tanis, J., Harrison, J., Herman, J., & Keisling, M. (2011). *Injustice at every turn: A report of the national transgender discrimination survey.* National Center for Transgender Equality and National Gay and Lesbian Task Force. Retrieved December 21, 2022, from http://www.thetaskforce.org/downloads/reports/reports/ntds_full.pdf

Gray, A. C., & Parker, K. F. (2019). Race, structural predictors, and police shootings: Are there differences across official and "unofficial" accounts of lethal force? *Crime & Delinquency, 65*(1), 26–45.

Gruenewald, J. (2012). Are anti-LGBT homicides in the United States unique? *Journal of Interpersonal Violence, 27*(18), 3601–3623.

Gruenewald, J., & Allison, K. (2018). Examining differences in bias homicide across victim groups. *Crime & Delinquency, 64*(3), 316–341.

Gruenewald, J., & Kelley, K. (2014). Exploring anti-LGBT homicide by mode of victim selection. *Criminal Justice and Behavior, 41*(9), 1130–1152.

Herek, G. M. (2002). Heterosexuals' attitudes toward bisexual men and women in the United States. *Journal of Sex Research, 39*(4), 264–274.

Hesse-Biber, S., & Griffin, A. J. (2013). Internet-mediated technologies and mixed methods research: Problems and prospects. *Journal of Mixed Methods Research, 7*(1), 43–61.

Ijoma, S. (2018). False promises of protection: Black women, transgender people & the struggle for visibility as victims of intimate partner and gendered violence. *University of Maryland Law Journal of Race, Religion, Gender & Class, 18*, 255.

Jones, M., & Williams, M. L. (2015). Twenty years on: Lesbian, gay and bisexual police officers' experiences of workplace discrimination in England and Wales. *Policing and Society, 25*(2), 188–211.

June, K. (2017). *Representations of transgender murder victims in digital US news media: A framing analysis* (Masters thesis). University of South Florida.

Retrieved December 21, 2022, from https://digitalcommons.usf.edu/mastersheses/143/

Leppel, K. (2016). The labor force status of transgender men and women. *International Journal of Transgenderism, 17*(3–4), 155–164.

Litwin, K., & Xu, Y. (2007). The dynamic nature of homicide clearances: A multilevel model comparison of three time periods. *Homicide Studies, 11*, 94–114.

MacKenzie, G., & Marcel, M. (2000). Media coverage of the murder of U.S. transgenderwomen of color. In L. M. Cuklanz & S. Moorti (Eds.), *Local violence, global media: Feminist analyses of gendered representations* (pp. 79–106). Peter Lang.

Mazur, E. (2010). Collecting data from social networking web sites and blogs. In S. D. Gosling & J. A. Johnson (Eds.), *Advanced methods for behavioral research on the Internet* (pp. 77–90). American Psychological Association.

McBride, B. (2018, February 9). *HRC mourns loss of Celine Walker, a transgender woman murdered in Florida*. Human Rights Campaign. Retrieved May 2, 2020, from https://www.hrc.org/blog/hrc-mourns-loss-of-celine-walker-a-transgender-woman-murdered-in-florida

McKeiver, D. (2018, February 9). *Police ID victim killed at hotel near St. Johns town center*. News4Jax. Retrieved May 2, 2020, from https://www.news4jax.com/news/2018/02/09/police-id-victim-killed-at-hotel-near-st-johns-town-center/

Miles-Johnson, T. (2013, April–June). LGBTI variations in crime reporting: How sexual identity influences decisions to call the cops. *Sage Open, 3*, 1–15.

Miles-Johnson, T. (2015). Perceptions of group value: How Australian transgender people view policing. *Policing and Society: An International Journal of Research and Policy, 26*(6), 605–626.

Miles-Johnson, T. (2016). Policing diversity: Examining police resistance to training reforms for transgender people in Australia. *Journal of Homosexuality, 63*(1), 103–136.

Miles-Johnson, T. (2019). Police recruit perception of transgender officers: Inclusion, diversity and transgender people. *Journal of Criminological Research, Policy and Practice, 6*(3), 2189–2201.

Miles-Johnson, T., & Death, J. (2020). Compensating for sexual identity: How LGB and heterosexual Australian police officers perceive policing of LGBTIQ+ people. *Journal of Contemporary Criminal Justice, 36*(2), 251–273.

Momen, R., & Dilks, L. (2021). Examining case outcomes in US transgender homicides: An exploratory investigation of the intersectionality of victim characteristics. *Sociological Spectrum, 41*(1), 53–79.

Osborn, M. (2022). US news coverage of transgender victims of fatal violence: An exploratory content analysis. *Violence against Women, 28*(9), 1–24.

Panter, H. (2018). *Transgender cops: The intersection of gender and sexuality expectations in police cultures*. Routledge.

Parkin, W. S., & Gruenewald, J. (2017). Open-source data and the study of homicide. *Journal of Interpersonal Violence, 32*(18), 2693–2723.

Patterson, C., Emslie, C., Mason, O., Fergie, G., & Hilton, S. (2016). Content analysis of UK newspaper and online news representations of women's and men's 'binge' drinking: A challenge for communicating evidence-based messages about single-episodic drinking? *British Medical Journal Open, 6*(12), 1–9.

Platt, L. F., & Bolland, K. S. (2017). Transgender* partner relationships: A qualitative exploration. *Journal of GLBT Family Studies, 13*(2), 163–185.

Puckett, J. L., & Lundman, R. J. (2003). Factors affecting homicide clearances: Multivariate analysis of a more complete conceptual framework. *Journal of Research in Crime and Delinquency, 40*, 171–193.

Regoeczi, W. C., Jarvis, J. P., & Riedel, M. (2008). Clearing murders: Is it about time? *Journal of Research in Crime and Delinquency, 45*, 142–162.

Rief, R. M., & Clinkinbeard, S. S. (2020). Exploring gendered environments in policing: Workplace incivilities and fit perceptions in men and women officers. *Police Quarterly, 23*(4), 427–450.

Roberts, A. (2007). Predictors of homicide clearance by arrest: An event history analysis of NIBRS incidents. *Homicide Studies, 11*, 82–93.

Roberts, A., & Lyons, C. (2011). Hispanic victims and homicide clearance by arrest. *Homicide Studies, 15*, 48–73.

Roberts, M. (2018, February 9). *Number 4-rest in power and peace Celine Walker*. TransgenderGriot. Retrieved May 2, 2020, from https://www.news4jax.com/news/2018/02/09/police-id-victim-killed-at-hotel-near-st-johns-town-center/

Rodriguez, M. (2017, January 6). Virginia trans woman India Monroe shot to death in December, misgendered in early reports. Retrieved from Mic.com: https://www.mic.com/articles/164502/virginia-trans-woman-indiamonroe-shot-to-death-in-december-misgendered-in-early-reports

Rodrıguez-Madera, S. L., Padilla, M., Varas-Dıaz, N., Neilands, T., Vasques Guzzi, A. C., Florenciani, E. J., & Ramos-Pibernus, A. (2017). Experiences of violence among transgender women in Puerto Rico: An underestimated problem. *Journal of Homosexuality, 64*, 209–217.

Seely, N. (2021). Reporting on transgender victims of homicide: Practices of misgendering, sourcing and transgenderparency. *Newspaper Research Journal, 42*(1), 74–94.

Sevelius, J. M. (2013). Gender affirmation: A framework for conceptualizing risk behavior among transgender women of color. *Sex Roles, 68*(11–12), 675–689.

Seymour, K. (2022). Women in the criminal justice system. In *Women, crime and justice in context: Contemporary perspectives in feminist criminology from Australia and New Zealand* (pp. 57–72). Routledge.

Silverman, R. A., & Kennedy, L. W. (1997). Uncleared homicides in Canada and the United States. In *Lethal violence: Proceedings of the 1995 meeting of the Homicide Research Working Group* (pp. 81–86). National Institute of Justice.

Silvestri, M. (2017). Police culture and gender: Revisiting the 'cult of masculinity'. *Policing: A Journal of Policy and Practice, 11*(3), 289–300.

Sloop, J. M. (2000). Disciplining the transgendered: Brandon Teena, public representation, and normativity. *Western Journal of Communication (Includes Communication Reports), 64*(2), 165–189.

Tajfel, H., & Turner, J. (1979). An integrative theory of intergroup-conflict. In W. Austin & S. Worchel (Eds.), *The social psychology of intergroup relations* (pp. 33–47). Brooks/Cole.

Talusan, M. (2016). *Unerased: Counting transgender lives.* Mic, National Coalition of Anti-Violence Programs, GLAAD. Retrieved May 2, 2020, from https://mic.com/unerased

Teal, J. L. (2015). *"Black transgender bodies are under attack": Gender non-conforming Homicide Victims in the US 1995–2014* (Doctoral dissertation). Humboldt State University.

Thomas, D. M., Amburgey, J., & Ellis, L. (2016). Anti-transgender prejudice mediates the association of just world beliefs and victim blame attribution. *International Journal of Transgenderism, 17*(3–4), 176–184.

Turner, R., & Kosa, R. (2003). *Cold case squads: Leaving no stone unturned.* Bureau of Justice Assistance.

Waters, E., Pham, L., Convery, C., & Yacka-Bible, S. (2018). *A crisis of hate: A report on LBGTQ hate violence homicides in 2017*. National Coalition of Anti-Violence Programs. Retrieved May 2, 2020, from http://avp.org/wp-content/uploads/2018/01/a-crisis-of-hate-january-release.pdf

Wellford, C., & Cronin, J. (1999). *An analysis of variables affecting the clearance of homicides: A multistate study*. Justice Research and Statistics Association.

Williams, M. L. (2009). *Making of a monster: Media construction of gender non-conforming homicide victims* (Doctoral dissertation). Washington State University.

Wood, F., Carrillo, A., & Monk-Turner, E. (2019). Visibly unknown: Media depiction of murdered transgender women of color. *Race and Justice, 12*(2), 1–19.

7

Disorder in the Court: Trans Folx Experiences of Criminal Legal Practitioner Failings

April Carrillo

Introduction

Typically, discussions of how trans folx[1] are unfairly treated by the criminal legal system focus on the police or on the correctional system. There is limited research in how they experience the court systems, with most of the information being found in grey literature.[2] Make no mistake, transgender folx are also targeted within the confines of the courtroom, which takes the form of upholding archaic views about dress codes,

[1] A variation on the word folks, folx is meant to be a gender-neutral way to refer to members of or signal identity in LGBTQ+ communities (Peters, 2017).

[2] Grey literature refers to works from, "government, academics, business, and organization in electronic and print formats not controlled by commercial publishing, i.e., where publishing is not the primary activity of the producing body" (GreyNet International, 2020, para. 3).

A. Carrillo (✉)
Department of Political Science, Criminal Justice, College of Arts and Sciences, University of South Dakota, Vermillion, SD, USA
e-mail: april.carrillo@usd.edu

H. Panter and A. Dwyer (eds.), *Transgender People and Criminal Justice*, Critical Criminological Perspectives, https://doi.org/10.1007/978-3-031-29893-6_7

behavior, and acceptable gender presentation (Goodmark, 2013; James et al., 2016; Lambda Legal, 2015). These insistences on specific standards by definition excludes those who are outside of the inaccurate gender binary in terms of existence and presentation, which places them at a disadvantage, as they are held to an ideal that has no room for them. Transgender folx in this study reported their own experiences with general incompetency, described targeted attacks from legal practitioners, and even sometimes how this affected the outcome of their proceedings, often negatively.

Even before entering the courtroom, participants expressed fear or uneasiness of how they would be perceived by practitioners, even if they had no previous experience with the courts (Goodmark, 2013). This apprehension took different forms, as some chose to hide their identity by entirely and even not correcting someone when they were repeatedly misgendered. The anticipation and even expectation that they would receive unfair treatment is then mitigated by their own behavior to not disrupt the court and practitioners. Thus, the title of this chapter, *Disorder in the Court*, is to note the disruption that legal practitioners see in transgender folx in the courtroom, a disruption to "normal proceedings" that do not include a nuanced understanding of gender identity and expression. This should not affect their cases or treatment, but the reality is that it does. Yet, attorneys misgendering their own clients, judges making judgements based on their personal biases, etc., are the true disorder and disruption.

This chapter will discuss the experiences of transgender folx in the courtroom, as they are vital to understanding the realities that these folx often face. Criminal activity, real or perceived, is needed to start interactions with police or the correctional system, but courts can be for anyone who needs to file legal paperwork, has a parking ticket, filing for divorce, facing eviction, etc. Providing an avenue for these narratives to live permanently is essential, as the treatment of trans folx in court needs to be highlighted and discussed. At the end of this chapter, I also provide recommendations of how to avoid these instances in the future to aid legal practitioners in avoiding being disruptive if a trans person happens to be in the room that day.

Trans Experiences in Court

Goodmark (2013) specifically notes the lack of trust in the legal system from transgender folx, who despite may be needing services or help, may avoid the system altogether because of their fear. Court staff has been found to refuse to use correct names and pronouns, verbally harass trans folx, and even make disparaging remarks in open court (James et al., 2016; Lambda Legal, 2015). And, in extreme cases, judges have even quoted the bible, calling their gender identity a choice, and another threatened to eliminate "visitation/custody rights to a transgender parent if she followed through with her plans for gender [affirming] surgery" (Lambda Legal, 2015, p. 1a). Generally, though, misconduct most often took the form of negative comments that referred to people's gender identity, sexual orientation, or gender expression.

Specifically, within Lambda Legal's (2015) study, 20% of those who had been in court heard damaging comments from a professional, such as a judge, attorney, or another courtroom employee, with most of those participants who overheard the comment being people of color. Further, it was found that other instrumental people in the courtroom would also make these comments: witnesses (28%), jurors (12%), and other folx in the courtroom (22%), respectively. However, courtroom professionals would even take this one step further and publicly out[3] transgender folx in open court, even though there are rare exceptions where this information would be relevant (Lambda Legal, 2015). The motivation for such gross misconduct would be to alter the outcome of the case by equating being LGBTQ+ with criminality, an attempt to shame them in a packed courtroom, or even to exclude them from jury duty (Lambda Legal, 2015). It cannot be understated how unprofessional such a weaponization of identity is, but it can be tactical, as they can work on a jury or necessary professionals, if played up to the right audience.

Even when the matters are not criminal, coming to court can still be a hassle for transgender folx, as going to court could mean that transgender folx have to discuss any legal dissonance between their lived identity and

[3] To out someone is to disclose a person's LGBTQ+ identity without their permission (Maidment, 2018).

their legal gender (Goodmark, 2013). James et al. (2016) found that in their example of over 27,000 transgender folx in the United States, 23% of them had been addressed incorrectly in the court (e.g., using he and not she) and was addressed with the wrong honorific (Mr. instead of Ms/Mrs.). Further, 19% of folx were asked specifically about the physical aspects of their transition, which included hormone use and surgeries, which was more common than reported verbal harassment (3%) or unequal treatment (9%). So, unsurprisingly, there is a large discrepancy between folx who reportedly had their paperwork completed (11%) and 68% who had not changed anything. While paperwork does not validate the gender identity of any person, having it aligned with how you identify is vital, as 32% of folx were harassed, denied services or benefits, and even physically attacked when there was a dissonance between their paperwork and their identity (James et al., 2016).

Courtroom Perceptions of Trans Folx

To further understand how trans folx are treated in the courtroom, it is vital to discuss the perceptions of legal practitioners. Previous findings have aligned with the above section concerning transgender experiences. The attitudes of individual practitioners can influence case outcomes, and even fuel negative interactions between practitioners themselves. Even being a lawyer does not protect transgender people from discrimination, as Blanck et al. (2021) found in a survey of 3,590 legal professionals in the United States, that being LGBQ+ and transgender increased the likelihood that a person would experience discrimination. Other characteristics such as age, disability, and identifying as a woman also increased this risk, as these intersectional identities compounded the amount of discrimination a person faced (Blanck et al., 2021). Alarmingly, if a person who works within the system is treated poorly for being transgender because of negative interactions with colleagues, it stands to reason that this applies to those coming to court as well.

Concerning judges, Honorée and Juban (2020) examined specific demographics (political party, race, sex) of judges in cases of employment discrimination in the United States where the plaintiff was transgender.

While the race of the judge did not play a factor in whether there would be a determination in favour of the transgender plaintiff, if the judge was a member of the Democratic party and identified as female, they were almost twice as likely to rule in favor of transgender plaintiffs (Honorée & Juban, 2020). Even though employment discrimination is not a criminal legal issue, it is vital to understand that judges work in the same system, and thus, their perceptions are valid to understand the attitudes around transgender folx. When analysing jurors and if they have any LGBTQ+ bias, Woods (2019) points out that there is not a substantive method of addressing if such a concern for a bias exists. This is vital to systemically challenge and alter, as jurors have been found to hold poor views of LGBTQ+ people when they are the victims of hate crimes, interpersonal violence, and even when they are murdered (Woods, 2019).

Even transgender young people cannot escape this bias, as outlined by Marksamer (2008) in their policy analysis of how the law fails transgender young people. Specifically, Marksamer (2008) reveals how the risk factors that transgender young people face (such as family rejection, harassment, low self-esteem, experiences with transphobia, etc.) lead them to act out in understandable ways, such as running away, not going to school, and using substances. However, often when they go to the court, context does not matter, and juveniles, who need intervention, are instead sent to detention facilities. Specifically, Marksamer (2008) highlights the story of Destiny (not her real name), who fell along this trajectory, committing crimes that were not violent or egregious, but rather to deal with difficult circumstances, as children often do. In Destiny's case, her criminal activity was directly tied to difficulties in her personal life that she was dealing with because of coming out as transgender. However, after being repeatedly assaulted at a facility meant for cisgender boys, during the hearing to have her transferred, her attorney called her a "young man" and told the judge that he thought that Destiny "overblows a lot of the incidents" (Marksamer, 2008, p. 77). The treatment of transgender folx within the courtroom highlights a fundamental flaw in the most "just" part of the criminal legal system: If your identity places you at a higher risk of being negatively perceived and unfairly treated, is this justice?

Current Study

This chapter uses data from 44 qualitative interviews with folx who identified under the transgender umbrella (transgender, non-binary, genderqueer) and their experiences with the three branches of the criminal legal system (law enforcement, courts, corrections). From these narratives, this analysis will be of their experiences in the courtroom, especially in terms of general incompetency and targeted attacks. Limited literature has even reported on these narratives; thus, the intent of this work is to add the voices of transgender folx to necessary discussions of discrimination in the criminal legal system. This data is intended to show this disorder in courtrooms after a transgender person enters is a result of legal professionals in the criminal legal system being woefully unequipped with accurate vocabulary and basic knowledge, and they are not held accountable when they actively discriminate.

Methods and Sample

Sampling Procedures

The design of this study is rooted in a community-based approach, where it was created alongside a local community of transgender folx that I had sustained contact with. As I emphasise in all my works, I want to note that without community guidance and trust, I would not have been able to interview the amount of people I did with questions that were respectful, and have successful, narrative-rich interviews. To assume that I, a queer, white Latinx person, would be privy to these deeply personal stories, then claim I am an expert in their experiences is extremely privileged and does not acknowledge the burden that this can actually place on marginalised communities (Huckins, 2021). Because I conducted myself by being community informed, it allowed me to interview a diverse group of transgender people who possessed multiple intersections of identity, such as differences of race, disability, income, age, and so on.

Interviews

In terms of qualifiers, participants just had to be 18, live in the state of Virginia, identify under the transgender umbrella (transgender, non-binary, genderqueer, genderfluid, etc.), and have an experience with the criminal legal system. These experiences ranged from changing their name in court, to being pulled over in a car by police, all the way to incarceration. The diversity of experiences of these participants allowed for a broad understanding of the separate parts of the criminal legal system and the treatment of transgender folx in a variety of ways. The questions were open ended and started with basic information, then phased to life history and daily experiences, and then rounded out with their narratives concerning any interactions with the criminal legal system.

All interviews took place between November 2018 and December 2019, either in person or online, depending on the preference of the participant. Folx were paid $15 for their time, which varied from 42 minutes to 3 hours. The interviews themselves placed the participant in a seat of control, as they determined what was recorded, how long the interview was, and if anything needed to be off the record. Everything was done with explicit consent, with the comfort of the participant being my main concern. All participants chose a pseudonym at the time of the interview that has served as their name when discussing their narratives to protect their privacy.

Analytical Method

The analytical method of this study is reflective of the abductive method described by Timmermans and Tavory (2012), where the researcher is informed by their own thoughts and positions but uses a rigorous epistemological method for analysis. Thus, while there is an expectation that certain findings will be apparent, it leaves room for organic discoveries through observation and data collection (Timmermans & Tavory, 2012). For this study, the themes that centre around experiences in the courtroom were rooted from the following questions from the interview guide: (a) Have you ever been to court for any reason? (b) Can you tell me about court professionals' reactions to your gender identity? (c) Have you ever had a negative interaction with court professionals *because of* your gender identity or expression?

Participant Characteristics

The participants in this study had an average age of 35, and their ages ranged from 19 to 65. While most participants identified as white (66%), 34% were people of colour, which was made up of a number of different races and ethnicities. Concerning gender identity, most participants identified as transgender women (57%), with transgender men and non-binary/genderqueer folx following behind at 23% and 20%, respectively. Table 7.1 has specific information concerning additional participant characteristics, which can be found in Appendix.

Findings

Participants revealed their court system experiences in their interviews, with experiences ranging from ignorance and misgendering, all the way to their gender identity being weaponized by legal practitioners to alter case outcomes. These instances are important to highlight, as the blatant disregard of these experiences diminishes the legitimacy. As previously mentioned, there have been non-profits that have conducted the necessary work to try and have a base of knowledge, but if the goal of the field of criminology is to incorporate each aspect of the system, this is a failure. When reflecting on this topic, specifically concerning the interviews I conducted, there is a sentence from a participant that underscores the importance of discussing these issues. During the interview, Grace described how practitioners during a hearing would not acknowledge her with her name or pronouns, even though all the paperwork[4] had been changed and her presentation matched her gender identity. She told me that "[n]obody stood up for the fact that I was a woman except for

[4] This is not to say that trans folx have to have their paperwork to be valid; this is more of a criticism of how even when trans folx follow the "rules," they still face discrimination.

me," and then she took a pause, tearing up about the memory of having to fight back against everyone in the courtroom who had done her the disservice of not acknowledging her identity. What is also alarming here is that Grace had done everything "right." Her paperwork was changed, her presentation was changed, and she lived her life as a woman, yet her gender identity was instead used as an excuse to treat her poorly.

For this chapter, the findings are centring around the specific experiences and the misconduct on behalf of the legal practitioners in the courtroom when it came to transgender folx. The intended purpose is to not only highlight the narratives of the transgender folx who experienced these wrongs, but to also hold practitioners accountable and prepare folx for the sometimes-sad reality of the courtroom. These will be analysed and categorised in the two dimensions of general Incompetency and targeted attacks.

General Incompetency

Discussions of targeted attacks of transgender folx because of their gender identity are important, but not every experience is rooted in an obvious, malicious event. Participants also described instances where they experienced ignorance in accordance with their gender identity in the courtroom, and these experiences are just as valid and vital to understand. These instances have been labelled as general incompetency, where practitioners did not have the vocabulary, training, or even life experience to successfully interact with someone who is outside the gender binary. Further, participants noted that to take control of interactions with practitioners, they would have a handle on their physical appearance, as they were aware of the stigmatisation of being transgender. Zelda captured this sentiment as noting that being transgender would complicate her visits to court as she said:

> Walking through to [the] courthouse, am I going to get stereotyped as a hooker going to their court case? And [then] I've already lost it [the case] because that's what everybody's already making up. Because that's the biggest thing for transgender people, it is hooking. The easiest one [to be arrested for] and it's the hardest one to prove you're not doing.

> Walking down the street, a cop pull[s] you over. How are you going to prove you're not a hooker?

This hyperawareness of how transgender people are perceived in the criminal legal system informed folx on how to interact with practitioners. The conscious choice to step back in the closet to try and not be disruptive is purposeful to make it out of the situation unscathed. Tobias described how he did not argue with the police officer or the judge when he was in court for a traffic incident.

> They [police and judge] did use female pronouns, but in the face of the court system, it's very much… I revert back to [she/her pronouns], 'cause it's scary. I don't want any trouble. I don't want any trouble, you know? The cop gave a different side of the story and he was like um, well [he][5] was very cooperative.

This reverting that Tobias is describing came out of his fear and the clear ignorance of the practitioners to not ask about pronouns, even though Tobias had a clear masculine presentation. Their use of incorrect pronouns signalled to Tobias that this may not be a safe environment, and he was even scared. Notably, Tobias was there for a traffic violation where he ended up just having to pay court costs, but he was still struck by the possibility that he might face more dire consequences. However, to prevent this from happening, he allowed himself to be misgendered for a small period of time, without correcting the judge and the police officer.

Even when they are not the one on trial, just watching criminal legal practitioners unable to respect pronouns can damage the perceptions of other people who are present. For instance, when asking Emily how they think courtroom professionals perceive transgender folx, they described an instance when they sat in court to support folx who were in the J20 trials after being arrested during Donald Trump's inauguration. Emily repeatedly watched a judge and courtroom misgender a defendant, and their attorney repeatedly correcting the court, and described that this

[5] The police officer used "she" here instead.

had been happening for months, all throughout the trial. This is an obvious instance where the court practitioners should have been held accountable, as pronouns are important, or to at least use the defendant's name, as this is an issue of respect and dehumanisation. The defendant was never addressed properly while there was a jury trial, and Emily describing this instance of how they believed courtroom professionals perceived transgender folx is indicative of their view of courtroom professionals' behaviour. While Emily never explicitly told me that their perception was poor of courtroom professionals, I find it interesting that this was their go-to example.

Moreover, even to preempt being misgendered, when a participant gave previous notice, the courts still actively misgendered, deadnamed, and even made it very obvious in open court that there was a transgender person in the room. Julian, when heading to court, did his research ahead of time, and ensured that he could let the courts know of the name and pronouns he used and presentation, as well as other accommodations for the hearing. When he went to court, Julian watched the court clerk hand the judge the letter he had previously sent, which was the policy at the time, and he watched the judge read the letter. Then, in a practice that seems counterintuitive, the court took attendance before proceedings started and when they got to Julian's name, they called his deadname.

> They just called everybody's name and ask[ed] them to raise their hands. And I raised my hand when I heard my [dead]name called. So, they just like stared at me for a full minute and I was like [laughs] like this is very awkward.

Not only did they use the incorrect name, but the incorrect pronouns as well. Thus, when they called his legal name, Julian had to raise his hand to a name that, under the binary understanding of gender in the United States, was different from his presentation, effectually outing him in the entire courtroom, which could have compromised his safety.

Another participant's experience, Wolf's, noted that the ignorance of the court practitioners was probably the reason why his case had such a positive outcome. After going to court following being harassed by a roommate who then threatened to kill him, Wolf and his wife went to file for a protective order. When he arrived at the court for his case, Wolf's paperwork concerning his name and his gender marker was correct, so when the roommate tried to weaponise transphobia against him, the court practitioners were confused. The roommate's court-appointed attorney actually approached Wolf and asked him about the misgendering and accusations.

Attorney: "He's talking about that you're um, trans sexual."
Wolf: [laughs] Um, I'm like, "Yeah, that's not what people are called."
Attorney: "Are you this or that?"
Wolf: I'm like, "No, he's just calling me that because he wants to." (aside) Like, I was just lying my ass off just to get past that. Can we just go [on] with the court case, you know?

The case continued, and at some point, when the roommate tried to continue to misgender and degrade Wolf, the judge stopped the proceedings until the defendant properly addressed Wolf and even apologised to him in open court. Now, it should be noted that Wolf was not lying about his identity. Wolf IS a man, he lives his life as a man, and he does not identify as a transexual. He identifies as a man.

As Wolf put it, "They just saw a guy being harassed by another guy," with the advantage of not being seen as transgender, but for the man he lives his life as. This is a common survival tactic that transgender people have been found to employ in terms of utilising passing privilege in their everyday lives and the criminal legal system in order to move freely. And in terms of this case, Wolf was in the right, but his inclination and fear was that the court would not have ruled in his favour. Wolf's experience highlights a sinister duality that transgender folx often have to walk between as a result of incompetence and hatred, that of happiness and safety. To be safe, Wolf told the lawyer "no" and did not reveal his transness in order to receive a positive outcome. However, for other participants, they did not fare as well in their interactions with the court system, as they were actually targeted for their gender identity.

Targeted Attacks

Participants who experienced targeted attacks in the courtroom effectually understood that without their gender identity being an issue, they most likely would not have had to endure their events. For instance, as earlier mentioned, Grace described that she was the only one who stood up for herself in the courtroom. To give context to her particular case, Grace had started her transition later in life, and her marriage did not survive, as her partner of over 30 years rejected her, and then falsely made a report of assault against Grace in order to get a restraining order to get her out of their house. Grace was not aware of this until after she arrived home from work one day, and then was placed in handcuffs. Fast forward to divorce proceedings and in the courtroom, Grace's ex-wife and the ex-wife's attorney repeatedly used the incorrect pronouns, wrong name, and kept referring to Grace as a man. When Grace had to take the stand, she attempted to correct the attorney.

> The ex [and] the lawyer kept referring to me as him, him, him, him. And I was under oath, and I says look, I am a woman. My driver's license was correct. My anatomy was correct, my mind was correct, everything says woman, but because I used to be the husband, [they] kept saying him, him, him, him. And I said under oath to the judge, I says I am a woman and I said that twice. [The judge] could care less, he didn't care. He didn't, he didn't chastise the lawyer, didn't chastise my ex, didn't say a word one way or the other. He just let it go, just water under the bridge.

Following the divorce, Grace went into a substantial amount of debt, which was combined with medical debt of over $100,000, and at the time of the interview (10 years later), she still had about $6,000 left to pay.

In Grace's case, there was the attorney and ex-wife's blatant disrespect of her identity, as well as the judge allowing it to happen, and Grace's own lawyer not defending her. This created a hostile atmosphere, where any previous wrongdoing by the ex-wife (previous cases of abuse) or evidence seemed to be set aside for the sake of arguing that the divorce was Grace's fault for transitioning. The fixation on her gender identity and the allowance let the judge make Grace the villain, but also made Grace liable for the costs associated with the separation and subsequent divorce. It is hard to imagine that without Grace's gender identity being the root cause of the entire set of the above circumstances, that someone retired from the military, with a steady, prestigious job, extensive education, and was a religious figure in their community would have been given the same treatment if they were cisgender.

Djinni also experienced similar misgendering and targeted attacks in the courtroom during her divorce from her ex-wife. Djinni's experience paralleled those of Grace's, in that the ex-wife was filing for divorce because she had an issue with Djinni's gender identity. In the courtroom, while she reported that the judge treated her fairly, the ex's lawyer misgendered and deadnamed her, even though Djinni's name was changed before the divorce was finalised, with the new case paperwork even having the incorrect name. However, Djinni's wife took it one step further and claimed that the mental stress from taking care of Djinni caused her to lose her job, and thus, she needed financial support. The ex-wife did not disclose in the courtroom that a fight between them concerning gender identity was the catalyst for the event where she had to take care of Djinni in the first place.

In the courtroom, Djinni's ex-wife received the order of $1,000 a month for three years, had the survivors benefit plan, and split the savings account. After the decree went through, Djinni was forced out of the military since after her hospitalisation, her commanding officers emphasised that they did not want her to come out and be public, even though legally, she had every right to at the time. One officer told her, "I don't have to tolerate LGBT shit," and, following several incidents, she decided to leave the service with a severance after serving 12 years, eight years shy of her plan to do the full 20 years for a retirement benefit. After leaving the service, she went into arrears (behind on her payments) and was harassed daily by her ex-wife for the money, and then the court reassessed the payments to be $1,250 a month to the ex-wife, even after Djinni's income had changed. At the time of the interview, she was behind on her mortgage, had found another LGBT-friendly lawyer, but was having a hard time retaining her due to the lack of income, and was only making $1,600 a month. After the ex-wife filed a complaint with the court, the judge responded, “Well, this individual is bringing in 1,600 dollars a month. Why can’t this individual pay the ex?” To which Djinni replied, “I repeatedly told her [ex-wife], ‘Look, I am not paying for your luxuries at the sacrifice of my necessities.’” What is even more damning is the fact that after Djinni found an LGBT-centred lawyer who stood up for her, the lawyer was shocked at the outcome of the first proceedings where the ex-wife was awarded so much money. However, based on the hostile treatment from the original lawyer, to Djnni, it was not surprising.

On the criminal court side of things, participants were also faced with targeted harassment from courtroom practitioners. Vanessa, who was charged with an accessory to sex work, unknowingly, was treated with hostility from her arrest and all throughout her court proceedings. Vanessa did not know the friend she was giving a ride to a hotel and waiting for was engaging in sex work, but police did not ask her anything as they dragged her to the ground after getting her to step out of her truck. She was then taken to court and charged, and even though, like Grace, her paperwork was changed and accurate, the courts misgendered her and treated her poorly.

> A big part of it was also they took pictures of me and put me in [the system], to keep track of me. Just in case I’m [a] repeat offender and involved in stuff. Yeah, I was kind of annoyed, especially when they misgendered me on the court documents. They asked me if I was pre or post op.

Even if Vanessa was guilty of the crimes they had accused her of, any status of surgeries she may or may not elect to receive are none of the courts’ business. The presence of certain body features does not indicate guilt or innocence, and equating Vanessa to her body parts is an example of perpetuating harmful stereotypes of transgender folx by assuming that she would be involved in sex work *because* she is transgender.

Jasmine also described while attending mental health court, that even though the rest of the court called her by her name and used she/her pronouns, her assigned caseworker refused to give her the same respect.

> I see the same judge every Tuesday. Okay, so he refers to me as Mrs., although the mental health specialist refers to me as Mr. because that's what the stenographer has to put on the paperwork. But the judge said, the commonwealth attorney, she refers to me as Mr., but she was corrected in court said, "No, miss." The judge told me I could do that, this is his courtroom. He can do whatever he wants. But if she says Mister, then she's doing it for legal reasons. Well, doesn't she got to uphold the same legal reasons as the commonwealth attorney? Why does she get to call me her? My caseworker says mister. So she's my caseworker that's supposed to work with me on one on ones and everything.

Thus, even though the caseworker used the excuse of being legally correct, Jasmine's assertion is also correct. Why does she get to ignore Jasmine's name and pronouns when all the other people in the court are not following suit? Jasmine further described that the commonwealth attorney (the prosecutor) was working with her to change her name faster so the mental health specialist would not have a viable excuse to continue to deadname and misgender her. This event is very telling in that Jasmine, without her paperwork, was being respected by those in the courtroom, but her own representative was actively choosing to not respect the fact that she is a woman and lived her life that way.

Lucky and Julian even faced negative court outcomes because of the targeted *transgenderphobia* in the courtroom during their own proceedings. Julian, as mentioned above, was going through eviction proceedings where he was deadnamed in front of an entire courtroom. However, while the first judge seemed surprised at Julian not appearing to align with the name on his legal paperwork, he described the second judge as looking "more disgusted".

> [She] like squinted and like just like I said, [looked] kind of disgusted both when I was called up and when she made her judgment. Like she just gave me like this one final disgusted look and like that was my judgment. You get to pay $700 'cause the landlord didn't do his job.

Julian and this judge also had a back and forth in accordance with the judgement, as Julian was told to pay $700 for painting the walls pastel colours after living in the building for two years under the new landlord, who never painted. When Julian tried to argue with the receipts for the paint and the proof of the light colours, the judge cut him off asking him, "Are you a painter?" even though a decent paint job for the apartment would not cost nearly as much as $700. Further, because of the judge finding Julian at fault for the paint job and liable for the $700, he was evicted on this basis.

Lucky, on the other hand, was charged in court on the basis of her ex-boyfriend's lie. After the ex-boyfriend filed a protective order against Lucky, the boyfriend then attacked her in her own home, but Lucky was summoned to court for violating the protective order. She noted that she did not bring a lawyer because she didn't think she would need one because he was lying. She also noted that

> I don't know if [it] was to save face with his family or I don't know why, but he told a lie and that I attacked him, and the judge found me guilty and gave me 30 days. [chuckles] I did 30 days in jail for that and it was a damn lie. A damn lie.

When I asked her what evidence the ex-boyfriend had, Lucky remarked that the judge just went on his word and he did not have any evidence. Lucky went on to note that she figured

> The fact that I was dressed as a female in the courtroom got me found guilty. Really it did. I am almost sure [of] that because that man had no reason to put me in jail.... I mean actually. I am so sure that, that old judge looked down on me [laughs] and said I'm gonna lock that ass up. [laughs] I could see I, he was seething... I know they can't hide it.

Lucky noted that there was no other reason to lock her up for 30 days than the judge's own bias, and the way she perceived him looking at her was the basis for such an unreasonable sentence. Despite no evidence, and a story that likely did not add up, being a defendant who did not fit into a cisgender, heteronormative mold was a recipe for Lucky to experience active discrimination and targeted transphobia by the judge.

Overall, participants had several different experiences with the criminal legal system in terms of the courtroom, which can affect their case outcomes in particularly negative ways. The court system is often touted as this objective place that does not hold room for personal opinion alongside the objectivity of the law. However, this is not the case, as these folx have shown, which is vital to continue and showcase these experiences, as they are not only damaging to folx: these instances allow such bigotry to propagate throughout the system. While the system does indeed need an overhaul, it cannot be understated that the people within that system need to do better in terms of their individual actions.

Recommendations

So, how should the criminal legal system actually address these cases of legal professional cultural incompetency and hostility in order to diminish the chances of them happening in the future? First, there must be acknowledgement that while these recommendations can go a long way to alleviate some of the instances found in this chapter as well as others, there will be pushback. This resistance has already been demonstrated when the incorporation of transgender folx in public spaces draws undue attention alongside uninformed opinions of media personalities (Hughto et al., 2021), states taking up hostile legislations against including transgender folx (ACLU, 2022), and, concerning the criminal legal system, drawing hate from the likes of so-called women's liberation groups who weaponise their transphobia in the name of protecting "real women[6]" (WoLF, 2021). Entire groups of people are constantly being politicised, discriminated against, and attacked for being who they are, and this cannot stand. Transgender folx are here, they have always existed, and they deserve equitable treatment.

The three main recommendations to grapple with these negative experiences in the courtroom are that of cultural competency training, paperwork changes, and accountability for courtroom practitioners (This should be good for any form of bigotry within the courtroom, but the point remains the same). Cultural competency has already been shown to bridge gaps in criminal legal practitioner understanding (Engelman &

[6] They really mean cisgender women.

Deardorff, 2016),[7] and is seen by practitioners themselves as having a practical value (Whitfield, 2019). Further, the exact need for cultural competency training lies in its name, in that it would help those who are culturally ignorant of the nuances of being LGBTQ+, show them how LGBTQ+ people experience life and move through space, and teach them how to interact with LGBTQ+ folx. Many folx in the United States are still receiving most of their information about transgender folx from the news media (Lipka, 2016) rather than educated, nuanced discussion about these topics. Thus, logically, most of the legal professionals described here also probably received their information in this manner. It needs to be stated that training is not the end all be all, but teaching people to treat transgender folx with respect is necessary, as the default setting in America is exclusion and seeing transgender people as disposable.

Concerning paperwork changes, some of the narratives discussed in the chapter could have been prevented with just a couple of lines on paperwork that would have stopped practitioners from outing them in the courtroom. While legal records can be notoriously hard to change (some states still require proof of gender confirmation surgery for a changed birth certificate—Transgender Law Center, 2017), a line on the specific paperwork entering court would inform the court of who is standing in front of them without changing the legal record. This is necessary, as even when Julian described that he previously contacted the court to inform them of his name change and presentation, they still used the legal name. This could have been avoided if there was a precedent where next to the person's name, their pronouns and name they go by, were written, with the legal name only placed on the necessary filings. With the use of other official documents like a Social Security or ID number, the use of a legal name in open court is obsolete.

There has already been precedent for courts to accept transgender folx by their accurate names and pronouns. A U.S. Supreme Court clerk reprimanded two lawyers who filed in support of the Gloucester County School Board vs. Gavin Grimm in 2017 (Walsh, 2014), and the U.S. Army Court of Criminal Appeals made a ruling that in any future

[7] It should be noted that in this study, the recommendation is to shift attitudes away from ableist understandings; the authors explicitly noted that further training was needed.

proceedings after Chelsea Manning came out, she should be referred to as such and with accurate pronouns (Salpietro, 2017). Further, the judiciary for England and Wales has already considered pronoun use and accurate name use. As of December 2021, judges were given the guidance to respect and use "a person's gender identity and their present name for nearly all court and tribunal purposes, regardless of whether they have obtained legal recognition of their gender by way of a Gender Recognition Certificate" (Quinn, 2021, para. 4). For folx where this does not apply, there would only be the legal name filled in, and the practitioners could just use that form with the pronouns listed, thus normalising the practice of ensuring that everyone is acknowledged accurately within the confines of the courtroom. There also needs to be a paperwork amendment where folx can file before their court date, which would be an additional note before their date in court, letting the court know if it was not made clear at the first contact of the incident, filing, etc.

The last recommendation that I have concerning the experiences of these participants centres on holding bad actors accountable. As Goodmark (2013, p. 98) states, "[a] responsive system would require fundamental changes to both the law itself and to those who enforce it". There needs to be a formal, simplified way that folx can file complaints against bad actors, as well as those who were complacent in the same courtroom and did not stop the proceedings or remove the offender from the courtroom, if they had that power. This expansion of holding folx accountable is in an effort to ensure that folx are actually receiving the fair treatment that they are promised in the American Constitution. There are already notes of this in the literature, as Neumeier and Brown (2021) already call out leadership in legal workplaces for not holding bad actors accountable for their actions. They further elaborate that queer and disabled attorneys, if they are even told about these environments, are only told in private conversations by those who wish to keep their heads down (Neumeier & Brown, 2021). Further, when someone acts in a discriminatory manner so blatantly, oftentimes, their actions are not out of nowhere: they are either emboldened by the lack of consequences or the quiet conversations behind the scenes, and they are just saying what a lot of actors are thinking (Neumeier & Brown, 2021). Thus, those who stand there and do nothing are just as capable as the person who directly caused the harm. These complaints also need to be public, as folx need to be aware of the kind of practitioners they are dealing with, as well as an open discussion to the larger legal profession. Keeping things behind closed doors and in secret has allowed bigotry to thrive, so it should be dragged screaming into the light so people like Grace do not have to be the only ones to stand up for themselves in the courtroom.

Appendix

See Table 7.1.

Table 7.1 Descriptive characteristics of participants ($n = 44$)

Mean age (range 19–65)	35
Gender identity	
Transwoman	57%
Transman	23%
Non-binary or genderqueer	20%
Race	
Black	21%
Latinx	5%
AAPI[a]	2%
Indigenous	5%
Mixed Brown[b]	2%
White	66%
Employment status	
Employed	71%
Unemployed	11%
Social Security Income (SSI)	9%
Underground Economy	9%
Education	
Less than high school	7%
High school/GED	11%
Some college	41%
College/technical degree	41%
Incarceration experience	
No	86%
Yes (2 days to 8 years)	14%
Homelessness experience	48%
Military service	14%

Note [a]Asian American Pacific Islander
[b]This was a self-identifying term used by the participant

References

ACLU. (2022, January 21). *Legislation affecting LGBTQ+ rights across the country.* ACLU. https://www.aclu.org/legislation-affecting-LGBTQ+-rights-across-country

Blanck, P., Hyseni, F., & Wise, F. (2021). Diversity and inclusion in the American legal profession: Discrimination and bias reported by lawyers with disabilities and lawyers who identify as LGBTQ+. *American Journal of Law & Medicine, 47*(1), 9–61.

Engelman, A., & Deardorff, J. (2016). Cultural competence training for law enforcement responding to domestic violence emergencies with the deaf and hard of hearing: A mixed-methods evaluation. *Health Promotion Practice, 17*(2), 177–185.

Maidment, A. (2018, May 22). "It feels like someone's taken your identity away"—Why it's never OK to 'out' someone as LGBTQ+. *Cosmopolitan.* Retrieved December 21, 2022, from https://www.cosmopolitan.com/uk/love-sex/a20771316/outing-someone-LGBTQ+/

Goodmark, L. (2013). Transgender people, intimate partner abuse, and the legal system. *Harvard Civil Rights-Civil Liberties Law Review, 48*, 51.

GreyNet International. (2020). *Grey literature network service.* GreyNet International. http://www.greynet.org

Honorée, A. L., & Juban, R. (2020). Is there transgender bias in the courtroom? *Employee Relations, 42*(6), 1531–1545.

Huckins, G. (2021, January 6). For marginalized groups, being studied can be a burden. *Wired.* Retrieved December 21, 2022, from https://www.wired.com/story/for-marginalized-groups-being-studied-can-be-a-burden

Hughto, J. M., Pletta, D., Gordon, L., Cahill, S., Mimiaga, M. J., & Reisner, S. L. (2021). Negative transgender-related media messages are associated with adverse mental health outcomes in a multistate study of transgender adults. *LGBT Health, 8*(1), 32–41.

James, S. E., Herman, J. L., Rankin, S., Keisling, M., Mottet, L., & Anafi, M. (2016). *Executive summary of the report of the 2015 U.S. Transgender Survey.* National Center for Transgender Equality. Retrieved December 21, 2022, from https://transgenderequality.org/sites/default/files/docs/usts/USTS-Full-Report-Dec17.pdf

Lambda Legal. (2015). *Protected and served?* Lambda Legal. Retrieved December 21, 2022, from https://www.lambdalegal.org/protected-and-served

Lipka, M. (2016, October 3). *Americans are divided over which public bathrooms transgender people should use*. Pew Research. Retrieved December 21, 2022, from https://www.pewresearch.org/fact-tank/2016/10/03/americans-are-divided-over-which-public-bathrooms-transgender-people-should-use

Marksamer, J. (2008). And by the way, do you know he thinks he's a girl? The failures of law, policy and legal representation for transgender youth in juvenile delinquency courts. *Sexuality Research & Social Policy, 5*(1), 72–92.

Neumeier, S. A., & Brown, L. X. (2021). Beyond diversity and inclusion: Understanding and addressing ableism, heterosexism, and transgendermisia in the legal profession: Comment on Blanck, Hyseni, and Altunkol Wise's national study of the legal profession. *American Journal of Law & Medicine, 47*(1), 76–87.

Peters, M. (2017, May 9). Womyn, wimmin, and other folx. *The Boston Globe*. Retrieved December 21, 2022, from https://www.bostonglobe.com/ideas/2017/05/09/womyn-wimmin-and-other-folx/vjhPn82ITGgCCbE12iNn1N/story.html

Quinn, B. (2021, December 27). Transgender people: Judges advised to use preferred personal pronouns. *The Guardian*. Retrieved December 21, 2022, from https://www.theguardian.com/law/2021/dec/27/transgender-people-judges-advised-to-use-preferred-personal-pronouns

Salpietro, F. G. (2017). RESPECT: Transgender pronoun preference and the application of the Model Code of Judicial Conduct. *Court Review, 53*, 162.

Timmermans, S., & Tavory, I. (2012). Theory construction in qualitative research: From grounded theory to abductive analysis. *Sociological Theory, 30*(3), 167–186.

Transgender Law Center. (2017). *State-by-state overview: Changing gender markers on birth certificates*. Transgender Law Center. Retrieved December 21, 2022, from https://transgenderlawcenter.org/resources/id/state-by-state-overview-changing-gender-markers-on-birth-certificates

Walsh, M. (2014, March 3). A supreme court rebuke over use of proper pronouns in transgender case. *Education Week*. Retrieved December 21, 2022, from https://www.edweek.org/education/a-supreme-court-rebuke-over-use-of-proper-pronouns-in-transgender-case/2017/03

Whitfield, M. (2019). *Influence of implicit-bias training on the cultural competency of police officers* (Doctoral dissertation). Walden University.

WoLF. (2021, August 12). *Women's liberation front responds to Scott Weiner*. Women's Liberation Front. Retrieved December 21, 2022, from https://www.womensliberationfront.org/news/wolf-responds-to-scott-wiener-sb132

Woods, J. B. (2019). LGBTQ+ in the courtroom: How sexuality and gender identity impact the jury system. In C. Najdowski & M. Stevenson (Eds.), *Criminal juries in the 21st century: Psychological science and the law* (pp. 61–83). Oxford University Press.

8

"Never Let Anyone Say That a Good Fight for the Fight for Good Wasn't a Good Fight Indeed": The Enactment of Agency Through Military Metaphor by One Australian Incarcerated Trans Woman

Sherree Halliwell, Andrew Hickey, Carol du Plessis, Amy B. Mullens, Tait Sanders, Jessica Gildersleeve, Tania M. Phillips, Joseph Debattista, Kirsty A. Clark, Jaclyn M. W. Hughto, Kirstie Daken, and Annette Brömdal

Introduction

This case study examines a public archive of letters written by Natasha Keating, a trans woman housed in two Australian male carceral settings between 2000 and 2007 (when Natasha was aged 23–30 years old). As is common with many trans persons' experiences of incarceration in Australia and elsewhere, Natasha experienced violence and

S. Halliwell (✉) · J. Gildersleeve
Faculty of Business, Education, Law and Arts, School of Humanities and Communication, Institute for Resilient Regions, Centre for Health Research, University of Southern Queensland, Toowoomba, QLD, Australia

A. Hickey
Faculty of Business, Education, Law and Arts, School of Humanities and

H. Panter and A. Dwyer (eds.), *Transgender People and Criminal Justice*, Critical Criminological Perspectives, https://doi.org/10.1007/978-3-031-29893-6_8

sexual mistreatment by other incarcerated persons and correctional officers, including denial of gender-affirming supports and care, being misgendered and misnamed (often intentionally), and denial of gender-appropriate accommodations (Brömdal et al., 2019a, 2019b, 2023; Brown, 2014; Brown & McDuffie, 2009; du Plessis et al., 2023; Halliwell et al., 2022; Hughto et al., 2022; Sanders et al., 2022; U.S. Department of Justice, 2012). The effects of this mistreatment resulted in Natasha experiencing suicidal ideation, depression, and social marginalisation. Incarcerated transgender persons, especially trans

---

Communication, University of Southern Queensland, Toowoomba, QLD, Australia

C. du Plessis · A. B. Mullens · T. Sanders · T. M. Phillips · K. Daken
Faculty of Health, Engineering and Sciences, School of Psychology and Wellbeing, Institute for Resilient Regions, Centre for Health Research, University of Southern Queensland, Ipswich, QLD, Australia

A. B. Mullens
Faculty of Health, School of Psychology and Counselling, Queensland University of Technology, Kelvin Grove, QLD, Australia

J. Debattista
Metro North Public Health Unit, Metro North Hospital and Health Service, Brisbane, QLD, Australia

K. A. Clark
Department of Medicine, Health and Society, Institute for Public Policy Studies, Vanderbilt University, Nashville, TN, USA

J. M. W. Hughto
Departments of Behavioural and Social Sciences and Epidemiology, School of Public Health, Centre for Health Equity Research, Brown University, Providence, RI, USA

A. Brömdal (✉)
Faculty of Business, Education, Law and Arts, School of Education, Institute for Resilient Regions, Centre for Health Research, University of Southern Queensland, Toowoomba, QLD, Australia
e-mail: Annette.Bromdal@usq.edu.au

women, remain a vulnerable group (Brömdal et al., 2019b; Clark et al., 2023; Hughto et al., 2022; U.S. Department of Justice, 2012) who experience significant and disproportionate violence, harassment, and sexual mistreatment by other incarcerated persons and correctional staff due to having a gender identity and/or expression that misaligns with socially constructed norms rooted in cisnormativity and heteronormativity (Brömdal et al., 2019b; Franks et al., 2022; Halliwell et al., 2022; Jenness & Fenstermaker, 2016; Lynch & Bartels, 2017; Phillips et al., 2020; Rosenberg & Oswin, 2015; Sanders et al., 2022; Stanley & Smith, 2015; Swan et al., 2023; Van Hout et al., 2020). This case study is written to honour Natasha and demonstrates how, despite these hardships, she was able to advocate fiercely for herself and others whilst incarcerated. It forms part of a trio of papers exploring Natasha's experiences and honouring her legacy (see also du Plessis et al., 2023; Halliwell et al., 2022).

Within this chapter, we also respond to Tebes et al.'s (2004) call for further research exploring the relationship between personal narratives and cognitive transformation. We highlight how Natasha utilised letter writing to embody an aspirational identity as an activist and agent of social change and justice for trans incarcerated persons. Furthermore, this chapter draws attention to the ways that Natasha leveraged a deliberately framed discourse—a discourse we cast under the guise of *military metaphor*—to mediate her self-identity (Opsal, 2011). Through this, she was able to subvert the homogenising effects of the prison as a "total institution" (Goffman, 1961, p. 4); one overtly designed to strip its inhabitants of their capacity for self-determination.

Identity Management Within Carceral Settings

Current sociological definitions of "agency" acknowledge the importance of macro contexts in exerting influence upon the person's ability to think, act and affect their social and physical environment (see for example Adams, 2006; Ross & Mirowsky, 2013; Twenge et al., 2012). As argued by Erizikova et al., the project of identity management within the incarceration context is "profoundly complicated" (2014, p. 143), owing to the incarcerated person's poverty of agentic choice within a system designed to homogenise its inhabitants and stigmatise the person as a "social deviant." The habitude required by the carceral context is designed to reduce the individual's status to that of the *inmate* (Goffman, 1963).

The significant harms obtruded upon incarcerated trans women are well documented. However, we draw attention to literature that identifies that when institutional impositions are excessively degrading, or experiences particularly traumatic, people often report transformative changes in response to these adversities (Clark et al., 2023; du Plessis et al., 2023; Halliwell et al., 2022; McCorkel, 1998; Mehta et al., 2021; Tebes et al., 2004; Tedeschi & Calhoun, 1995). Such changes can be understood in terms of the *cognitive transformation* provoked by the situation and the strategies applied by the individual for coping in these circumstances. In these situations, cognitive transformation occurs as attempts are made to rationalise the place of the person within the oppressive context, with this in turn resulting in the reconstitution of the person's sense of self to accommodate the demands of the situation.

As explained by Tebes et al. (2004), *cognitive transformation* "involves a turning point in a person's life characterised by: (1) the recognition that coping with adversity results in new opportunities; and (2) the reevaluation [sic] of the experience from one that was primarily traumatic or threatening to one that is growth promoting" (pp. 769–770). This re-evaluation, or reinterpretation of prior experiences "occurs in one or more of three domains – how one views oneself, others, or life in general" (Tebes et al., 2004, p. 771), with Tebes et al. (1995) explaining that *cognitive transformation* in the aftermath of threatening, challenging, or traumatic events may give rise to enhanced adaptation that could be characterised as evidence of resilience. Although such situations and adversities would usually predict poor outcomes, in some circumstances, people are able to respond by adopting one of:

> four potential protective processes that may be promotive of resilience:

(1) reduction of the risk impact, either directly by altering the meaning of the risk factor or through altering one's exposure to or involvement in the risk factor;
(2) reduction of the likelihood of negative chain reactions following exposure to the risk factor;
(3) the promotion of self-esteem and self-efficacy through successful task accomplishment or the availability of secure and supportive personal relationships; and
(4) the opening up of opportunities. (Tebes et al., 2004, p. 772)

Where experiences are reinterpreted through the guise of metaphor, evidence of cognitive transformation can take form in enacted and embodied life narratives. Indeed, in the case of Natasha, it was through the process of drafting and compiling her letters of complaint and advocacy that she was able to engage a process of cognitive transformation that resulted in her reframing the traumas and adversities of her past and present. Natasha developed a self-affirming persona within her letters, via the application of military metaphors, that emphasised Natasha's resilience and personal growth, at the same time articulating her criticisms of the carceral system and advocacy for transgender people.

In his seminal work on identity management within "total institutions," Irving Goffman (1961, p. 4) wrote:

> The self, in this sense, is not a property of the person to whom it is attributed but dwells rather in the pattern of social control that is exerted in connection with the person by himself and those around him. This special kind of institutional arrangement does not so much support the self as constitute it.

Goffman explained that total institutions such as prisons, psychiatric institutions, and boot camps function as "forcing houses for changing persons" (1961, p. 12), wherein the overarching purpose is to reshape the flawed identities of incarcerated persons in order to produce compliant and socially acceptable citizens. The high degree of control that total institutions exert over the choices available to their inhabitants, coupled with forced participation in practices of regulation and re-education, fundamentally shape incarcerated persons' identities. Yet, despite their redemptive and rehabilitative goals, carceral systems do little to change society's perceptions of incarcerated persons as irredeemable others (Maruna, 2001). The practice of incarcerating people is itself intended to reduce the incarcerated person to "othered" status, stigmatising their worst acts and reducing the person "from a whole and usual person to a tainted, discounted one" (Goffman, 1963, pp. 2–3).

Goffman's (1963) framing of stigma as a socially created construct suggests that while the convict stigma is a product of interaction with dominant, normalised carceral structures and cultural sensibilities, it may also be resisted and contested. One way this can be achieved is through the construction of *alternative* narratives (Opsal, 2011; Snow & Anderson, 1987). Previous studies examining identity management within total institutions have focused on how narrative identity work involves the use of strategies through which people express accounts of self beyond that of "incarcerated individual." These alternative narratives are positioned in opposition to dominant institutional narratives and offer the basis for new conceptions of self (see Maruna, 2001; McAdams & Bowman, 2001; McCorkel, 1998; Opsal, 2011; Riessman, 2000; Singer, 1997; Snow & Anderson, 1987). The alternative narrative provides a crucial platform upon which critique and interrogation of dominant narratives might occur. As Mumby (1987) argued, "because of their embeddedness in the everyday practices of organisations, [dominant] narratives...often articulate an organisational reality that is accepted as 'the natural order of things'" (pp. 113–114). The challenge represented by the alternative narrative is evidenced in the possibilities that it presents, thus drawing into question the authority assumed by the dominant narrative.

Van Dijk (2006) identified two main discursive strategies used by institutions to exercise power and dominance; the declaration of *positive self-representation* and *negative other representation.* This model demonstrates how emphasis is placed on the valuable attributes and characteristics of normative identity locations while contrasting those associated with the Other as undesirable, or simply put, by emphasising *the* "good" inherent to normative identity locations, the "bad" associated with the incarcerated Other is also drawn into view (Karimi & Tabrizi, 2015).

Dominant discourses within the carceral context frame the incarcerated person as requiring of punitive discipline *and* rehabilitative intervention, in turn emphasising the appropriateness of normative identity characteristics. This not only implicates a view of the incarcerated person as deviant Other, but also the requirement for the incarcerated person's rehabilitation. Therefore, it is common in carceral settings for focus to be given to narratives of redemption, self-transformation, and societal repatriation (Maruna, 2001; McAdams & Bowman, 2001). But as demonstrated by Andrews et al. (1997), letter writing provides a means for incarcerated persons to declare accounts of an *alternative* Self. By enabling articulations of the self beyond that of the "incarcerated person," letter writing provides "critical space" (McCorkel, 1998, p. 245) for the letter writer to articulate expressions of self-identity that emphasise widened accounts of the incarcerated person. We turn now to examine Natasha's use of letter writing to challenge, reject and refashion her stigmatised identity. In the analyses that follow, we demonstrate how the enactment of military metaphors enabled Natasha to resist and supplant an identity defined by her incarceration and detail the cognitive transformation that she underwent during this process.

Military Metaphor as a Mobilising Concept

Metaphors are particularly useful in ordering the cognitive transformation of self. Lakoff and Johnson (1980) argued that although metaphors are commonly thought of as merely explanatory devices or linguistic flourishes, they exert an important cognitive function in shaping "a person's conceptual system" (Lakoff & Johnson, 1980, p. 6). Metaphors reveal the processes by which a person sees the world. Accordingly, by examining how metaphors are used in the development of descriptions of self, insight into how an identity is defined by a person is also revealed (Beckett, 2003).

Natasha applied what we define here as a "military metaphor" in her letters. She invoked a confrontational logic, wherein her experience was cast as a "battle" and in which she confronted an "opposition" and faced "adversity." As Steinert (2003, p. 266) noted, military metaphor has "...invaded the public discourse in economics, international relations, sport, even some medical specialties—and, of course, crime policy and policing". Often used by those in power to mobilise, legitimise and universalise support for their position, military metaphor is omnipresent in situations where humans encounter a challenge, resistance or threat (Steinert, 2003). It is notable that in this instance, Natasha used the military metaphors to destabilise the institution of the prison and criminal processing system by appealing to convictions towards justice and what is fair. Far from being associated with all that is *good* and *right*, the institution in Natasha's experience was the perpetrator of injustices and the cause of her marginalisation. This inversion provided Natasha with critical space to detail accounts of her experiences and articulate what Giordano et al. (2002) define as her *replacement self*.

Much of the scholarly literature[1] pertains to applications of military metaphor in the field of medicine, where medical institutions

---

[1] There is significant debate within the medical field as to the desirability and utility of the hegemonic *military metaphor* in relation to life-threatening conditions such as cancer and HIV/AIDS. Violence metaphors such as "battling" and "fighting" the "enemy" are dominant within oncology and HIV management (Miller, 2010; Penson et al., 2004; Reisfield & Wilson, 2004; Semino et al., 2018; Sontag, 1979). Framed as a universal call to action, *military metaphor* has prompted "whole societies to mobilize, human, economic and social resources for health care and medical research" (Nie et al., 2016, p. 3). Tate and Pearlman (2016) note that the use of *military metaphor* within oncology treatment regimens can empower patients; the *cognitive transformation* process involved in personifying the illness as the enemy, the patient as the besieged and the treatment as weaponry/arsenal, evokes resilience, determination and inner strength. However, as Shapiro (2018) argues, where patients internalise the war and come to embody the battle ground itself, this can lead to depression as they courageously fight down feelings of distress and despair, rather than finding acceptance of their circumstances and reaching out for support. Fuks (2010) and Hendricks et al. (2018) have also criticised the use of *military metaphor* within the medical field, arguing that the absolutism of "winning" or "losing" a war can negate anything short of an outright victory. For patients in remission from cancer or living with chronic or progressive diseases such as HIV/AIDS, "the battlefield remains occupied and the patient's suffering remains unknown to all but the patient" (Fuks, 2010, p. 62). Fuks (2010, p. 57) proposes a "natural" metaphor as an alternative to military lexicon, using terms such as "renewal", "blooms" and "springtime" to frame health and well-being in terms of season. Similarly, Hendricks et al. (2018) suggest "journeys" as a metaphor for the cancer experience, arguing that "there is no winning or losing on a journey. The emphasis is instead on a larger process, since life itself is often compared to a journey" (Hendricks et al., 2018, p. 269). The polemic framing of suffering via *military metaphor* contrasts with the obscurantic, gentler metaphors advanced by its detractors. While there is a growing body of clinicians and academics who advocate for the retirement of the military metaphor within medicine (see Fuks, 2010; Hendricks et al., 2018; Mutch, 2006; Nie et al., 2016; Shapiro, 2018; Tate & Pearlman, 2016), the emergence of COVID-19 as a global threat has rather reinforced the supremacy of

wage war on their patients' illnesses. Where military metaphor is leveraged in the public sphere, it is mobilised to explain the policies and practices employed by public institutions and their agents, rather than exploring the experiences of those affected (Beckett, 2003). As a persuasive "weapon" in governments' "arsenals," military metaphor invokes unifying and legitimising claims which call for and justify extraordinary responses. Steinert notes that this invocation of a "universal experience of war" (2003, p. 275) indicates how military metaphor mobilises the masses and justifies calls for civic duty and the sacrifice of personal freedoms for the greater good. Extending this further, Flusberg et al. (2018, pp. 1, 3, 8) describe how governments have effectively utilised military metaphors to invoke senses of moral panic and collective outrage. The "Wars on drugs," the "war against crime," the "war on poverty" and the "war on inflation" are invoked to identify an object for public outcry and to generate support for policies that are intended to confront such problems. As Steinert (2003) explained, pledging oneself to war is an honourable way of overcoming fear, helplessness, and powerlessness, particularly when faced with unknowable and uncontrollable threats.

Considering the adversarial context in which prison life is constituted, is not surprising that Natasha invoked military metaphors to illustrate her experiences of prison life. What is rather notable is that these metaphors were deployed by a person who would typically be positioned as the focus of its mediating intention (i.e. the subject of society's "War on Crime"). This detournement of the military metaphor by Natasha reveals how the mobilisation of critique can challenge dominant systemic narratives. In using these metaphors, Natasha's letters co-opted a narrative usually deployed by the institution to instead position herself as the locus of moral virtue.

military metaphor in how the medical profession, communities and governments reference and respond to universal health threats (Gillis, 2020).

Methodology

Biographical Context

Natasha Keating was born in regional Victoria, Australia, in 1977. From an early age, she eschewed normative social expectations of gender, seeking to emulate popular singer and actress, Madonna. Natasha's mother, Peggy, was supportive of her attempts to navigate and affirm her gender. However, victimisation and bullying at school resulted in Natasha withdrawing from formal education aged 13, and quickly becoming involved in illicit drug use, sex work, shoplifting and other minor criminal offenses (Australian Transgender Support Association of Queensland [ATSAQ] 2008: interview with Krissy & Gina 2021, interview with Peggy 2021). Natasha's illicit drug-related offending escalated to armed robbery in 2000, for which she served seven years in two male carceral settings in Queensland, Australia. It was during this period that the letters in focus here, were written.

Sadly, upon her release, Natasha's placement in the same suburb that had been the site of her previous offending led to a recommencement of her illicit drug-taking and deterioration in her mental health. Following a tumultuous period of adjustment to life post-incarceration, Natasha moved into the care of her mother and stepfather. In August 2008, Natasha's mother found that her daughter had passed away in her bed in the family home, having taken her own life (interview with Krissy & Gina 2021, interview with Peggy 2021).

Consistent with Natasha's wishes, ATSAQ gifted the archive of personal correspondence to a library in Australia, where it remains publicly accessible. This archive is utilised here in accordance with Natasha's hope that scholarly interest in her experiences would effect social change, and we have crafted this analysis with this aspiration in mind.

Dataset

The dataset (see Table 8.1 on page 202) contains an archive of letters that Natasha Keating wrote to and received from people within and outside the law enforcement, and criminal processing system in Australia, including correctional staff/managers, medical health practitioners, support organisations, lawyers, anti-discrimination representatives and friends. For this chapter, the letters were initially accessed from the library archive by the last author (AB) and were subsequently digitised, copied and de-identified prior to sharing with the research team. These digital copies were then used as the basis of the analysis contained in this paper. It consists of 270 pages, 121 documents authored by Natasha Keating, and 41 documents provided/sent to Natasha between the 6th March 2006 and 2nd March 2007. Consistent with Natasha's wish to translate her experiences into an autobiography, this project seeks to honour this wish by shedding some light on her accounts:

> I Ms. Shannon Keating, also known by the alias of "NATASHA" give you...The Australian Transgender Support Association of Queensland... full permission and release you of any liability to use my known alias of "NATASHA" for the purpose of the following: Use in the ATSAQ monthly newsletters; Interviews (oral/written/recorded/videotaped/emailed); And/or anyway you see fit to better educate and inform people on the issues, facing transgender people and the transgender community. From this, the 13th day of February 2006 to the 13th day of February 3016.

The dataset was also subject to ethical clearance, with approval provided by the University of Southern Queensland's Human Research Ethics Committee (H19REA236). This approval included permission, per Natasha's wishes, to use her real name and identifiable information in the future publications. The decision to use Natasha's real name was further reinforced by ATSAQ and her mother, who relayed (personal communication, January 2021) that doing so would provide a tribute to Natasha's legacy. In addition, permission to name organisations mentioned in the letters was also provided by the same Human Research Ethics

Committee. However, to protect the privacy of other named people in the letters, these names have been de-identified.

Data Analysis and Limitations

Archival data in the form of personal documentation, such as letters of correspondence, has several advantages: it is contextually grounded; it exists a priori to research inquiry; it contains rich personal information; and it reveals the thought processes and knowledge of their producers (Prior, 2011). However, it also holds limitations. When applied to research scrutiny—particularly when the archive is accessed posthumously—the data remains "non-interactive" (Miller & Alvarado, 2005). This can pose challenges in terms of the reliability of the data and analyses made of included artefacts. As Ritchie and Spencer (1994) argue, archival data of this type makes the *precise* interpretation of their producers' meanings a central concern for researchers. Further, letters of correspondence comprise stories narrated by the producer to an assumed audience, an audience not immediately recognisable to researchers. The narrator's positionality is anchored and expressed through their intentionality to appeal to this audience, with the observations, comments and self-definitions drawn in the text configured by this perspective (Bogren, 2010). As Charon (2001) explains, written narrative storytelling meaning is divined via the reader, with the positionality of the reader crucial to this act of interpretation. With these points in mind, we came first to Natasha's letters as readers and accordingly acknowledge our role in mediating her accounts as researchers.

This chapter forms part of a larger body of work focusing on the discriminatory and inhumane policies and practices governing transgender incarcerated persons in Australia and the US. Recognising and inspired by the scholarly work of trans scholars and activists/advocates that have sought to campaign for social change within the carceral system (Stanley & Smith, 2015; Stanley et al., 2012), the authors of this paper comprise a research team collectively committed to documenting the lived experiences of trans persons, and dismantling the oppressive policies and injustices still practiced in our carceral institutions. Our scholarship spans disciplines of gender and trans studies, sociology, clinical and health psychology, education, epidemiology, behavioural sciences, public health, medical anthropology, criminology and critical policy analysis. Our authorship team includes researchers of trans and cisgender lived and embodied experiences spanning sexual orientations and includes both trans and cis persons with incarceration experiences. Accordingly, our analyses of the archival data derive from multiple disciplinary and epistemic perspectives to enable a wide reading of this material and scope to the interpretative claims made in the analysis.

To activate this analysis, we flexibly employed Braun and Clarke's (2019) thematic analysis approach alongside Fairclough's (1992, 1995) critical discourse analysis framework. In the first step of thematic analysis, the first (SH) and last (AB) authors reviewed the documents independently, ascertaining and verifying their chronology, removing duplicate correspondence and assigning identified general codes to themes evident in the letters. This initial review process was inductive in nature, and there were no predetermined codes. The first (SH) author then undertook a critical analysis of the documents within NVivo analytics software, focusing on highlighting recurring codes and from which a coding frame of short descriptors grouping similar ideas was produced (Owen, 1984). These codes were inspected, collated and reviewed by the full research team and were used to confirm, reinterpret and refine the analyses made of Natasha's letters.

Building on Van Dijk's (1993, 2001) analytic methodology, which reveals relationships between discourse and identity construction, social reality and power, the first author undertook a critical discourse analysis of key themes identified from the data, utilising Fairclough's (1992, 1995) framework. The critical discourse analysis sought to identify the strategies utilised by Natasha to legitimise, persuade and effect social change through her discourse. At the first level of analysis, attention was given to defining the dynamics inherent to Natasha's experiences as a transgender incarcerated woman and the institutional context of this situatedness. The second level of analysis focused on the structure, word selection and epistemic authority of Natasha's letters of complaint.

The third level of analysis sought to construct a sense of the ontological condition of Natasha's lived experience from which her letter-writing activities could be contextualised. At the final level of analysis, we critiqued the carceral system and experiences of trans-identifying women.

Analysis and Discussion

This case study focuses on Natasha Keating's letters of complaint and replies from authorities, those engaged with Natasha in support roles and organisations during the two years preceding her release. This period of her incarceration (2005–2007) marked a change in her discursive strategy, whereby she exponentially increased the quantity and sophistication of her correspondence, expanded her external support network, and escalated her complaints and appeals to higher authorities. As argued by Kidd and Carel (2017), the inherent weakness in any letter of complaint is the epistemic asymmetry between complainant and authority, which often manifests in terms of an inequality of knowledge and a systemic power imbalance. In her early years of incarceration, Natasha corresponded via handwritten letters, frequently used informal upper case and repeated exclamation points for emphasis and adopted a submissive positionality in both personal communications and official communications. This is particularly evident in letters addressed to the General Managers of the institutions in which she was incarcerated, and representatives of the Australian Council for Civil Liberty. In the latter years of her incarceration, Natasha assiduously ameliorated her letter-writing strategies by adopting a formal, typed manner of address, utilising the institutional instruments of change (complaints procedures), acquiring an extensive knowledge of the legal statutes and policies pertaining to incarcerated persons' (and specifically transgender) rights, and escalating her grievances to higher authorities. During this period, Natasha made increasing use of *military metaphors* in her personal communications with ATSAQ, a state-specific trans support organisation, to construct a heroic sense of self-identity in the face of an intractable institution. From this, a dualism emerged, cast as a "battle" or "fight" between Natasha and the bureaucracy of the carceral system.

Cognitive Transformation Enacted via a Narrative of "Protective Process" Related to Partner Anton

Early 2006 was a particularly prolific period in Natasha's correspondence history, with 29 letters of complaint pertaining to February 2006 alone. It is also notable that Natasha began to increase her network of external agents during that month, adding the Queensland Ombudsman, Brunswick Street Medical Centre, Brisbane Gender Clinic, Information Commissioner and Prisoners' Legal Service to her contacts. She also increasingly leveraged these higher channels of legal redress, including representing herself in the Queensland Supreme Court. We suggest that the escalation in Natasha's letter writing can be viewed as a "protective process" (Rutter, 1987) in response to a series of particularly stressful and threatening events that occurred in late 2005 and early 2006 relating to her carceral relationship with her partner Anton (pseudonym).

Natasha referred to Anton—an incarcerated man—as her "husband" in several of her letters to ATSAQ and styled him "de-facto" in correspondence with the Queensland Government Department of Corrective Services. For a period of almost two years, Natasha and Anton had been engaged in an intimate relationship, and latterly accommodated in the same cell. In December 2005, a Sentence Management Review recommended that Anton be removed to another carceral institution. This action was interpreted by Natasha as a highly irregular response to her refusal to sign a conciliation agreement document pertaining to unrelated grievances. She confided in her lawyer of her reliance on Anton remaining within the same correctional facility, characterising his support as critical at a time when she was suffering emotional and mental trauma:

> it is not unreasonable for us to draw the conclusion that the Management of [the correctional centre] are transferring [Anton] to try and punish me personally for bringing the complaint...With the emotional and mental trauma that I am presently going through with the discrimination action I have commenced (quite correctly in my opinion), I really do need [Anton] to remain at [the correctional centre] with me. This is

> a fact that the Staff and Management are aware of and by the transferring of [Anton] away from here, they are counting on his lack of ongoing support as having a detrimental effect on my case. (Letter to Natasha's lawyer, 10th January 2006)

Between January and March 2006, Natasha complained of several grievances relating to the institution's denial of hers and Anton's "couple" status, including one incident that escalated to a "Section 38" placement, which she called a "slanderous allegation" and "treacherous" action, resulting in her removal to a separate detention unit. In a letter of complaint to her lawyer shortly after Anton's transfer, Natasha alleged that the prison service had taken this action as a punitive measure:

> the reason he was being transferred, I believe, has a lot to do with them punishing both of us, but doing it through him, as they're too scared to directly attack me to that extent, as I will fight back of course… I would like to know, where has that 'Duty of Care' been for the past 3 years while they've been mentally torturing me every single day of my sentence, over such issues as the 'Women's runners', 'Bras', 'Female underwear', and everything else. (Letter to Commissioner, Anti-Discrimination Commission Queensland, 20th March 2006, asterisks in original)

The matter of Anton's transfer became a focus for Natasha's "war" with the Department of Corrective Services for the remainder of her term of incarceration. On 21 March 2006, she wrote to the Ombudsman requesting documentary evidence of the Section 38 particulars and details pertaining to Anton's transfer. In her letter to ATSAQ on 8 May 2006, she advised that her lawyer had "taken up the WAR with me on my inter-facility contact with [Anton]". She reported in her correspondence with ATSAQ on 15 May 2006 that "I am finally getting somewhere with my application for visits and calls with my husband. PHEW!!! I knew I would, but as with everything, it just takes a little time and a lot of patience". In late May 2006, Natasha was denied inter-facility contact with Anton on the grounds that they did not satisfy the conditions for a de-facto partnership, a decision that she challenged in a letter directed to the Director General of the Department of Corrective Services:

> I was informed on the FORM 4, notification to prisoner form... that my application was declined due to not fulfilling the criteria of section 32DA of the Acts Interpretation Act 1954, wherein it provides the relevant information in relation to De FACTO PARTNER/S. I would like to know on whose authority does the management of this Correctional Centre, and any other Correctional Centre take their instruction on advising someone of this decision and where exactly does the management gain their authority to do so? (Natasha Keating letter to Director General, Department of Corrective Services, 25 May 2006)

Her emotional request for telephone contact with Anton following the loss of his mother was also denied on 6 June 2006: "All official-ness aside, I hope you can put yourself in my position and treat my application as you yourself would hope to be treated in these circumstances... and find it within yourself to allow this one-off phone call and see it for what it is". Natasha received a letter dated 2 June 2006, confirming an appointment for a Supreme Court direction hearing for statement of reasons application concerning her request for an explanation of the denial of inter-facility contact with Anton, which prompted her to write to the General Manager of Anton's carceral facility for documents pertaining to the decision:

> I would now appreciate very much if you could please, pursuant to section 32 (1) of the Judicial Review Act 1991, provide me with the list of material used in determining the decision to decline a special circumstances phone call, and provide me with a statement of reasons as to how you arrived at your decision to decline a special circumstances phone call between [Anton] and myself, Ms Shannon Keating, within the 28 day time limitation as prescribed by the Act. (Natasha Keating letter to General Manager of Anton's carceral facility, Department of Corrective Services, 13 June 2006)

The matter of inter-facility contact with Anton was not resolved within the remaining term of Natasha's incarceration. However, the fight for her right to pursue an intimate and loving "de-facto" relationship with her partner of almost two years provided an emotionally charged focus for Natasha's war with the Department of Corrective Services. Faced with the threat of Anton's transfer, and then confronted with his removal and the denial of inter-facility contact, Natasha's coping strategy involved a "protective process" of cognitive transformation whereby the demands of her role and requirements for task accomplishment strengthened her self-esteem and self-efficacy (Rutter, 1987). Despite experiencing setbacks and further traumas in pursuing legal recognition of her relationship with Anton, Natasha was able to transform her life trajectory by finding resilience and meaning in her fight for justice.

Cognitive Transformation Enacted via a Narrative of Military Metaphor

Natasha positioned her experiences of conflict, assault and trauma as a battle or fight with a carceral system with whom she came to view herself as being at war. She penned a "war ditty" as a rallying cry to her supporters: "Never let anyone say that a good fight for the fight for good wasn't a good fight indeed" (Natasha Keating, ATSAQ, 14th December 2005). Her motivational framing in writing this and similar calls-to-action was that they were intended to be read by wider trans communities in the ATSAQ newsletter. It positions Natasha as a role model and champion, even while incarcerated, for those also fighting for recognition and justice.

Table 8.1 (originally in Halliwell et al., 2022) particularises the semantic categories and words that Natasha used to construct a holistic concept of the correctional experience as war. She employed military metaphors to variously describe the physical place, actors and agents associated with the carceral system and the actions taken by herself, corrections officers, institutional representatives, her support system and the wider community. Adopting Lakoff and Johnson's (1980) framework, we propose the following underlying conceptual metaphors derived from Natasha's accounts provide useful guiding indicators of her use of military metaphor: "CORRECTIONAL FACILITIES ARE BATTLE-GROUNDS" and "PRISON LIFE IS WAR" (Halliwell et al., 2022). In her writings to her trans support organisation, ATSAQ Natasha uses fighting language on 22 occasions. Within these discourses, we have identified three semantic categories (micro-propositions), which inform ideational and interpersonal macro propositions (Fairclough, 1995; Halliday & Matthiessen, 2013). Table 8.1 references these instances as derived from the dataset.

Natasha most frequently referred to her engagement with the Department of Corrective Services as a "battle" or "war", with this functional language establishing a contextual framing of the carceral system as "adversarial." Within this context, all actions taken by Natasha and agents of the Department of Corrective Services are depicted as heightened, militarised and confrontational:

> I could take on the Department of Corrective Services for them to allow me to have surgery... Although with the battle I've had just trying to purchase a pair of women's runners and some basic toiletries, it would definitely be bigger than Ben Hur! (Letter to Discrimination Lawyer, 2nd February 2006)

Metaphor not only exposes underlying thought processes but as we observe through Natasha's use of metaphors to re-write her narrative, it also possesses a transformative property. Her visualisation of her incarceration as a "war" created a lived reality that reframed her punitive experience as a "Righteous Cause" to be fought against a tyrannous enemy, rather than a just punishment to be endured. She characterised her interactions with the Department of Corrective Services as a "good fight" in several letters, reaffirming her conceptualisation of her actions as just and warranted. This lexicon became a mantra that Natasha used to galvanise support and legitimise her claims: "take care and keep up the good fight! (I even have mum saying that now! GOD bless her)" (Letter to ATSAQ, 15th May 2006).

By conceptualising her struggles while incarcerated as a "good fight," Natasha also reframed her individual struggle as a universal cause that righteously demanded participation by all in defending against *the* enemy. Her letters to her trans support organisation in 2006 increasingly featured the inclusive formation "we" rather than the singular "I" of earlier letters: "The battle hasn't quite been won, and the war is really only beginning…We've taken the beach at Normandy and France

Table 8.1 Military metaphor lexicon

Date	Semantic category	Language	Ideational/interpersonal function
07/12/05	Carceral system	"Mammoth" battle	Adversarial
07/12/05	Values	good fight/fight for good	Righteous cause
14/12/05	Values	'War Ditty' Never let anyone say That a good fight for the 'fight for good' Wasn't a good fight Indeed	Righteous cause
17/01/06	Actions and Agency	"Battle of the Bras"	Righteous cause
24/01/06	Values	good fight	Righteous cause
30/01/06	Actions and agency	The battle hasn't quite been won, and the war is really only beginning… We've taken the beach at Normandy and France still lies up ahead!!!	Adversarial
30/01/06	Action and agency	take the fight on	Adversarial
02/02/06	Action and agency	battle I've had bigger than Ben Hur	Adversarial
20/02/06	Action and agency	have to battle have to battle	Adversarial
Undated (Feb 2006)	Action and agency	STRIKES AGAIN fight never ends the battle continues we battle on hear me roar! I will not be stood over we battle on the battle for them was nowhere near the BATTLE I had for…	Adversarial

(continued)

Table 8.1 (continued)

Date	Semantic category	Language	Ideational/interpersonal function
30/03/06	Action and agency	for me to fight	Adversarial
	Values	they were hoping to 'cripple' me emotionally, but enough to stop me fighting them	Righteous cause
21/03/06	Action and agency	they're a little bit too scared to attack me directly and so they should be!"	Adversarial
08/05/06	Adversarial system	taken up the WAR	Adversarial
08/05/06	Action and agency	fighting their B/S	Adversarial
	Action and agency	pick that battle back up off its backside ad kick them down on theirs!!	Adversarial
	Carceral system	these battles and wars against the system	Adversarial
15/05/06	Carceral systems	another battle	Adversarial
		isn't everything a battle!	Adversarial
	Action and agency	feisty little battler	Adversarial
	Values	keep up the good fight	Righteous cause
15/06/06	Action and agency	WAR!!!!!! WE TAKE NO PRISONERS	Adversarial
			Adversarial
		I am hoping to appeal to you both and your sense of "WARRIORESS-NESS"	Adversarial
		waging a war	
17/06/06	Action and agency	battle for 'pink & cute' runners	Adversarial

still lies up ahead!!!" (Letter to ATSAQ, 30th January 2006)*;* and as headlined in her letter of 15th June 2006: "WAR!!!!!! WE TAKE NO PRISONERS." In the same letter, she also included motivational rally-cries and appeals for support: "I am hoping to appeal to you both and your sense of 'WARRIORESS-NESS'". Through its inherent legitimacy, universalisation elevates the individual *case* to a universal *cause*. Natasha not only used the implicit naming device "good fight" to infer the righteousness of her position—she also used explicit contrasting language to describe her actions *vis à vis* those taken by agents of the carceral system:

> First were the Bras, then the panties, and the battle for them was nowhere near the "BATTLE" I had for the size 9's but with a lot of help from my friends, we got them too!... and now we battle on, to get them to recognize that yes, I am a woman, hear me roar! I will not back down; I will not be stood over by anyone just because they believe the colour of the shirt on their back gives them power to do what they want without being answerable to anyone, because we all have to answer for what we do, we are not GOD. And so the battle continues, now, I believe that the use of words; Inmate; Offender and Prisoner is not conducive to our rehabilitation, and the general consensus of the "residents" of this establishment, is in agreement. So now we battle on... (Letter to ATSAQ, undated February 2006)

Examining the thought processes that inform the semantic micro-propositions contained within this letter to ATSAQ, we identify the central argument in Natasha's narrative that the carceral system is unjust, unbending, unrelenting, and its agents tyrannous in their operationalisation of prison protocols and practices. Natasha represented these oppressive systemic factors as being mobilised against incarcerated trans persons, ostensibly depicting the carceral system as waging an unjust civil war against its charges. In contrast, she positioned herself as a heroic fighter for justice: "I'll not lower myself to their level!!!… 'Staff' shouldn't be in a position of power if they're going to ABUSE that power and the trust that has been put in them…" (Letter to ATSAQ, 30th March 2006). Indeed, in the later months of her incarceration, she entirely flipped the convict stigma narrative (Goffman, 1963) and accused the carceral system of criminality: "I want to reiterate the possibility and probability of CRIMINAL CHARGES for this type of interference with my mail" (Letter to General Manager of Correctional Centre, 23rd June 2006).

As Vanhooren et al. (2015) argue, many incarcerated persons struggle to reconcile the convict stigma with their aspirational identity. Many choose to deny the existential challenge that their situation presents. Escalating individual struggles to a "war" created the opportunity for a heroic identity to emerge, one positioned by Natasha as engaged in leading the fight against the enemy. Natasha reconstructed her identity by casting herself as a heroic warrior in the "good fight" against the carceral system: "...so this will be another battle! But hey, what's new isn't everything a battle! Lucky [I'm] a feisty little battler hey loves!" (Letter to ATSAQ, 15th June 2006). By adopting military metaphors to contextualise her situation, Natasha overcame the existential challenge of the convict stigma, constructing an identity that was agentic, resilient, just and good.

Conclusion: On the Limits of Agency and Alternative Narratives

We return to the consideration of "agency" as outlined in the early sections of this chapter (Adams, 2006; Ross & Mirowsky, 2013; Twenge et al., 2012), and the example that Natasha's experiences provide in context of the prison as "total institution" (Goffman, 1963, p. 4). It appears that within the deliberate and constraining structures of the prison, Natasha was able to create "critical space" (McCorkel, 1998, p. 245) to express a sense of self-identification, with letter writing providing a tangible medium upon which this reclamation of the Self was enacted.

The letters written by Natasha were significant for her capacity to articulate an alternative conception of Self. The letters represented an act of resistance, within which direct claims were made by Natasha in response to the oppressive setting of the prison. As Natasha's repertoire for writing these letters developed and her skill in questioning the legitimacy of actions drawn against her increased, she demonstrated a growing sophistication for understanding the workings of this "total institution." This is where Natasha's reading of the prison structure, and its systems emerged as most evident. The letters represented a tangible form for this understanding and the accompanying realisation of the circumstances within which she was positioned. Natasha's letters and the increasing focus they took on defining and illustrating the everyday violence she experienced provided this rallying point towards this "good fight" for human rights. In this sense, Natasha's archive of letters is far more than *just* a chronicle of events and circumstances; it is also a chronicle of her emerging self-identification.

Yet we remain cautious in suggesting that such acts of resistance represent an idealised expression of agency. The total institution (Goffman, 1963) remains an oppressive context, defined precisely in terms of its capacity to limit such agency. That Natasha was able to generate these letters speaks to her convictions and the specific circumstances within which she found herself. This is notable, but it did also bear costs. She was marginalised and targeted for her activism. She was separated from her partner. She was denied basic rights. The letter writing, while an act of agentic self-identification, was also a provocation for further marginalisation. Invoking Goffman (1961, p. 4) once more, we highlight that "the self in this sense is not a property of the person to whom it is attributed, but dwells rather in the pattern of social control".

It remains that Natasha's agency was still performed in context of the prison. Natasha's invocation of her "replacement self" (Giordano et al., 2002)—one defined in terms of her "warrioress-ness" and the war she waged with the carceral system—was writ-large as a *response* to the conditions within which she found herself. In this sense, the experience of incarceration remained central to her identity, and although her transformation in response to these adversities (McCorkel, 1998) activated her agency for calling out the abuses she experienced, these actions were nonetheless performed within the context of the carceral setting, and the experience of incarceration. In this sense, we speculate as to the limits of the identity transformation possible in such contexts and note that Natasha's demonstration of agency remained bound to her emplacement within a prison positioned as a "forcing house for changing persons" (Goffman, 1961, p. 12).

Acknowledgements The authors would like to acknowledge the feedback of Gina Mather, past President, and Kristine Johnson, past Secretary, of the

Australian Transgender Support Association of Queensland Inc. (ATSAQ) and Peggy Keating, Natasha's mother, for reviewing and endorsing the manuscript.

Funding Acknowledgements The authors disclosed receipt of the following financial support for the research, authorship and/or publication of this article: This work was supported by the Centre for Health, Informatics, and Economic Research Internal Funding Bid (2019) at the University of Southern Queensland with the last author (AB) as the lead investigator. This work was also supported by the University of Southern Queensland through an Internal Research Capacity Grant with the last author (AB) as the lead investigator [Project ID 1007573, 2020].

References

Adams, M. (2006). Hybridizing habitus and reflexivity: Towards an understanding of contemporary identity? *Sociology, 40*(3), 511–528.

Andrews, J., Clark, D. J., & Baird, F. (1997). Therapeutic letter writing: Creating relational case notes. *The Family Journal, 5*(2), 149–158.

Australian Transgender Support Association of Queensland [ATSAQ]. (2008). *ATSAQ: The update*. ATSAQ Newsletter.

Beckett, C. (2003). The language of siege: Military metaphors in the spoken language of social work. *The British Journal of Social Work, 33*(5), 625–639.

Bogren, A. (2010). Studying social power in textual data: Combining tools for analyzing meaning and positioning. *Critical Discourse Studies, 7*(1), 73–84.

Braun, V., & Clarke, V. (2019). Reflecting on reflexive thematic analysis. *Qualitative Research in Sport, Exercise and Health, 11*(4), 589–597.

Brömdal, A., Clark, K. A., Hughto, J. M. W., et al. (2019a). Whole-incarceration-setting approaches to supporting and upholding the rights and health of incarcerated transgender people. *International Journal of Transgenderism, 20*(4), 341–350.

Brömdal, A., Halliwell, S., Sanders, T., et al. (2023). Navigating intimate transgender citizenship while incarcerated in Australia and the United States. *Feminism & Psychology, 33*(1), 43–64.

Brömdal, A., Mullens, A. B., Phillips, T. M., et al. (2019b). Experiences of transgender prisoners and their knowledge, attitudes, and practices regarding sexual behaviors and HIV/STIs: A systematic review. *International Journal of Transgenderism, 20*(1), 4–20.

Brown, G. R. (2014). Qualitative analysis of transgender inmates' correspondence. *Journal of Correctional Health Care, 20*(4), 334–342.

Brown, G. R., & McDuffie, E. (2009). Health care policies addressing transgender inmates in prison systems in the United States. *Journal of Correctional Health Care, 15*(4), 280–291.

Charon, R. (2001). The patient-physician relationship. Narrative medicine: A model for empathy, reflection, profession, and trust. *JAMA, 286*(15), 1897–1902.

Clark, K. A., Brömdal, A., Phillips, T., et al. (2023). Developing the "oppression-to-incarceration cycle" of Black American and First Nations Australian transgender women. *Journal of Correctional Health Care, 29(1),* 27–38.

du Plessis, C., Halliwell, S., Mullens, A., et al. (2023). A transgender agent of social change in incarceration: A psychobiographical study of Natasha Keating. *Journal of Personality, 91*(1), 50–67.

Erzikova, E., Mills, C. B., & Sparks, J. V. (2014). Identity management in HIV-positive prisoners in Russia: A case study. *Russian Journal of Communication, 6*(2), 143–154.

Fairclough, N. (1992). *Discourse and social change*. Polity Press.

Fairclough, N. (1995). *Critical discourse analysis: The critical study of language.* Longman.

Flusberg, S. J., Matlock, T., & Thibodeau, P. H. (2018). War metaphors in public discourse. *Metaphor and Symbol, 33*(1), 1–18.

Franks, N., Mullens, A. B., Aitken, S., et al. (2022). Fostering gender-IQ: Barriers and enablers to gender-affirming behavior amongst an Australian general practitioner cohort. *Journal of Homosexuality*, 1–24. https://doi.org/10.1080/00918369.2022.2092804

Fuks, A. (2010). The military metaphors of modern medicine. In Z. Li & T. L. Long (Eds.), *The meaning management challenge: Making sense of health, illness and disease* (pp. 55–68). Brill.

Gillis, M. (2020). Ventilators, missiles, doctors, troops ... the justification of legislative responses to COVID-19 through military metaphors. *Law and Humanities, 14*(2), 135–159.

Giordano, P. C., Cernkovich, S. A., & Rudolph, J. L. (2002). Gender, crime, and desistance: Toward a theory of cognitive transgenderformation. *American Journal of Sociology, 107*(4), 990–1064.

Goffman, E. (1961). *Asylums. Essays on the social situation of mental patients and other inmates*. Aldine.

Goffman, E. (1963). *Stigma: Notes on the management of spoiled identity*. Prentice Hall.

Halliday, M. A. K., & Matthiessen, C. (2013). *Halliday's introduction to functional grammar*. Routledge.

Halliwell, S., du Plessis, C., Hickey, A., et al. (2022). A critical discourse analysis of an Australian incarcerated transgender woman's letters of complaint and self-advocacy. *Ethos, 50*, 208–232.

Hendricks, R. K., Demjén, Z., Semino, E., et al. (2018). Emotional implications of metaphor: Consequences of metaphor framing for mindset about cancer. *Metaphor and Symbol, 33*(4), 267–279.

Hughto, J. M. W., Clark, K. A., Daken, K., et al. (2022). Victimization within and beyond the prison walls: A latent profile analysis of transgender and gender diverse adults. *Journal of Interpersonal Violence, 37*(23–24), NP23075–NP23106.

Jenness, V., & Fenstermaker, S. (2016). Forty years after Brownmiller: Prisons for men, transgender inmates, and the rape of the feminine. *Gender & Society, 30*(1), 14–29.

Karimi, M., & Tabrizi, H. H. (2015). Critical discourse analysis of two letters of complaint and manipulation of people in power. *Mediterranean Journal of Social Sciences, 6*(4), 486–492.

Kidd, I. J., & Carel, H. (2017). Epistemic injustice and illness. *Journal of Applied Philosophy, 34*(2), 172–190.

Lakoff, G., & Johnson, M. (1980). *Metaphors we live by*. University of Chicago Press.

Lynch, S., & Bartels, L. (2017). Transgender prisoners in Australia: An examination of the issues, law and policy. *Flinders Law Journal, 19*(2), 185–231.

Maruna, S. (2001). *Making good: How ex-convicts reform and rebuild their lives*. American Psychological Association.

McAdams, D. P., & Bowman, P. J. (2001). Narrating life's turning points: Redemption and contamination. In D. P. McAdams, R. Josselson, & A. Lieblich (Eds.), *Turns in the road: Narrative studies of lives in transgenderition* (pp. 3–34). American Psychological Association.

McCorkel, J. A. (1998). Going to the crackhouse: Critical space as a form of resistance in total institutions and everyday life. *Symbolic Interaction, 21*(3), 227–252.

Mehta, D., Bruenig, D., Pierce, J., et al. (2021, May). Recalibrating the epigenetic clock after exposure to trauma: The role of risk and protective psychosocial factors. *Journal of Psychiatric Research, 149*, 374–381.

Miller, F. A., & Alvarado, K. (2005). Incorporating documents into qualitative nursing research. *Journal of Nursing Scholarship, 37*(4), 348–353.

Miller, R. S. (2010). Speak up: 8 words & phrases to ban in oncology! *Oncology times, 32*(12), 20.

Mumby, D. K. (1987). The political function of narrative in organizations. *Communication Monographs, 54*(2), 113–127.

Mutch, A. (2006). Organization theory and military metaphor: Time for a reappraisal? *Organization, 13*(6), 751–769.

Nie, J.-B., Gilbertson, A., de Roubaix, M., et al. (2016). Healing without waging war: Beyond military metaphors in medicine and HIV cure research. *The American Journal of Bioethics, 16*(10), 3–11.

Opsal, T. D. (2011). Women disrupting a marginalized identity: Subverting the parolee identity through narrative. *Journal of Contemporary Ethnography, 40*(2), 135–167.

Owen, W. F. (1984). Interpretive themes in relational communication. *Quarterly Journal of Speech, 70*(3), 274–287.

Penson, R. T., Schapira, L., Daniels, K. J., et al. (2004). Cancer as metaphor. *The Oncologist, 9*(6), 708–716.

Phillips, T., Brömdal, A., Mullens, A. B., et al. (2020). "We don't recognise transgenderexuals...and we're not going to treat you": Cruel and unusual and the lived experiences of transgender women in US prisons. In M. Harmes, M. Harmes, & B. Harmes (Eds.), *The Palgrave handbook of incarceration across popular culture* (pp. 331–360). Palgrave Macmillan.

Prior, L. (2011). Using documents in social research. In D. Silverman (Ed.), *Qualitative research: Issues of theory, method and practice* (3rd ed., pp. 93–100). Sage.

Reisfield, G. M., & Wilson, G. R. (2004). Use of metaphor in the discourse on cancer. *Journal of Clinical Oncology, 22*(19), 4024–4027.

Riessman, C. K. (2000). Stigma and everyday resistance practices: Childless women in South India. *Gender & Society, 14*(1), 111–135.

Ritchie, J., & Spencer, L. (1994). Qualitative data analysis for applied policy research. In A. Bryman & B. Burgess (Eds.), *Analyzing qualitative data* (pp. 173–194). Routledge.

Rosenberg, R., & Oswin, N. (2015). Transgender embodiment in carceral space: Hypermasculinity and the US prison industrial complex. *Gender Place and Culture, 22*(9), 1269–1286.

Ross, C. E., & Mirowsky, J. (2013). The sense of personal control: Social structural causes and emotional consequences. In C. S. Aneshensel, J. C. Phelan, & P. A. Bierman (Eds.), *Handbook of the sociology of mental health* (pp. 379–402). Springer.

Rutter, M. (1987). Psychosocial resilience and protective mechanisms. *American Journal of Orthopsychiatry, 57*(3), 316–331.

Sanders, T., Gildersleeve, J., Halliwell, S., et al. (2022). Transgender architecture and the prison as archive: "Don't be a queen and you won't be arrested". *Punishment & Society*, 1–24. https://doi.org/10.1177/14624745221087058

Semino, E., Demijén, Z., Hardie, A., et al. (2018). *Metaphor, cancer and the end of life: A corpus-based study.* Routledge.

Shapiro, J. (2018). "Violence" in medicine: Necessary and unnecessary, intentional and unintentional. *Philosophy, Ethics, and Humanities in Medicine, 13*(1), 7.

Singer, J. A. (1997). *Message in a bottle: Stories of men and addiction.* Free Press.

Snow, D. A., & Anderson, L. (1987). Identity work among the homeless: The verbal construction and avowal of personal identities. *American Journal of Sociology, 92*(6), 1336–1371.

Sontag, S. (1979). *Illness as metaphor*. Farrar.

Stanley, E. A., & Smith, N. (2015). *Captive genders: Transgender embodiment and the prison industrial complex* (2nd ed.). AK Press.

Stanley, E. A., Spade, D., & Queer (In)Justice. (2012). Queering prison abolition, now? *American Quarterly, 64*(1), 115–127.

Steinert, H. (2003). The indispensable metaphor of war: On populist politics and the contradictions of the state's monopoly of force. *Theoretical Criminology, 7*(3), 265–291.

Swan, J., Phillips, T. M., Sanders, T., et al. (2023). Mental health and quality of life outcomes of gender-affirming surgery: A systematic literature review. *Journal of Gay & Lesbian Mental Health, 27*(1), 2–45.

Tate, T. P., & Pearlman, R. A. (2016). Military metaphors in health care: Who are we actually trying to help? *The American Journal of Bioethics, 16*(10), 15–17.

Tebes, J. K., Irish, J. T., Puglisi Vasquez, M. J., et al. (2004). Cognitive transgenderformation as a marker of resilience. *Substance Use and Misuse, 39*(5), 769–788.

Tebes, J. K., Kaufman, J. S., Bronstone, A. B., et al. (1995). Coping with adversity: The case for resilience over prevention. In Symposium (Ed.), *Symposium, promoting resilience vs. preventing disorder: The case for resilience over prevention. Biennial meeting of the Society for Community Research and Action.*

Tedeschi, R. G., & Calhoun, L. G. (1995). *Trauma & transgenderformation: Growing in the aftermath of suffering.* Sage.

Twenge, J. M., Campbell, W. K., & Gentile, B. (2012). Generational increases in agentic self-evaluations among American college students, 1966–2009. *Self and Identity, 11*(4), 409–427.

U.S. Department of Justice. (2012). *National Standards to prevent, detect, and respond to prison rape: Final rule.*

Van Dijk, T. A. (1993). Principles of critical discourse analysis. *Discourse & Society, 4*(2), 249–283.

Van Dijk, T. A. (2001). Critical discourse analysis. In D. Tannen, D. Schiffrin, & H. E. Hamilton (Eds.), *Handbook of discourse analysis* (pp. 352–371). Blackwell.

Van Dijk, T. A. (2006). Politics, ideology, and discourse. In K. Brown (Ed.), *Encyclopedia of language & linguistics* (2nd ed., pp. 728–740). Elsevier.

Van Hout, M. C., Kewley, S., & Hillis, A. (2020). Contemporary transgender health experience and health situation in prisons: A scoping review of extant published literature (2000–2019). *International Journal of Transgender Health, 21*(3), 258–306.

Vanhooren, S., Leijssen, M., & Dezutter, J. (2015). Posttraumatic growth during incarceration: A case study from an experiential–existential perspective. *Journal of Humanistic Psychology, 58*(2), 144–167.

9

Concluding Thoughts and Future Directions

Heather Panter and Angela Dwyer

Neglected Victimhood

Throughout this book, transgender victimhood has been presented and contextualised to better understand the various levels of victimisation that transgender people face within criminal justice systems around the globe. From international social-legal and political perspectives, transgender people are delegitimised, dehumanised, and often face a criminalised existence. As such this book walked readers through each step of the criminal processing system from creation of laws based on

H. Panter (✉)
School of Justice Studies, Liverpool Centre for Advanced Policing Studies, Liverpool John Moores University, Liverpool, UK
e-mail: h.a.panter@ljmu.ac.uk

A. Dwyer
School of Social Sciences, Tasmanian Institute of Law Enforcement Studies, University of Tasmania, Glen Waverley, VIC, Australia
e-mail: angela.dwyer@utas.edu.au

H. Panter and A. Dwyer (eds.), *Transgender People and Criminal Justice*, Critical Criminological Perspectives, https://doi.org/10.1007/978-3-031-29893-6_9

social-legal discourses, policing of laws, criminal investigations involving transgender victims, transgender experiences in courtrooms, to experiences in prison. During this exploration, what became apparent was the politicisation of gender and how this politicisation allows for legal neglect of equality and basic human rights.

Shockingly despite LGBTQ+ steps towards better equality, transgender people specifically appear to have been neglected and further victimised. This can be seen in the UK, for example, where transgender hate crimes have increased 56%, notably the biggest increase across all types of hate crimes since 2021 (Home Office, 2022). Or, in Poland where conservative and populist PiS-party has politically targeted transgender communities specifically (see Chapter 2). Or, as explored in Chapter 3, transgender people are legally criminalised in 14 various regions across the world: with 11 countries imposing death penalties. But the victimisation does not just end on the legal level, it continues through the policing of transgender people (see Chapter 5), the marginalisation of transgender homicide victims (see Chapter 6), unequal treatment in courtrooms (see Chapter 7), and oppression that exists in carceral settings for transgender people (see Chapter 8).

These narratives fall into easy alignment with critically queer criminological ideas. Even at the fringes of criminal processing systems, schools, political rhetoric, and legislative frameworks structure up entry points through which transgender young people and adults flow effortlessly into the machinations of criminal processing systems. Legislative frameworks physically expunge transgender people from the human population through death penalties. Political rhetoric moves them out of public spaces. Cisnormative social expectations undoubtedly drive the behaviours of school staff, and apparently court practitioners. The gatekeepers of these systems, police, shore up public expectations of cisnormativity, interacting with and criminalising transgender people as non-cisnormative bodies taking up public spaces. This pattern continues with transgender people even upon their deaths when police are investigating their homicides. Policing interactions, evidently also court interactions, and arguably schools, engage in implicit and explicit processes of dehumanisation and delegitimisation of transgender people, with these emerging as end goals in themselves.

New Challenges

Different interdisciplinary exploration pertaining to victimhood have been explored within this book. By relying upon authors from various disciplines, the overall aim of this book was to further development of studies surrounding transgender victimhood with an international scope. This unique approach was warranted as transgender victimhood does not exist in silos within criminal justice systems. Yet, it is acknowledged that that book serves as a critical starting point for future researchers to examine topics further.

Transgender studies are constantly evolving due to political discourses and the challenges these discourses present. For example, members of the criminal justice system should be effectively educated on transgender people, their lives, their challenges, and their experiences while their unique victimhood is acknowledged. Legislative framework should ensure that transgender people are protected in public places with respect to human rights and anti-discrimination laws, particularly where conservative politicians are in positions of power to sway public discourse. As such, global criminal justice systems should ensure that nation-states bar legislation that impinge upon the lives, or bring about the deaths of, transgender people.

Notably the shift in political discourses is only the starting point for change. Foundationally and with continuity, police organisations should work to establish clear guidelines for interacting with transgender victims, witnesses, and suspects. This might involve the development of specialist death investigation guidelines to ensure transgender people are treated with respect and dignity even in death. But at the most basic policing level, officers should be trained around issues related to transgender lives. Further, within the courtroom, legislation mandating respectful and dignifying behaviours for courtroom practitioners and other court system workers should be implemented. This would involve constant auditing to ensure that transgender people are protected throughout the criminal court process (whether victims, witnessed, accused, or convicted) all the way through to the penal system.

Reference

Home Office. (2022). *Hate crime, England and Wales, 2021 to 2022*. Retrieved November 1, 2022, from https://www.gov.uk/government/statistics/hate-crime-england-and-wales-2021-to-2022/hate-crime-england-and-wales-2021-to-2022

Index

H. Panter and A. Dwyer (eds.), *Transgender People and Criminal Justice*, Critical Criminological Perspectives, https://doi.org/10.1007/978-3-031-29893-6

FSC
www.fsc.org
MIX
Papier | Fördert gute Waldnutzung
FSC® C083411

Kolibri 360 GmbH
Ferdinand-Jühlke-Straße 7
99095 Erfurt, Deutschland
produktsicherheit@kolibri360.de